RIGHTS
•

David Lyons
Cornell University

Wadsworth Publishing Company, Inc.
Belmont, California

For Emily,
Matthew, and
Jeremy

Philosophy Editor: Kenneth King
Designer: Dare Porter

Printed in the United States of America
  2 3 4 5 6 7 8 9 10—83 82 81 80 79

Library of Congress Cataloging in Publication Data
Main entry under title:

Rights.

  Bibliography: p.
  CONTENTS: Hart, H. L. A. Are there any natural rights?—Rawls, J. Constitutional liberty and the concept of justice.—Wasserstrom, R. Rights, human rights, and racial discrimination. [etc.]
  1. Civil rights—Addresses, essays, lectures.
I. Lyons, David, date
JC571.R54   323.4   78-17497
ISBN 0-534-00600-0

Contents

Preface

The essays in this collection seek an understanding of rights, which are central to our social practices as well as to our moral and political principles. The authors seek to understand what rights we have, what rights are, and why they are important.

I would like to thank Stephen Massey, Richard Wasserstrom, and Kenneth King, my editor at Wadsworth Publishing Company, for their helpful ideas and suggestions, and Emily, Matthew, and Sandy for their help in proofreading.

I am especially grateful to the authors of these essays for permitting us to reprint them. The essays are presented in the order in which they were first published.

Introduction

•

David Lyons

Rights are centers of controversy. We stand on them, jealously guard them, demand their recognition and enforcement. Though we cannot claim charity, mercy, or generosity as our due, we can demand our rights. Being denied them warrants complaint and indignation. Respect for rights does not signify kindness nor call for gratitude, for it is merely what justice requires.

Rights are the principal currency of moral, political, and legal dispute. Decisions affecting war and peace, race and sex discrimination, birth control, civil disobedience, and a host of other socially divisive issues are defended or attacked on the ground that they respect or encroach upon our rights. Rights are involved in the most routine as well as sensational litigation. The winner of a legal battle over property, contracts, or damages for injuries, for example, is understood to have a right thereby confirmed, while the opponent's contrary claim is thereby denied. Political constitutions acknowledge, establish, and secure rights. Anyone protected by criminal prohibitions, any party to a legal process (including one who is charged or convicted of a crime), and any occupant of a public office is understood to have corresponding rights. Individuals also appeal to rights when public notice or intervention is not anticipated—as a consequence, for example, of promises made, debts unpaid, cooperative undertakings, or relationships of trust, consent, and dependence.

Disputes concerning rights often represent the clash of different individuals' interests; but sometimes they reflect differing conceptions of justice. We might agree that each person has some basic rights concerning, say, security of one's person, of the means to survive, and of free and fair agreements. But the limits of these rights are controversial. Suppose, for example, that a free and fair agreement has been made between the two of us. Under what circumstances would others have the right to intervene because that agreement threatens to affect their interests adversely? Answers might vary considerably. And more fundamental disagreement exists about other claims of right. Does one have the right to exact others' cooperation not just to prevent human suffering and deprivation but in order to raise living standards above a comfortable subsistence level? Does one have the right to claim a share of economic rewards based on the financial risks that one has taken or based on one's skill, productivity, effort, or need? The differing answers given to these and similar questions suggest that practical controversies cannot always be settled by our deciding on a single way to serve our common values; not, at any rate, when our values differ.

Some persons believe that disagreements about rights cannot be rationally settled. This view stems from philosophical skepticism about values in general—the doctrine that value judgments (including moral principles, but unlike judgments about "facts") are ultimately arbitrary, relative to culture, and without objective validity. Skepticism about values, like skepticism about the possibility of human knowledge, merits attention because it challenges us to justify our deeply held convictions, which we often find embarrassingly difficult to do. But value skepticism itself is often asserted dogmatically, as if in conformity with intellectual fashion and without regard to the absence or failure of supporting arguments.

Rights have also generated theoretical controversy apart from the general skepticism about values or substantive disagreement about what rights we have. The word "right" is a relative newcomer to our vocabulary, one which the ancients lacked—and in some quarters it is still looked on as a vagrant term, at least when applied outside the law. To some extent, this sort of skepticism about rights is a reaction to naive or parochial claims on behalf of "natural" or "human" rights; for example, that such rights are "self-evident" or that each member of the human race (past, present, and future) has the right to a two-week paid vacation. Two centuries ago, Jeremy Bentham labored to deflate the exaggerated rhetoric of human rights, but in doing so he assumed that rights are simply creatures of coercive laws. Perhaps for this reason, modern skepticism about rights has tended to reject any idea of "moral" rights—that is, rights that are independent of positive law and its powers of enforcement.

The contributors to this volume are primarily (though not exclusively) concerned with moral rights, those rights which do not owe their very existence to the law. They take for granted (rather than argue) that speaking of rights that are independent of the law makes perfectly good sense. In view of traditional skepticism about moral rights, however, we should examine this shared assumption. I will offer an account of it in the following section. This will lead naturally to a consideration from various viewpoints of the general theme presented by the essays collected in this volume: the distinctive importance of rights.

First we shall consider the connections between rights and enforcement. Then we shall examine a closely related point—the argumentative significance of rights. Finally we shall discuss the relations between rights and other values: justice, benefits and free choice, and dignity, equality, and respect for the moral law.

I. Rights and Enforcement

Positive law provides a home and regular employment for the concept of a right. Despite the law's hospitality, however, rights refuse to be confined within it. They insist on populating frontiers beyond the law. We appeal to them in our appraisal of the law, and we invoke them when we do not expect the law to intervene. Are these ideas nonsensical?

We can best begin with the law itself. Our legal rights are understood to derive from Constitutional provisions, legislative enactments, case law, executive orders, and the like. The legal rules and principles derived from such sources are not automatically enforced but constitute standards by which to judge official practice. And it is indisputable that, because of overwork, human limitations, incompetence, or corruption, officials sometimes fail to follow valid and binding standards, clear legal mandates that create or protect rights. Police, prosecutors, and judges sometimes stumble in their judgments; juries sometimes err in their verdicts; and legislatures sometimes fail to create machinery for protecting rights. Thus even within the law, rights can be conferred or acknowledged without being enforced.

This is not just a matter of imperfect enforcement when enforcement has been authorized. Rights can be recognized by the law in the absence of machinery for enforcement. Consider, for example, those civil rights of U.S. citizens that are based upon provisions of the Constitution, such as the equal protection clause. The Civil Rights Act and the Civil Rights Division of the Department of Justice are intended to secure these rights—specifically for members of minorities such as blacks—who have suffered systematic, persistent discrimination from both officials and private citizens. Enforcement machinery enhances those rights but does not create them.

Thus legal rights are not necessarily enforced; their enforcement need not even be authorized. It follows that neither enforcement nor its authorization is an essential feature of rights. But the idea that rights are creatures of enforcement is the main basis for rejecting the idea of moral rights. What other reason (aside from general skepticism about values) would warrant the notion that there cannot be rights independent of the law?

The argument so far has not proved that moral rights *do* exist. But acceptance of the idea of such rights might be reinforced by considering the way we often look at important issues. Consider the U.S. Constitution once again. That document is valued not least because it commits the government to a respect of certain rights, such as the right to equal protection of the laws, to fair treatment under the laws, and to political dissent, privacy, and religious freedom. But Constitutional recognition of these rights could be ended by a lawful process of amending the document. Indeed, proposals to eliminate some of them are periodically advanced. Now if one believes that such a change would be not just unwise but wrong; if one thinks it morally imperative that the law secure such rights; if, most importantly, one maintains that injustice is done and individuals are *wronged* unless governments are limited in such ways; then one is, in effect, assuming and invoking rights that are independent of the law. But one cannot have it both ways: One cannot assume rights independent of the law (the violation of which constitutes a moral wrong) in arguments for their legal recognition and also hold that such rights are simply creatures of the law. Furthermore, our views about justice, however much they differ, generally imply that human beings have some moral rights. No sound argument for dismissing this idea has yet been advanced.

But the idea that rights are closely connected with enforcement cannot itself be dismissed. It can, however, be developed in ways that do not seek to confine rights within the limits of the law.

II. Rights and Moral Arguments

One reason why rights are important is that claims of right are argumentatively powerful. The rhetoric of rights raises the moral stakes and obliges one's opponent to discredit one's claim or else provide strong arguments to outweigh it. One's right is not a mere desire, interest, or preference. As Richard Wasserstrom observes in *Rights, Human Rights, and Racial Discrimination,* to invoke a right is to demand a special justification for decisions that are seen as encroaching upon it. One way of understanding this idea brings us back to the idea of enforcement.

John Stuart Mill held that a claim of right is a claim for some protection by society, to guarantee a benefit or liberty.[1] A similar view is suggested by H. L. A. Hart, who argues in *Are There Any Natural Rights?* that "to have a right entails having a moral justification for limiting the freedom of another person and for determining how he should act." According to this view, though rights do not entail enforcement, they *justify* it.

Hart does not assume that rights are creatures of the law. But his theory could explain why even moral rights are so closely associated with the law, since law is one of the chief human instruments for limiting freedom. Law employs systematic threats and penalties called punishments as well as physical force and so exercises what Mill called "compulsion and control" over human conduct.[2] Hart's theory could also be extended to account for the connection between rights and enforcement in the law: If one substitutes the word "legal" for "moral," it says that legal rights provide legal justifications for limiting others' freedom.

Is this sound? Do valid claims of right automatically justify coercive measures against others? We must distinguish two elements in Hart's account. One is the idea that if I have a right, then *others require* a special justification for limiting *my* freedom. The second idea is that if I have a right, then *I have* a justification for limiting *others'* freedom (in order, say, to secure some service or benefit that is due me or to block some threatened interference with my own behavior). These two elements concern justified interference quite differently. The second idea positively

---

[1]John Stuart Mill, *Utilitarianism,* Chap. V, par. 24.
[2]John Stuart Mill, *On Liberty,* Chap. I, par. 9.

connects rights with justified interference, but the first does not. The first idea says that rights create obstacles in the way of justified interference; thus if only the first point were part of a true account of rights, then valid claims of right would not automatically provide grounds for enforcement.

We must therefore concentrate on Hart's second point, that my right justifies limiting another's freedom. This should be compared with a commonly accepted idea about rights, that they are "correlative" with obligations. At its minimum, the doctrine of correlativity asserts that when I have a right, some other person or persons are under an obligation to me (to provide some service or benefit, for example, or to refrain from interfering with my behavior). We should note in passing that this doctrine does not clearly hold for all rights. The right of Congress to regulate interstate commerce, for example, does not entail that others have any obligations; it concerns what Congress is constitutionally "competent" to do. Let us suppose, however, that such exceptions involve determinate species of rights and that the rights with which we are concerned do imply others' obligations, as the doctrine of correlativity asserts.

Let us now compare the claim that if I have a right, some other person or persons are under an obligation to me, with the claim that if I have a right, I have a justification for limiting others' freedom. If a man is bound to me by a tie of obligation, such a tie makes a difference to the propriety of behavior between us. I am justified in claiming that he should behave toward me in certain ways; I may be justified in demanding that he do so. I am justified in exhorting him and remonstrating with him in ways that others would not be. I am also justified in complaining to or about him and perhaps in denouncing him for his failure to provide the service or the benefit owed me or for interfering with me. I am justified in sustaining an adverse moral judgment of his failure as well as justified in expressing my disapproval, indignation, and so on. But it does not follow that I have a justification (or that a justification exists) for limiting his freedom. Nor is it clearly true. To see this, we must display a distinction that expressions like "limiting another's freedom" and "interfering with another" can obscure.

It is one thing to disapprove of another's behavior and to express one's disapproval strenuously. It is quite another thing to use physical force, threats, or penalties to regulate another person's conduct. The justification for one is not justification for the other. No sharp line, of course, can be drawn between insistent expression of one's moral disapproval and coercive interference with another's behavior—just as no sharp line can be drawn between being bald and having a full head of hair. But there is nevertheless a difference, which in this case seems morally significant. When others are under an obligation to me and threaten to default, there are actions I might appropriately take which I would not otherwise be justified in taking. But in many such cases I do not think that one of those things is for me to use force or to have others (whether private individuals or public officials) use force on my behalf. (Compare Hart, n. 6, p. 16)

And yet it may be said that rights are *relevant* to arguments for enforcement. Many would maintain that enforcement is justified whenever legal rights are threatened or attacked. Others would accept the use of physical force, threats, or penalties to secure basic rights concerning one's survival, say, or one's dignity as a human being.

We can look at this in two alternative ways. Rights may provide a justification for enforcement that is "prima facie"; that is, a sound argument that can nevertheless be overridden by high stakes on the other side, such as more important rights. If enforcement of rights is *un*justified in some cases, that is because the argument they provide is outweighed by conflicting considerations. Alternatively we might suppose that enforcement becomes warranted for rights only when the stakes are very high or when other factors are present.

If we should decide to give up Hart's idea that my right justifies limiting another's freedom, we would not strip rights of all argumentative significance. We would be left with the idea that when I have a right, others require a special justification for interfering with me or for withholding some benefit or service. This means that interference with me that might be justified if I had no relevant right could not be justified on the same minimal grounds. Some special, extraordinary grounds would then be needed.

Ronald Dworkin develops a similar point in *Taking Rights Seriously*. When I have a certain right against the government, the government requires a special justification for decisions that would encroach upon that right by, say, limiting my liberty. Thus Dworkin assumes that the government's decisions can routinely be justified by showing that they serve the general welfare. Such an argument justifies changing Lexington Avenue from a two-way to one-way street, even though some persons will be inconvenienced by the change, if overall inconvenience will be lessened or other benefits secured. But the right to speak one's mind freely on political matters entails that restrictions on political speech cannot be justified by showing that they would lessen overall inconvenience or otherwise serve the general welfare. The stakes must be much higher. In this sense, Dworkin says, rights "trump" ordinary arguments for limiting liberty. Unless we treat rights with such respect, we fail to take them seriously.

III. Rights and Justice

Now we must ask why rights are so important that they might be thought to justify the use of coercion. Is this just a brute fact about rights? Or can it be explained by reference to some other goods that rights secure?

Rights are closely associated with justice, and the stringency of justice might explain the importance that is attached to rights. As justice is given priority over other values, so it is said that rights must be served ahead of mere desires, preferences, or interests.

Utilitarianism is the view that benefits should be maximized and burdens minimized, where benefits and burdens are functions of individuals' interests, desires, and preferences. Utilitarianism is widely believed to be defective because it reverses the priorities of morality. It is not concerned to distribute benefits and burdens fairly, to respect rights, or to give people what they as individuals deserve.

Dworkin argues that utilitarianism fails to "take rights seriously," and this point is assumed by John Rawls and Robert Nozick in the development of their theories of justice.

In *Constitutional Liberty and the Concept of Justice,* Rawls argues for two basic principles: first, that one has "an equal right to the most extensive liberty compatible with a like liberty for all"; and secondly, that socially distributed goods must be attached to social roles that are open to all (that is, one has a right to fair equality of opportunity) and must be distributed equally except where inequalities work to everyone's advantage (that is, one has a right to institutions that are so arranged). Rawls employs these principles to argue for the Constitutional protection of certain fundamental rights or liberties (of the person, of conscience, and so on). Rawls thus rejects utilitarianism because it is prepared to compromise basic liberties for the sake of economic goods and to impose trade-offs between individuals, making some pay, in effect, for others' benefits. He believes, moreover, that his principles provide a much firmer foundation than does utilitarianism for our prized Constitutional rights.[3]

Robert Nozick's *The Entitlement Theory* appears to attach even greater importance to individual rights. Justice is presented as a function of certain basic rights (to life, liberty, and so on)—and of three further principles: One concerns acquisition (the creation of new rights to goods); another regulates transfers of goods already owned between individuals; and a third rectifies injustice (that is, violations of personal rights). In Nozick's view, Rawls's conception of "justice as fairness" is, like utilitarianism, mistakenly committed to imposing "patterns" of distribution without regard to individual rights. Social justice is obtained, Nozick says, not by designing institutions to maximize benefits or secure some preferred distributional pattern such as equality, but by minimizing restrictions, allowing people to acquire goods and transfer them freely so long as they do not encroach upon another person's rights. Resulting distributions are morally irrelevant. Justice is determined not by outcomes but by processes that are legitimate because they respect rights.

Human Rights and the General Welfare, the final essay in this volume, challenges the assumption that respect for rights is incompatible with utilitarianism. According to David Lyons, Mill accepts the general welfare criterion but does not regard it as directly establishing the requirements of morality. Moral conduct essentially involves respect for moral rights and obligations (this is part of the logic of the moral concepts). Lyons argues that Mill's analysis of justice and morality is not vitiated by his commitment to the general welfare. In other words, Mill does not regard the maximizing of welfare as one's overriding moral obligation. Mill holds that to argue for a right is to justify a social rule calculated to secure some benefit or liberty. To have a right is thus to have a valid claim to such protection. Therefore the adequacy of the resulting theory of justice turns not just on the substantive foundation for such arguments but on the analysis of rights.

[3]Rawls's essay in this volume anticipates and sketches the more elaborate argument of his celebrated book, *A Theory of Justice* (Cambridge, Mass.: Harvard University Press, 1971).

Thus one might try to explain the importance of rights by reference to their connection with the principles of justice. For these principles are generally assumed to have absolute priority. This view, however, presents some problems.

First, one might ask whether principles of justice truly take precedence over all other values, as assumed. Nozick assumes this, Rawls seems to argue for it, Mill believes it generally true—but room for doubt remains. A related point is this: One might argue that the principles of justice have priority because they concern rights. Since the idea of justice is relatively abstract while the idea of rights more obviously concerns individuals, the argument would not be implausible. But that would mean that the priority of justice could not account for the importance of rights, which would still need explaining.

Second, Mill and others may be mistaken in supposing that questions about justice and questions about rights are interchangeable. On the one hand, some matters of justice do not directly involve rights. I can judge that some nasty man *deserves* the bad luck that he suffers without being committed to the view that he has a right to it or that someone else must have had a right to make sure that he suffered for his nastiness. His bad luck may be judged morally fitting—a matter of justice—even if rights are not in question. On the other hand, to suppose that some rights lie outside the realm of justice makes sense. Consider, for example, when it seems most appropriate to say that someone has been done an injustice. I do a man injustice if I cheat, defraud, or exploit him, or perhaps if I manipulate or oppress him. But what if I assault him, treat him cruelly, or kill him? Do I then do him an injustice? I do not mean to suggest that such acts are not wrongs or that they do not violate his rights—only that some wrongs may not also be injustices. (Hart might say that these are "idle" uses of the term "right.") If some rights lie outside the realm of justice in this way, the importance that supposedly attaches to all rights cannot be explained by reference to the alleged priority of justice. So there must be another explanation if rights are important as assumed—or only some classes of rights are so important.

IV. Rights, Benefits, and Choices

Even if we think that questions about rights are coextensive with questions of justice, we may still ask why they are assumed to be important. We may wish to dig beneath the surface of these moral concepts and uncover the root idea of a right. Such an approach to understanding rights was first laid out by Bentham and has resulted in various theories about the nature of rights. These include Bentham's own beneficiary theory discussed by Hart in *Bentham on Legal Rights* and by Lyons in *Rights, Claimants, and Beneficiaries;* Hart's choice theory; and Joel Feinberg's analysis of rights in terms of claiming in *The Nature and Value of Rights.*

It is commonly assumed that the root idea of a right is some sort of advantage. It is also supposed that rights imply others' obligations. Bentham's theory is a natural combination of these two presumptions. He held that I have a right just when some other person is required to serve some interest of mine—just when I am the intended beneficiary of another's obligation.

Certainly most of the rights that we claim are understood to be advantageous in some way, and they are often rights to specific benefits or services. This theory seems, however, to have exceptions. To claim that I have a right to gamble away my earnings (at least when others are not dependent upon me) makes perfectly good sense, and neither this right nor its exercise seems to involve any advantage.

This theory cannot adequately be appraised without taking into account some important distinctions among rights, especially those described and systematized by Hohfeld.[4] He identified four elemental categories of rights (from which more complex rights could be compounded). My right to gamble away my earnings fits into one category, while Bentham's theory seems applicable to another. Looking briefly at Hohfeld's system will be worthwhile in any case, since so many discussions of rights take his distinctions for granted (for better or worse) while other discussions suffer from a failure to consider any such distinctions.

Hohfeld's categories correspond to four distinct questions, on the answers to which litigation can hinge. Since legal rights depend upon these answers, Hohfeld reasoned in effect that a positive answer to each type of question constitutes the necessary and sufficient condition for the existence of a distinct type of right (a useful working assumption is that similar distinctions can be made within the moral sphere, and my summary allows for this):

1. Must another person behave toward me in a certain way? If so, it will be said that I have a certain right. In Hohfeld's system, this situation describes a "claim-right," which may be thought of as the other side of an obligation owed to me. A claim-right is typically a right to specific benefits or services such as the payment of a debt, compensation for an injury done, and so on. But note that though Hohfeld thought vaguely of rights as advantages, he did not build that idea into his definitions.

2. May I behave in a certain way? If I do no wrong in behaving so, then I am said to have a right; in Hohfeld's system, I have a "liberty" (not his preferred term, but the one most frequently used). This type of right is thus the absence of a restriction upon my conduct (or, more narrowly, the absence of an obligation owed to some other person).

3. Am I capable of effecting certain changes in normative relations by, say, making agreements, getting married, or transferring property? If so, I am said to have a right of the sort that Hohfeld called a "power" or "capacity."

4. Can my own normative condition not be changed in a certain respect? If so, then I am said to have a right, one that is here called an "immunity."

[4]Wesley Newcomb Hohfeld, *Fundamental Legal Conceptions* (New Haven: Yale University Press, 1919; reprinted 1964).

Now it is undoubtedly true that these four questions are directly relevant to the determination of rights. Nevertheless Hohfeld's scheme appears defective as it stands, because in some cases, at least, other conditions must be met if rights are to exist. For example, the scheme implies that I have a right when I am able to change my normative relations. But if I negligently damage another's property or violate the penal code, I make myself liable to civil damages or to criminal prosecution and thus change my normative condition. Yet I have not exercised a right. Perhaps a Hohfeldian power is not a full-fledged right unless a liberty is attached. Again, suppose I am disqualified from inheriting some property. This constitutes a Hohfeldian immunity and thus counts within his system as a right—another implausible consequence. It suggests that rights must be advantageous and brings us back to the beneficiary theory.

One trouble with that theory, from the standpoint of the Hohfeldian system, is that it cannot aspire to account for all types of right. For it assumes that rights have corresponding obligations. But Hohfeld's scheme denies this. Only claim-rights come with obligations. Perhaps, however, this is another defect of his system. Perhaps all rights *do* have correlative obligations. If so, those obligations would most likely restrict others' interference with the exercise of the right.

Consider once again my right to gamble away my earnings. Is it just a liberty? If so, the beneficiary theory does not apply. My right cannot then serve as a counterexample to the theory; but the theory pays the price of very limited applicability. A right to do something is, however, taken by many to imply that others have an obligation to refrain from interfering. If this is correct, then a right to do something (such as gamble away my earnings) is not a mere liberty, since the mere absence of a restriction upon my behavior does not imply that restrictions exist on others' behavior. Hart, Wasserstrom, Dworkin, and others take this view. [5] In their approach, my right to gamble away my earnings has at its core a liberty (or perhaps two complementary liberties, so that I have a choice), which is protected by restrictions upon others' interference. Such a right may be thought to involve benefits in two ways. First, the restrictions upon others' interference serve interests such as personal security. These have nothing especially to do with the specific right in question, but they do concern factors that (in the view we are considering) turn mere liberties into rights. Second, it may be claimed that one has an interest generally in the freedom of choice that such rights protect. That is plausible, but it also seems concessionary to Hart, who holds that rights can be analyzed more generally and accurately in terms of respected choices rather than protected interests.

Hart argues that even claim-rights are not adequately interpreted by the beneficiary theory. For example, when an agreement is made for the benefit of a third party, the intended direct beneficiary of the promise and resulting obligation cannot press or waive the claim, since the promise has not been made to that person; thus, Hart argues, that person should not be regarded as having the right;

[5]For discussions of this point, see David Lyons, "The Correlativity of Rights and Duties," *Nous* 4 (1970): 45–55; and Marcus G. Singer, "The Basis of Rights and Duties," *Philosophical Studies* 23 (1972): 48–57.

while the person to whom the promise is made is the one who is owed performance of the promise, the one who can press or waive the claim, and the one who has the right, though not a beneficiary. The person with the right is the one with the option to insist upon the performance of the obligation or, alternatively, to release the other party from it. Similarly, the rights that are built from liberties have freedom of action and thus choice at their cores. The rights constructed from powers give one's decisions (to make a contract or a will, to marry, and so on) normative effect.

The choice theory is initially promising. But Hart finally concludes that it must be restricted to "ordinary" rights. The theory does not adequately account for important classes of rights within the law, such as Constitutional immunities or the rights we appeal to when we criticize the law. Hart suggests that no unified illuminating analysis of rights is possible.

Hart's conclusion should be regarded as a challenge rather than a final verdict. Two questions, moreover, must be asked about his argument. First, to what extent does it suggest that established usage in the law diverges from the use of "right" in extralegal contexts? Second, to what extent is Hart *describing* actual usage (in or outside the law), and to what extent is he *prescribing* usage? His arguments appear to combine both elements, with refinements of usage proposed in order to ensure that words like "right" serve a unique linguistic function.

V. Rights and Human Dignity

Joel Feinberg, too, is skeptical that philosophical analyses of rights can be illuminating. He says that "right" can be given a "formal definition" as "a kind of claim," but that a claim is "an assertion of right"—which takes us in a barren circle. But, he argues, an examination of the social practice of claiming can help us understand the strategic importance of rights. Respect for rights involves respect for human beings.

As Wasserstrom and Feinberg observe, rights go beyond mere favors and privileges. One cannot claim a right to others' kindness, to their unselfish sacrifice, or to their compassionate benevolence. There are two sides to this important truism. Rights do *not* secure all that is valuable in human relations (that is, the world would be a much sadder place without human sympathy). But rights concern what we *can* rightfully claim.

Furthermore, rights may be said to concern not what is merely welcome and good but what *must* be done—including, in the case of human rights, what is vitally needed for human well-being. Now it is natural to associate rights with others' obligations because of the connection of rights with what is mandatory rather than optional on the part of others. But not all requirements correspond to rights. It is often said, for example, that one should be charitable and generous—that one has a duty to behave in that way. This appears to make good sense, even though no other person could have a right to one's charity or generosity (for if the other had a right, then what would be required of one would not be classifiable as charity or generosity). It has also been suggested that one has some duties that concern oneself primarily, such as the duty to develop one's talents and the duty not to take one's own life. The suggestion is not incoherent, even if there are no corresponding rights. To speak of one's having corresponding rights against oneself seems to make no sense at all; and it is at least highly questionable that anyone else has rights against one that are strictly implied by such obligations. Other examples are no doubt possible. Rights thus go beyond requirements as well as favors.

As we have seen, some writers claim that rights go beyond mere requirements because some desirable feature is present when one has a right—some interest is served or some choice respected. A different approach to the connection of rights with other values is suggested by several of the writers represented in this volume. They see rights as connected with such goods as dignity, equality, or self-respect. And the connections that they describe are different. These goods are served not so much by the performance of the obligation as by the recognition that individuals have, or are capable of having, rights.

This theme is developed systematically by Feinberg. To think of someone as capable of possessing rights is to think of that person as capable of making not obsequious requests or plaintive appeals nor mere demands with no valid claim on our attention—but legitimate claims on others, claims that deserve hearing and respect. To think of someone as possessing rights, Feinberg argues, thus accords a measure of respect to that person.

The person seen as capable of possessing rights might be another or might be oneself. "To think of oneself as the holder of rights is not to be unduly but properly proud, to have that minimal self-respect that is necessary to be worthy of the love and esteem of others," Feinberg writes. "To respect a person then, or to think of him as possessed of human dignity, simply *is* to think of him as a potential maker of claims." Thus a community in which individuals are regarded as capable of possessing rights is one in which the individuals possess a significant measure of human dignity. They accord each other at least minimal respect as beings capable of setting legitimate limits on each other's conduct and choices, and this in turn is conducive to the valued good of self-respect for each person. One who is treated by others as possessing, or as capable of possessing, rights—or one who sees oneself as having rights—is encouraged to hold one's head as high as other humans.

Wasserstrom, who is primarily concerned with universal human rights, naturally emphasizes their connection with equality. To regard all humans as possessing rights is not just to think of them as right holders but also to think of them as equal in a morally significant respect. Each has a legitimate claim to the conditions of freedom and human well-being. But Wasserstrom places the connections between rights and respect in a different light. With an eye to the United States, he observes that it is more offensive for a society to have the conception of human rights but deny that some individuals have them (because, say, they have black skins) than to lack the conception of human rights entirely. "It is to read certain persons, all of whom are most certainly human beings, out of the human race. This is surely among the greatest of all moral wrongs."

Dworkin makes a similar point. Important rights against one's government are predicated upon the protection of individual dignity, equality of consideration, or some comparable value. To encroach on such a right "means treating a man as less than a man, or as less worthy of concern than other men . . . . The institution of rights is therefore crucial, because it represents the majority's promise to the minorities that their dignity and equality will be respected."

Thomas E. Hill, Jr., views the respect for rights from a different angle, that of *Servility and Self-Respect*. Other writers tend to emphasize the individual consequences of others' regard or lack of regard for individual rights. But Hill is primarily concerned with one's failure to appreciate one's own rights by misunderstanding or undervaluing them. Drawing upon suggestions found in Kant, Hill argues that a certain kind of servility amounts to this depreciation of one's moral rights and that such servility is not just an unfortunate lack of self-respect but a positive moral failing. The failure to take one's own rights seriously is an affront to morality itself.[6]

[6]Some of the material in this essay is presented, in somewhat different form, in my "Apology for Rights," *Cornell Review* 3 (Spring 1978): 24–32.

Are There Any Natural Rights?[1]

•

H. L. A. Hart

I shall advance the thesis that if there are any moral rights at all, it follows that there is at least one natural right, the equal right of all men to be free. By saying that there is this right, I mean that in the absence of certain special conditions which are consistent with the right being an equal right, any adult human being capable of choice (1) has the right to forbearance on the part of all others from the use of coercion or restraint against him save to hinder coercion or restraint and (2) is at liberty to do (i.e., is under no obligation to abstain from) any action which is not one coercing or restraining or designed to injure other persons.[2]

From *The Philosophical Review*, Vol. LXIV (April 1955), 175–191. Reprinted by permission of the author and *The Philosophical Review*.

[1]I was first stimulated to think along these lines by Mr. Stuart Hampshire, and I have reached by different routes a conclusion similar to his.

[2]Further explanation of the perplexing terminology of freedom is, I fear, necessary. *Coercion* includes, besides preventing a person from doing what he chooses, making his choice less eligible by threats; *restraint* includes any action designed to make the exercise of choice impossible and so includes killing or enslaving a person. But neither coercion nor restraint includes *competition*. In terms of the distinction between "having a right to" and "being at liberty to," used above and further discussed in Section I, B, all men may have, consistently with the obligation to forbear from coercion, the *liberty* to satisfy if they can such at least of their desires as are not designed to coerce or injure others, even though in fact, owing to scarcity, one man's satisfaction causes another's frustration. In conditions of extreme scarcity this distinction between competition and coercion will not be worth drawing; natural rights are only of importance "where peace is possible" (Locke). Further, freedom (the absence of coercion) can be *valueless* to those victims of unrestricted competition too poor to make use of it; so it will be pedantic to point out to them that though starving they are free. This is the truth exaggerated by the Marxists whose *identification* of poverty with lack of freedom confuses two different evils.

I have two reasons for describing the equal right of all men to be free as a *natural* right; both of them were always emphasized by the classical theorists of natural rights. (1) This right is one which all men have if they are capable of choice; they have it *qua* men and not only if they are members of some society or stand in some special relation to each other. (2) This right is not created or conferred by men's voluntary action; other moral rights are.[3] Of course, it is quite obvious that my thesis is not as ambitious as the traditional theories of natural rights; for although on my view all men are *equally* entitled to be free in the sense explained, no man has an absolute or unconditional right to do or not to do any particular thing or to be treated in any particular way; coercion or restraint of any action may be justified in special conditions consistently with the general principle. So my argument will not show that men have any right (save the equal right of all to be free) which is "absolute," "indefeasible," or "imprescriptible." This may for many reduce the importance of my contention, but I think that the principle that all men have an equal right to be free, meager as it may seem, is probably all that the political philosophers of the liberal tradition need have claimed to support any program of action even if they have claimed more. But my contention that there is this one natural right may appear unsatisfying in another respect; it is only the conditional assertion that *if* there are any moral rights then there must be this one natural right. Perhaps few would now deny, as some have, that there are moral rights; for the point of that denial was usually to object to some philosophical claim as to the "ontological status" of rights, and this objection is now expressed not as a denial that there are any moral rights but as a denial of some assumed logical similarity between sentences used to assert the existence of rights and other kinds of sentences. But it is still important to remember that there may be codes of conduct quite properly termed moral codes (though we can of course say they are "imperfect") which do not employ the notion of *a* right, and there is nothing contradictory or otherwise absurd in a code or morality consisting wholly of prescriptions or in a code which prescribed only what should be done for the realization of happiness or some ideal of personal perfection.[4] Human actions in such systems would be evaluated or criticised as compliances with prescriptions or as *good* or *bad, right* or *wrong, wise* or *foolish, fitting* or *unfitting,* but no one in such a system would have, exercise, or claim rights, or violate or infringe them. So those who lived by such systems could not of course be committed to the recognition of the equal right of all to be free; nor, I think (and this is one respect in which the notion of a right differs from other moral notions), could any parallel argument be constructed to show that, from the bare fact that actions were recognized as ones which

---

[3]Save those general rights (cf. Section II, B) which are particular exemplifications of the right of all men to be free.

[4]Is the notion of *a* right found in either Plato or Aristotle? There seems to be no Greek word for it as distinct from "right" or "just" (δίκαιον), though expressions like τὰ ἐμὰ δίκαια are I believe fourth-century legal idioms. The natural expressions in Plato are τὸ ἑαυτοῦ (ἔχειν) or τὰ τινὶ ὀφειλόμενα, but these seem confined to property or debts. There is no place for a moral right unless the moral value of individual freedom is recognized.

ought or ought not to be done, as right, wrong, good or bad, it followed that some specific kind of conduct fell under these categories.

I

(A) Lawyers have for their own purposes carried the dissection of the notion of legal right some distance, and some of their results[5] are of value in the elucidation of statements of the form "X has a right to . . ." outside legal contexts. There is of course no simple identification to be made between moral and legal rights, but there is an intimate connection between the two, and this itself is one feature which distinguishes a moral right from other fundamental moral concepts. It is not merely that as a matter of fact men speak of their moral rights mainly when advocating their incorporation in a legal system, but that the concept of a right belongs to that branch of morality which is specifically concerned to determine when one person's freedom may be limited by another's[6] and so to determine what actions may appropriately be made the subject of coercive legal rules. The words "*droit*," "*diritto*," and "*Recht*," used by continental jurists, have no simple English translation and seem to English jurists to hover uncertainly between law and morals, but they do in fact mark off an area of morality (the morality of law) which has special characteristics. It is occupied by the concepts of justice, fairness, rights, and obligation (if this last is not used as it is by many moral philosophers as an obscuring general label to cover every action that morally we ought to do or forbear from doing). The most important common characteristic of this group of moral concepts is that there is no incongruity, but a special congruity in the use of force or the threat of force to secure that what is just or fair or someone's right to have done shall in fact be done; for it is in just these circumstances that coercion of another human being is legitimate. Kant, in the *Rechtslehre,* discusses the obligations which arise in this branch of morality under the title of *officia juris,* "which do not require that respect for duty shall be of itself the determining principle of the will," and contrasts them with *officia virtutis,* which have no moral worth unless done for the sake of the moral principle. His point is, I think, that we must distinguish from the rest of morality those principles regulating the proper distribution of human freedom which alone make it morally legitimate for one human being to determine by his choice how another should act; and a certain specific moral value is secured (to be distinguished from moral virtue in which the good will is manifested) if human relationships are conducted in accordance with these

[5]As W. D. Lamont has seen: cf. his *Principles of Moral Judgment* (Oxford, 1946); for the jurists, cf. Hohfeld's *Fundamental Legal Conceptions* (New Haven, 1923).

[6]Here and subsequently I use "interfere with another's freedom," "limit another's freedom," "determine how another shall act," to mean either the use of coercion or demanding that a person shall do or not do some action. The connection between these two types of "interference" is too complex for discussion here; I think it is enough for present purposes to point out that having a justification for demanding that a person shall or shall not do some action is a necessary though not a sufficient condition for justifying coercion.

principles even though coercion has to be used to secure this, for only if these principles are regarded will freedom be distributed among human beings as it should be. And it is I think a very important feature of a moral right that the possessor of it is conceived as having a moral justification for limiting the freedom of another and that he has this justification not because the action he is entitled to require of another has some moral quality but simply because in the circumstances a certain distribution of human freedom will be maintained if he by his choice is allowed to determine how that other shall act.

(B) I can best exhibit this feature of a moral right by reconsidering the question whether moral rights and "duties"[7] are correlative. The contention that they are means, presumably, that every statement of the form "X has a right to . . ." entails and is entailed by "Y has a duty (not) to . . . ," and at this stage we must not assume that the values of the name-variables "X" and "Y" must be different persons. Now there is certainly one sense of "a right" (which I have already mentioned) such that it does not follow from X's having a right that X or someone else has any duty. Jurists have isolated rights in this sense and have referred to them as "liberties" just to distinguish them from rights in the centrally important sense of "right" which has "duty" as a correlative. The former sense of "right" is needed to describe those areas of social life where competition is at least morally unobjectionable. Two people walking along both see a ten-dollar bill in the road twenty yards away, and there is no clue as to the owner. Neither of the two are under a "duty" to allow the other to pick it up; each has in this sense a right to pick it up. Of course there may be many things which each has a "duty" not to do in the course of the race to the spot—neither may kill or wound the other—and corresponding to these "duties" there are rights to forbearances. The moral propriety of all economic competition implies this minimum sense of "a right" in which to say that "X has a right to" means merely that X is under no "duty" not to. Hobbes saw that the expression "a right" could have this sense but he was wrong if he thought that there is no sense in which it does follow from X's having a right that Y has a duty or at any rate an obligation.

(C) More important for our purpose is the question whether for all moral "duties" there are correlative moral rights, because those who have given an affirmative answer to this question have usually assumed without adequate scrutiny that to have a right is simply to be capable of benefiting by the performance of a "duty"; whereas in fact this is not a sufficient condition (and probably not a necessary condition) of having a right. Thus animals and babies who stand to benefit by our performance of our "duty" not to ill-treat them are said *therefore* to have

[7] I write " 'duties' " here because one factor obscuring the nature of a right is the philosophical use of "duty" and "obligation" for all cases where there are moral reasons for saying an action ought to be done or not done. In fact "duty," "obligation," "right," and "good" come from different segments of morality, concern different types of conduct, and make different types of moral criticism or evaluation. Most important are the points (1) that obligations may be voluntarily incurred or created, (2) that they are *owed to* special persons (who have rights), (3) that they do not arise out of the character of the actions which are obligatory but out of the relationship of the parties. Language roughly though not consistently confines the use of "having an obligation" to such cases.

rights to proper treatment. The full consequence of this reasoning is not usually followed out; most have shrunk from saying that we have rights against ourselves because we stand to benefit from our performance of our "duty" to keep ourselves alive or develop our talents. But the moral situation which arises from a promise (where the legal-sounding terminology of rights and obligations is most appropriate) illustrates most clearly that the notion of having a right and that of benefiting by the performance of a "duty" are not identical. X promises Y in return for some favor that he will look after Y's aged mother in his absence. Rights arise out of this transaction, but it is surely Y to whom the promise has been made and not his mother who *has* or *possesses* these rights. Certainly Y's mother is a person concerning whom X has an obligation and a person who will benefit by its performance, but the person *to whom* he has an obligation to look after her is Y. This is something *due to* or *owed to* Y, so it is Y, not his mother, whose right X will disregard and to whom X will have done *wrong* if he fails to keep his promise, though the mother may be physically injured. And it is Y who has a moral *claim* upon X, is *entitled* to have his mother looked after, and who can *waive* the claim and *release* Y from the obligation. Y is, in other words, morally in a position to determine by his choice how X shall act and in this way to limit X's freedom of choice; and it is this fact, not the fact that he stands to benefit, that makes it appropriate to say that he has *a right*. Of course often the person to whom a promise has been made will be the only person who stands to benefit by its performance, but this does not justify the identification of "having a right" with "benefiting by the performance of a duty." It is important for the whole logic of rights that, while the person who stands to benefit by the performance of a duty is discovered by considering what will happen if the duty is not performed, the person who has a right (to whom performance is *owed* or *due*) is discovered by examining the transaction or antecedent situation or relations of the parties out of which the "duty" arises. These considerations should incline us not to extend to animals and babies whom it is wrong to ill-treat the notion of a right to proper treatment, for the moral situation can be simply and adequately described here by saying that it is wrong or that we ought not to ill-treat them or, in the philosopher's generalized sense of "duty," that we have a duty not to ill-treat them.[8] If common usage sanctions talk of the rights of animals or babies it makes an idle use of the expression "a right," which will confuse the situation with other different moral situations where the expression "a right" has a specific force and cannot be replaced by the other moral expressions which I have mentioned. Perhaps some clarity on this matter is to be gained by considering the force of the preposition "to" in the expression "having a duty to Y" or "being under an obligation to Y" (where "Y" is the name of a person); for it is significantly different from the meaning of "to" in "doing something to Y" or "doing harm to Y," where it indicates the person affected by some action. In the first pair of expressions, "to" obviously does not have this force, but indicates the person to whom the person morally bound is bound. This is an intelligible

[8]The use here of the generalized "duty" is apt to prejudice the question whether animals and babies have rights.

development of the figure of a bond *(vinculum juris: obligare)*; the precise figure is not that of two persons bound by a chain, but of *one* person bound, the other end of the chain lying in the hands of another to use if he chooses.[9] So it appears absurd to speak of having duties or owing obligations to ourselves—of course we may have "duties" not to do harm to ourselves, but what could be meant (once the distinction between these different meanings of "to" has been grasped) by insisting that we have duties or obligations *to* ourselves not to do harm to ourselves?

(D) The essential connection between the notion of a right and the justified limitation of one person's freedom by another may be thrown into relief if we consider codes of behavior which do not purport to confer rights but only to prescribe what shall be done. Most natural law thinkers down to Hooker conceived of natural law in this way: there were natural duties compliance with which would certainly benefit man—things to be done to achieve man's natural end—but not natural rights. And there are of course many types of codes of behavior which only prescribe what is to be done, e.g., those regulating certain ceremonies. It would be absurd to regard these codes as conferring rights, but illuminating to contrast them with rules of games, which often create rights, though not, of course, moral rights. But even a code which is plainly a moral code need not establish rights; the Decalogue is perhaps the most important example. Of course, apart from heavenly rewards human beings stand to benefit by general obedience to the Ten Commandments: disobedience is wrong and will certainly harm individuals. But it would be a surprising interpretation of them that treated them as conferring rights. In such an interpretation obedience to the Ten Commandments would have to be conceived as due to or owed to individuals, not merely to God, and disobedience not merely as wrong but as *a wrong to* (as well as harm to) individuals. The Commandments would cease to read like penal statutes designed only to rule out certain types of behavior and would have to be thought of as rules placed at the disposal of individuals and regulating the extent to which *they* may demand certain behavior from others. Rights are typically conceived of as *possessed* or *owned by* or *belonging to* individuals, and these expressions reflect the conception of moral rules as not only prescribing conduct but as forming a kind of moral property of individuals to which they are as individuals entitled; only when rules are conceived in this way can we speak of *rights* and *wrongs* as well as right and wrong actions.[10]

II

So far I have sought to establish that to have a right entails having a moral justification for limiting the freedom of another person and for determining how he should act; it is now important to see that the moral justification must be of a

---

[9]Cf. A. H. Campbell, *The Structure of Stair's Institutes* (Glasgow, 1954), p.31.

[10]Continental jurists distinguish between *"subjektives"* and *"objektives Recht,"* which corresponds very well to the distinction between *a* right, which an individual has, and what it is right to do.

special kind if it is to constitute a right, and this will emerge most clearly from an examination of the circumstances in which rights are asserted with the typical expression "I have a right to. . . ." It is I think the case that this form of words is used in two main types of situations: (A) when the claimant has some special justification for interference with another's freedom which other persons do not have ("*I have a right to be paid what you promised for my services*"); (B) when the claimant is concerned to resist or object to some interference by another person as having no justification ("*I have a right to say what I think*").

(A) *Special Rights.* When rights arise out of special transactions between individuals or out of some special relationship in which they stand to each other, both the persons who have the right and those who have the corresponding obligation are limited to the parties to the special transaction or relationship. I call such rights special rights to distinguish them from those moral rights which are thought of as rights against (i.e., as imposing obligations upon)[11] everyone, such as those that are asserted when some unjustified interference is made or threatened as in (B) above.

(i) The most obvious cases of special rights are those that arise from promises. By promising to do or not to do something, we voluntarily incur obligations and create or confer rights on those to whom we promise; we alter the existing moral independence of the parties' freedom of choice in relation to some action and create a new moral relationship between them, so that it becomes morally legitimate for the person to whom the promise is given to determine how the promisor shall act. The promisee has a temporary authority or sovereignty in relation to some specific matter over the other's will which we express by saying that the promisor is under an obligation *to* the promisee to do what he has promised. To some philosophers the notion that moral phenomena—rights and duties or obligations—can be brought into existence by the voluntary action of individuals has appeared utterly mysterious; but this I think has been so because they have not clearly seen how special the moral notions of a right and an obligation are, nor how peculiarly they are connected with the distribution of freedom of choice; it would indeed be mysterious if we could make actions morally good or bad by voluntary choice. The simplest case of promising illustrates two points characteristic of all special rights: (1) the right and obligation arise not because the promised action has itself any particular moral quality, but just because of the voluntary transaction between the parties; (2) the identity of the parties concerned is vital— only *this* person (the promisee) has the moral justification for determining how the promisor shall act. It is *his* right; only in relation to him is the promisor's freedom of choice diminished, so that if he chooses to release the promisor no one else can complain.

(ii) But a promise is not the only kind of transaction whereby rights are conferred. They may be *accorded* by a person consenting or authorizing another to interfere in matters which but for this consent or authorization he would be free

---

[11]Cf. Section (B) below.

to determine for himself. If I consent to your taking precautions for my health or happiness or authorize you to look after my interests, then you have a right which others have not, and I cannot complain of your interference if it is within the sphere of your authority. This is what is meant by a person surrendering his rights to another; and again the typical characteristics of a right are present in this situation: the person authorized has the right to interfere not because of its intrinsic character but because *these* persons have stood in *this* relationship. No one else (not similarly authorized) has any *right*[12] to interfere in theory even if the person authorized does not exercise his right.

(iii) Special rights are not only those created by the deliberate choice of the party on whom the obligation falls, as they are when they are accorded or spring from promises, and not all obligations to other persons are deliberately incurred, though I think it is true of all special rights that they arise from previous voluntary actions. A third very important source of special rights and obligations which we recognize in many spheres of life is what may be termed mutuality of restrictions, and I think political obligation is intelligible only if we see what precisely this is and how it differs from the other right-creating transactions (consent, promising) to which philosophers have assimilated it. In its bare schematic outline it is this: when a number of persons conduct any joint enterprise according to rules and thus restrict their liberty, those who have submitted to these restrictions when required have a right to a similar submission from those who have benefited by their submission. The rules may provide that officials should have authority to enforce obedience and make further rules, and this will create a structure of legal rights and duties, but the moral obligation to obey the rules in such circumstances is *due to* the co-operating members of the society, and they have the correlative moral right to obedience. In social situations of this sort (of which political society is the most complex example) the obligation to obey the rules is something distinct from whatever other moral reasons there may be for obedience in terms of good consequences (e.g., the prevention of suffering); the obligation is due to the co-operating members of the society as such and not because they are human beings on whom it would be wrong to inflict suffering. The utilitarian explanation of political obligation fails to take account of this feature of the situation both in its simple version that the obligation exists because and only if the direct consequences of a particular act of disobedience are worse than obedience, and also in its more sophisticated version that the obligation exists even when this is not so, if disobedience increases the probability that the law in question or other laws will be disobeyed on other occasions when the direct consequences of obedience are better than those of disobedience.

Of course to say that there is such a moral obligation upon those who have benefited by the submission of other members of society to restrictive rules to obey these rules in their turn does not entail either that this is the only kind of moral reason for obedience or that there can be no cases where disobedience will be morally justified. There is no contradiction or other impropriety in saying "I

[12]Though it may be *better* (the lesser of two evils) that he should: cf. Section (iii).

have an obligation to do X, someone has a right to ask me to, but I now see I ought not to do it." It will in painful situations sometimes be the lesser of two moral evils to disregard what really are people's rights and not perform our obligations to them. This seems to me particularly obvious from the case of promises: I may promise to do something and thereby incur an obligation just because that is one way in which obligations (to be distinguished from other forms of moral reasons for acting) are created; reflection may show that it would in the circumstances be wrong to keep this promise because of the suffering it might cause, and we can express this by saying "*I ought not* to do it though *I have an obligation to him* to do it" just because the italicized expressions are not synonyms but come from different dimensions of morality. The attempt to explain this situation by saying that our real obligation here is to avoid the suffering and that there is only a prima facie obligation to keep the promise seems to me to confuse two quite different kinds of moral reason, and in practice such a terminology obscures the precise character of what is at stake when "for some greater good" we infringe people's rights or do not perform our obligations to them.

The social-contract theorists rightly fastened on the fact that the obligation to obey the law is not merely a special case of benevolence (direct or indirect), but something which arises between members of a particular political society out of their mutual relationship. Their mistake was to identify *this* right-creating situation of mutual restrictions with the paradigm case of promising; there are of course important similarities, and these are just the points which all special rights have in common, viz., that they arise out of special relationships between human beings and not out of the character of the action to be done or its effects.

(iv) There remains a type of situation which may be thought of as creating rights and obligations: where the parties have a special natural relationship, as in the case of parent and child. The parent's moral right to obedience from his child would I suppose now be thought to terminate when the child reaches the age "of discretion," but the case is worth mentioning because some political philosophies have had recourse to analogies with this case as an explanation of political obligation, and also because even this case has some of the features we have distinguished in special rights, viz., the right arises out of the special relationship of the parties (though it is in this case a natural relationship) and not out of the character of the actions to the performance of which there is a right.

(v) To be distinguished from special rights, of course, are special liberties, where, exceptionally, one person is *exempted* from obligations to which most are subject but does not thereby acquire a *right* to which there is a correlative obligation. If you catch me reading your brother's diary, you say, "You have no right to read it." I say, "I have a right to read it—your brother said I might unless he told me not to, and he has not told me not to." Here I have been specially *licensed* by your brother who had a right to require me not to read his diary, so I am exempted from the moral obligation not to read it, but your brother is under no obligation to let me go on reading it. Cases where *rights*, not liberties, are accorded to manage or interfere with another person's affairs are those where the license is not revocable at will by the person according the right.

(B) *General Rights.* In contrast with special rights, which constitute a justification peculiar to the holder of the right for interfering with another's freedom, are general rights, which are asserted defensively, when some unjustified interference is anticipated or threatened, in order to point out that the interference is unjustified. "I have the right to say what I think."[13] "I have the right to worship as I please." Such rights share two important characteristics with special rights. (1) To have them is to have a moral justification for determining how another shall act, viz., that he shall not interfere.[14] (2) The moral justification does not arise from the character of the particular action to the performance of which the claimant has a right; what justifies the claim is simply—there being no special relation between him and those who are threatening to interfere to justify that interference—that this is a particular exemplification of the equal right to be free. But there are of course striking differences between such defensive general rights and special rights. (1) General rights do not arise out of any special relationship or transaction between men. (2) They are not rights which are peculiar to those who have them but are rights which all men capable of choice have in the absence of those special conditions which give rise to special rights. (3) General rights have as correlatives obligations not to interfere to which everyone else is subject and not merely the parties to some special relationship or transaction, though of course they will often be asserted when some particular persons threaten to interfere as a moral objection to that interference. To assert a general right is to claim in relation to some particular action the equal right of all men to be free in the absence of any of those special conditions which constitute a special right to limit another's freedom; to assert a special right is to assert in relation to some particular action a right constituted by such special conditions to limit another's freedom. The assertion of general rights directly invokes the principle that all men equally have the right to be free; the assertion of a special right (as I attempt to show in Section III) invokes it indirectly.

III

It is, I hope, clear that unless it is recognized that interference with another's freedom requires a moral justification the notion of a right could have no place in morals; for to assert a right is to assert that there is such a justification.

---

[13] In speech the difference between general and special rights is often marked by stressing the pronoun where a special right is claimed or where the special right is denied. "You have no right to stop him reading that book" refers to the reader's general right. "*You* have no right to stop him reading that book" denies that the person addressed has a special right to interfere though others may have.

[14] Strictly, in the assertion of a general right both the *right* to forbearance from coercion and the *liberty* to do the specified action are asserted, the first in the face of actual or threatened coercion, the second as an objection to an actual or anticipated demand that the action should not be done. The first has as its correlative an obligation upon everyone to forbear from coercion; the second the absence in anyone of a justification for such a demand. Here, in Hohfeld's words, the correlative is not an obligation but a "no-right."

The characteristic function in moral discourse of those sentences in which the meaning of the expression "a right" is to be found—"I have a right to . . . ," "You have no right to . . . ," "What right have you to . . . ?"—is to bring to bear on interferences with another's freedom, or on claims to interfere, a type of moral evaluation or criticism specially appropriate to interference with freedom and characteristically different from the moral criticism of actions made with the use of expressions like "right," "wrong," "good," and "bad." And this is only one of many different types of moral ground for saying "You ought . . ." or "You ought not. . . ." The use of the expression "What right have you to . . . ?" shows this more clearly, perhaps, than the others; for we use it, just at the point where interference is actual or threatened, to call for the moral *title* of the person addressed to interfere; and we do this often without any suggestion at all that what he proposes to do is otherwise wrong and sometimes with the implication that the same interference on the part of another person would be unobjectionable.

But though our use in moral discourse of "a right" does presuppose the recognition that interference with another's freedom requires a moral justification, this would not itself suffice to establish, except in a sense easily trivialized, that in the recognition of moral rights there is implied the recognition that all men have a right to equal freedom; for unless there is some restriction inherent in the meaning of "a right" on the type of moral justification for interference which can constitute a right, the principle could be made wholly vacuous. It would, for example, be possible to adopt the principle and then assert that some characteristic or behavior of some human beings (that they are improvident, or atheists, or Jews, or Negroes) constitutes a moral justification for interfering with their freedom; *any* differences between men could, so far as my argument has yet gone, be treated as a moral justification for interference and so constitute a right, so that the equal right of all men to be free would be compatible with gross inequality. It may well be that the expression "moral" itself imports some restriction on what can constitute a moral justification for interference which would avoid this consequence, but I cannot myself yet show that this is so. It is, on the other hand, clear to me that the moral justification for interference which is to constitute a *right* to interfere (as distinct from merely making it morally good or desirable to interfere) is restricted to certain special conditions and that this is inherent in the meaning of "a right" (unless this is used so loosely that it could be replaced by the other moral expres-. sions mentioned). Claims to interfere with another's freedom based on the general character of the activities interfered with (e.g., the folly or cruelty of "native" practices) or the general character of the parties ("We are Germans; they are Jews") even when well founded are not matters of moral right or obligation. Submission in such cases even where proper is not *due to* or *owed to* the individuals who interfere; it would be equally proper whoever of the same class of persons interfered. Hence other elements in our moral vocabulary suffice to describe this case, and it is confusing here to talk of rights. We saw in Section II that the types of justification for interference involved in special rights was independent of the character of the action to the performance of which there was a right but depended upon certain previous transactions and relations between individuals (such as promises, consent, authorization, submission to mutual restrictions). Two questions here suggest themselves: (1) On what intelligible principle could these bare forms of promising, consenting, submission to mutual restrictions, be either necessary or sufficient, irrespective of their content, to justify interference with another's freedom? (2) What characteristics have these types of transaction or relationship in common? The answer to both these questions is I think this: If we justify interference on such grounds as we give when we claim a moral right, we are in fact indirectly invoking as our justification the principle that all men have an equal right to be free. For we are in fact saying in the case of promises and consents or authorizations that this claim to interfere with another's freedom is justified because he has, in exercise of his equal right to be free, freely chosen to create this claim; and in the case of mutual restrictions we are in fact saying that this claim to interfere with another's freedom is justified because it is fair; and it is fair because only so will there be an equal distribution of restrictions and so of freedom among this group of men. So in the case of special rights as well as of general rights recognition of them implies the recognition of the equal right of all men to be free.

Constitutional Liberty and
the Concept of Justice
•
John Rawls

1.

An essential part of the political form of constitutional democracy is provision for certain fundamental liberties. These liberties may be contained in a bill of rights or in other clauses of a written constitution interpreted by a supreme court with the right of judicial review; or they may be secured by certain constitutional conventions and statutes which the supreme legislature would in no circumstances violate or override. There are, of course, various kinds of arguments which may be used to support the institutional forms embodying these constitutional liberties. In this essay, however, I should like to examine those arguments which derive from the concept of justice alone.

Justice is but one of many virtues of political and social institutions, for an institution may be antiquated, inefficient, degrading, or any number of other things without being unjust. The notion of justice is not to be confused with an all-inclusive vision of a good society; it is only one part of any such conception. When applied to an institution (or a system of institutions), justice requires the elimination of arbitrary distinctions and the establishment within its structure of a proper balance or equilibrium between competing claims. The principles of justice specify when the balance or share is proper and which distinctions are arbitrary; they do this by formulating restrictions as to how an institution may define offices

From *Nomos VI: Justice,* ed. C. J. Friedrich and J. Chapman (New York: Atherton, 1963), pp. 98–125. Copyright © 1963. All rights reserved. Reprinted by permission of the author and the publishers, Lieber-Atherton, Inc.

and positions and assign thereto powers and liabilities, rights and duties. Here, the concept of justice will be considered solely as it applies to (political) institutions, that is, publicly recognized systems of rules which are generally acted upon and which, by defining offices and positions, rights and duties, privileges and penalties, give social activity its form and structure. I shall not, then, discuss justice as it applies to particular persons or to their actions.

One may distinguish the various kinds of constitutional liberty as liberty of the person, liberty of conscience and freedom of thought, political liberty, freedom of movement, and equality of opportunity. It is characteristic of these liberties in a constitutional democracy that they are equal liberties; in respect to these liberties, no person is favored over another. Since the constitution is the foundation of the social and political structure, the highest-order system of positive rules regulative in relation to other institutions, the constitutional liberties define and establish an initial position of equal liberty for all citizens within the basic social system in which everyone must begin to have a place.

Our question, then, is the following: what arguments does justice provide for these constitutional liberties; what distinguishes these arguments from those which invoke other moral concepts and, in particular, from those which invoke the concept of social utility? I shall try to show that the concept of justice provides conclusive arguments for these liberties (although I shall consider only liberty of the person and of conscience), whereas the notion of social utility does not and, moreover, that the concept of justice represents the minimum and the most secure moral concept for achieving this result. In a free society, in which a wide divergence of religious and political belief is to be expected, the concept of justice is, therefore, the most rational ground for a common public understanding of the basis of these fundamental liberties.

To deal with our question, I shall formulate . . . a concept of justice which may be called "justice as fairness."[1] I shall then consider the manner in which this concept provides arguments for liberty of the person and freedom of conscience.

---

[1]For a more detailed discussion of this concept of justice, see "Justice as Fairness," *Philosophical Review,* LXVII (1958), 164–194. This concept of justice is closely related to the theory of the social contract; in particular, there are close similarities, as I have only recently come to realize, to Rousseau's concept of the general will in *Le Contrat social*. If space permitted, I should like to discuss briefly the relation of the argument of this essay to that of James Buchanan and Gordon Tullock in their book *The Calculus of Consent* (1962), which appeared after the meetings at which this paper was read. Both arguments are similar in that in each case an attempt is made to formulate a general principle to apply to the choice and design of a constitution, and the decision on a constitution is to be made first in the absence of certain kinds of information and is to regulate subsequent decisions and actions. The approaches differ in that Buchanan and Tullock use as the principle of choice Pareto's criterion as adjusted to apply to institutions, and they are mainly concerned with that part of the constitution having to do with legislative procedure, for example, with the advisability of majority rule; they take the fundamental constitutional liberties more or less as given. In this essay, I try to connect the principle of constitutional choice with the principles of justice (one part of the second principle having a formal resemblance to Pareto's criterion) and to illustrate their application to the basic constitutional liberties.

The discussion of these two forms will display a general method of argument which applies equally well to the other constitutional liberties and which illustrates the special aspects of the concept of justice.

2.

The concept of justice which I shall use may be stated, for the moment, in the form of two principles: first, each person participating in an institution or affected by it has an equal right to the most extensive liberty compatible with a like liberty for all; and, second, inequalities as defined by the institutional structure or fostered by it are arbitrary unless it is reasonable to expect that they will work out to everyone's advantage and provided that the positions and offices to which they attach or from which they may be gained are open to all. These principles express the concept of justice as relating three ideas: liberty, equality, and reward for services contributing to the common advantage.

The term "person" is to be understood in a general way as a subject of claims. In some cases, it means human individuals, but in others it refers to nations, corporations, churches, teams, and so on. Although there is a certain logical priority to the case of human individuals, the principles of justice apply to the relations among all these types of persons, and the notion of a person must be interpreted accordingly.

The first principle holds inviolably only given an assumption of *ceteris paribus*, that is, although there must always be a justification for departing from an initial position of equal liberty, and the burden of proof is on those who would depart from it, nevertheless, there can be and often is a justification for doing so. The principle does indeed imply, for example, that there is a presumption against the distinctions and classifications made by legal systems and other social institutions to the extent that they infringe on the original and equal liberty of the persons participating in them. The second principle defines how this presumption may be put aside by specifying the kinds of inequalities which are permissible.

By "inequalities," it is best to understand not any differences in the institutional structure between offices and positions and the rules defining their rights, duties, powers, and privileges, but differences in the benefits and burdens attached to them either directly or indirectly, such as prestige, wealth, and liability for taxation and compulsory services. Players in a game do not protest against there being different positions, nor do the citizens of a country object to there being different offices of government. It is not differences of this kind that are normally thought of as inequalities, but differences in the resulting distribution established by an institution or made possible by it of the things men strive to attain or avoid. Thus, they may complain about the pattern of honors and rewards set up by an institution (e.g., the privileges and salaries of government officials), or they may object to the distribution of power and wealth which results from the various ways in which men avail themselves of the opportunities allowed by it (e.g., the concentration of wealth which may develop in a free-enterprise economy allowing large entrepreneurial and speculative gains).

It should be noted that the second principle holds that an inequality is allowed only if there is reason to believe that the inequality will work to the advantage of every person engaged in or affected by the institution which defines or permits it. Since this principle applies to institutions, the representative man in every office or position defined by an institution, when he views it as a going concern, must find it reasonable to prefer his condition and prospects with the inequality to what they would be under the institution without it. The principle excludes, therefore, the justification of inequalities on the grounds that the disadvantages of those in one position are outweighed by the greater advantages of those in another position. It is at this point that the principles of justice differ from the principle of social utility, which incorporates no such restriction.

Finally, it is necessary that the various offices to which special benefits or burdens attach should be open to everyone. It may be, for example, to the common advantage, as just defined, to attach special benefits to certain offices. Perhaps by doing so the requisite talent can be attracted to them and encouraged to give its best efforts. But any offices having special benefits must be won in a fair competition in which contestants are judged on their merits. If some offices were not open, those excluded would normally be justified in feeling unjustly treated even if they benefited from the greater efforts of those who were allowed to compete for them. If one can assume that offices are open, it is necessary only to consider the design of institutions themselves and how they work together as a system. It is a mistake to focus attention on the varying relative positions and well-being of particular persons, who may be known to us by their proper names, and to require that every change of position and well-being, as a once-for-all transaction viewed in isolation, be in itself just. It is the system of institutions which is to be judged, and judged from a general point of view. Unless one is prepared to criticize the system of institutions from the standpoint of a representative man holding some particular office, one has no complaint against it.

Put another way, the principles of justice do not select specific distributions of desired things as just, given the wants of particular persons. This task is abandoned as mistaken in principle, and it is, in any case, not capable of a determinate answer. Rather, the principles of justice define the constraints which institutions and joint activities must satisfy if persons engaging in them are to have no complaint against them. If these constraints are satisfied, the resulting distribution, whatever it is, may be accepted as just (or at least as not unjust).

3.

These two principles may be interpreted as those which rational persons would acknowledge when the constraints of having a morality are imposed on them in circumstances which give rise to questions of justice, that is, in circumstances in which persons make conflicting demands on the design of their common institutions and in which they regard themselves as representing or possessing legitimate interests, the claims of which they are prepared to press on one another. Questions of justice and fairness arise when free persons, who have no authority over one another, are participating in their common institutions and settling or acknowledging among themselves the rules which define it and which determine or limit the resulting shares in its benefits and burdens. An institution is just or fair, then, when it satisfies the principle which those who participate in it could propose to one another for mutual acceptance in an original position of equal liberty. To see how the two stated principles are quite likely the best candidates for these principles, consider the following analytic construction.

Imagine a society of persons in which a certain system of practices is already established. These persons, let us suppose, are mutually self-interested, that is, their allegiance to their established practices is normally founded on the prospect of self-advantage. One need not suppose that, in all senses of the term "person," the persons in this society are mutually self-interested. The relations between nations, churches, and families is often mutually self-interested even though there is intense loyalty and devotion on the part of individual members. A more realistic conception of such a society might construe its persons as mutually self-interested families or some other association.

Imagine also that these persons are rational: they know their own interests more or less accurately; they are capable of tracing out the likely consequences of adopting one practice rather than another; they are capable of adhering to a course of action once they have decided on it; they can resist present temptations and the enticements of immediate gain; and the bare knowledge or perception of the difference between their condition and that of others is not, within certain limits and in itself, a source of great dissatisfaction. Only the last point adds anything to the usual definition of "rationality." Finally, assume that these persons have roughly similar needs and interests or needs and interests in various ways complementary, so that there exist schemes of cooperation which are mutually advantageous.

Since these persons are conceived as engaging in common practices which are already established, there is no question of our supposing them to be deciding how to set up their institutions from the start. Yet we can imagine them considering whether any of them has a legitimate complaint against their established institutions. Suppose that, in doing this, they try first to arrive at the principles by which complaints and thus institutions themselves are to be judged. They do not begin by registering complaints; instead, they try to settle on the standards by which a complaint is to be counted as legitimate.

Their procedure for this is the following: each person is allowed to propose the principles on which he wishes his own complaints to be tried, this privilege being subject to three conditions. It is understood (1) that, if the principles one proposes are accepted, the complaints of others will be similarly tried; (2) that no one's complaints will be heard until everyone is roughly of one mind as to how complaints are to be judged; and (3) that the principles proposed and acknowledged on any one occasion are binding, failing special circumstances, on all future occasions. Thus, each person will be wary of proposing a principle which would give him a peculiar advantage, in his present circumstances, supposing it to be accepted. Each knows that he will be bound by it in future circumstances, the peculiarities of which cannot be foreseen and which might well be such that the principle is then to his disadvantage. The main idea of the procedure is that everyone be required to make in advance a firm commitment which others also may reasonably be expected to make and that no one be given the opportunity to tailor the canons of a legitimate complaint to fit his own special condition and then to discard them when they no longer suit his purpose. Hence, each will propose principles of a general kind which preclude any attempt to take advantage of particular conditions as they may be known at one time or another. These principles will express the standards in accordance with which each person is the least unwilling to have his interests limited in the design of institutions, on the supposition that the interests of others will be limited in the same way. The restrictions which would so arise may be thought of as those a person would keep in mind if he were designing a social system in which his enemy were to assign him his place.[2]

The elements of this analytic construction can be divided into two parts with the following interpretations. The character and situations of the parties can be taken to represent the special features of circumstances in which questions of justice arise, for these questions arise when conflicting demands are made on the design of an institution and where it is assumed that each person will insist, so far as possible, on what he considers his rights—all of which sets the problem of finding a proper balance, or equilibrium, between these claims. On the other hand, the procedure whereby principles are proposed and acknowledged can be taken to represent the constraints of having a morality. A person who has a morality expresses in his thought and conduct an acceptance of general and universal principles which restricts the pursuit of his own interests. He regards these principles as conclusively binding on himself as well as on others in virtue of his and their nature as human persons. Thus, one's being subjected to the imagined procedure results in constraints analogous to those of having a morality.

There is the following argument for holding that the two principles would be acknowledged given the conditions of the analytic construction. Since there is no way for anyone to win special advantages for himself, each would consider it reasonable to acknowledge the first principle (that of equal liberty) as an initial principle. There is, however, no reason why one should regard this position as final, for, if there are inequalities which satisfy the second principle, the immediate gain which equality would allow can be considered as intelligently invested, in view of its future return. If, as is quite likely, these inequalities work as incentives to better efforts, the members of this society may look on them as concessions to human nature; they, like us, may think that people should ideally want to serve

[2]It will become clear later that this way of putting the matter is appropriate not because persons are assumed to avoid taking chances or to share a pessimistic view of the future, but rather because, in the case of the basic structure of the society in which each must begin, the possibility of a real and equal sharing of risk does not obtain; people have obligations, religious and familial, which restrict the acceptance of risk.

one another. But, since they are mutually self-interested, their acceptance of these inequalities is merely the acceptance of the relations in which they actually stand and a recognition of the motives which lead them to engage in their common practices. They have no title to complain of one another. Provided that the conditions of the principle are met, there is no reason why they should not allow such inequalities. Indeed, it would be shortsighted of them not to do so and could result, in most cases, only from their being dejected by the bare knowledge, or perception, that others are better situated. Each person will, however, insist on an advantage for himself and thus on a common advantage, for none is willing to sacrifice anything for the others.

4.

This argument is not, of course, sufficient to prove that persons conceived and situated as the conjectural account supposes and required to adopt the procedure described would settle on the two principles of justice. For such a proof a more elaborate argument would have to be given. There is, in particular, one natural objection which comes to mind. I wish to consider this objection as a way of introducing the arguments for liberty of the person and liberty of conscience which are founded on justice. Together with the argument of the analytic construction, the discussion of the natural objection is intended as a sketch of a proof of the proposition that, when the logical subject is the fundamental structure of the social system in which everyone must begin, the two principles of justice are those which would be acknowledged when the constraints of having a morality are imposed on rational persons in circumstances which give rise to questions of justice. Since the fundamental structure of the social system is the most important subject of questions of justice, being that part of the social order regulative of the rest, the two principles are not inappropriately referred to as the principles of justice, although there are other principles constitutive of the concept when it is applied to other subjects.

The natural objection to the argument for the two principles is roughly as follows. Suppose that a caste system is defined as one in which society is divided into a number of distinct groups arranged in a definite order of political authority and power, each group having its special occupations, and in which caste membership is hereditary and intermarriage forbidden. In particular, suppose such a system to include a caste of slaves. Given this definition, it does not seem impossible that rational individuals should acknowledge principles which allow of a caste system. Imagine that a group of such individuals finds a caste society already in being and that they are to decide whether to enter it. If the prospect of being in the upper caste greatly attracted them, might not they agree to contract into this society on the condition that their place in it be assigned by a chance device which gives them a certain likelihood of their being placed in the upper caste? It seems possible that they would prefer to take this option rather than to contract into a society satisfying the two principles of justice. (Such a society, I shall call an "open society," in view of the conditions stated in the second principle.) To be sure, such a preference between these two types of society may be unlikely, but it does not seem inconsistent with the notion of rationality. If not, there can be, one might think, no proof that the two principles are, in the sense explained, the principles of justice.

This natural objection rests, however, on a presupposition which does not obtain, namely, that there is the possibility of a real and equal sharing of risks in the case of one's initial place in the basic structure of the social system in which everyone begins. For this reason it fails. Before discussing the place of this presupposition in more detail, it is worthwhile to consider why the preference for a caste system is unlikely. Discussion of this matter will help clarify the nature of the two principles.

The preference for a caste system over an open society may be seen to be unlikely in the following way. Assume, as the first possibility, that the persons in question are human individuals without obligations to any other individuals and that they do not know their own talents and abilities. That is, they have no knowledge of how they will fare in the competition for positions in an open society. There are two main reasons against their agreeing to contract into a caste system. For one thing, whatever chance device is used, the chances must accord with the actual numbers of persons occupying the positions of the system. If but one person in a hundred is in the highest caste, there is but one chance in a hundred of entering it. On any realistic assumption, the likelihood of entering the upper caste is small, and the chance of being in one of the lower castes is high. The other consideration is that an open society may be assumed to be more efficient. Not only is this plausible on theoretical grounds, since a caste system will not place talent where it is most needed or encourage it to make its best contribution, but historical experience seems to support it. Thus, even if a caste society is not less affluent in all corresponding positions, a person's expectation of achieving well-being in a caste society must be less (taking this expectation as given by the expression $\Sigma p_i w_i$, where p_i is the percentage of persons in the ith position and w_i is an index of the average level of well-being of those in the ith position). If these individuals choose between the alternatives on the basis of this expectation, they would not prefer the caste system.[3]

A second possibility is that these individuals do know their talents and abilities. Before, the differences between persons did not enter, and the argument could be carried out from the standpoint of a single representative man. With the knowledge of talents, the case changes, since a gifted person will not evaluate the alternatives in the same way as an ungifted person. An open society must be evaluated according to the series of positions a person may expect to hold in it over time and not simply by the position in which he is likely to start. In the case of a talented person, since he can usually count on improving his place, his expectation

[3]It is not necessary to assume that rational individuals would decide between alternatives on this basis alone. They may well consider such other features of the distribution as variance and range. But making allowance for these possibilities would not, I think, affect the substance of the argument.

is greater than the expectation estimated by initial positions, whereas for the un-talented the opposite is true. Indeed, for one without talents, taking a chance in a caste system may be the only possible way of reaching the higher ranks. To sim-plify things, fix attention on two representative men, one for the upper and one for the lower ranges of ability. Between them there is a possible conflict of interest. If one assumes, in accordance with the conditions of the analytic construction, that unanimity is necessary before these individuals can contract into one society or the other, how is this conflict of interest to be resolved?

If the two principles of justice are acknowledged, the understanding is, in effect, that those favored in the natural lottery (that is, the lottery of native tal-ents and abilities) and who know that they have been favored undertake to gain from their good fortune only on terms that improve the condition of those who have lost out. They are not to win advantages simply because they are more gifted, but only to cover the costs of the necessary efforts of training and cultivating their endowments and for putting them to use in a way which benefits the losers. The more able propose, then, to the less able that the latter give up what is in any case a slight chance for an upper place in a caste system, and in return the more able agree that any inequalities they are to enjoy are for efforts which make a contri-bution to the less gifteds' well-being, so that the less gifted prefer the system with these inequalities. Accepting a society in which the two principles are satisfied is, then, the best way for the less gifted to overcome their misfortune in the natural lottery. The offer of the more gifted man to acknowledge the second principle would probably be accepted, since doing so would strike the ungifted as a fair way to take advantage of the natural fact of differing native endowments. There would, then, most likely be an agreement to contract into the open society.

5.

It is, however, a mistake to reply to the natural objection by showing that, even if it is true, an agreement to enter a caste society is unlikely. As previously noted, one of the assumptions of the natural objection is that there is a real and equal sharing of risks prior to the assignment of one's place in the caste society. But this assumption is not satisfied in the case of the social system in which every-one begins. Arguments which presuppose a real and equal risk are, therefore, without weight against the reasoning of the analytic construction.

That the natural objection does presuppose a real and equal acceptance of risks may be shown quite easily. Suppose that, in a society where slavery exists, a slaveholder were to try to justify his position to his slaves by claiming that, if given an option between a slave society and an open society, he would take his chance on becoming a slaveholder and willingly run the risk of becoming a slave. He may sincerely hold, although he is probably mistaken in doing so, that one's expectation of well-being (as previously defined) is higher for the slave society. On both these grounds, he says that slavery is not unjust and that he is not being unjust in holding slaves and in supporting the institution.

The reply to this is, first, that there has been no actual taking up of options to which everyone agreed and in which real and equal risks were shared. The slaves have had no chance to be anything but slaves, and therefore it is irrelevant what options the slaveholder would accept if certain real chances were offered. Since there has been no equal sharing of risks, the slaveholder's position is an inequality which could not be acknowledged from an original position of equal liberty. Again, it is irrelevant, even if it is true, that the expectation of well-being for a slave society is higher. If slaveholders are so well off that this is so, this is no justification to slaves who have never had any opportunity to reach that position. It is necessary in order for the slaveholder to make his case that, from an initial position of equal liberty, he (and his slaves) should have accepted, at the age of reason, the option of a slave society and should have submitted to the same real chances. One could imagine a society in which those who become slaves are chosen at birth or at some later time by some random device; but in this variant of slavery the slaveholder's case would not be any better. Finally, how is one to know whether the slaveholder is sincere in his claim? Indeed, how is he to know, given the manifest temptations to self-deception? Where sincerity of conviction is essential for the sense of community it cannot be gathered from opinions voiced from positions of secured advantage, but only by everyone's being in a real initial position of equal liberty from which, by reference to principles generally acknowledged, each can justify to every other the position in which he stands. This is the mark of a just society. In a free society, this initial position is represented in real institutions by that of equal citizenship.

It is possible to imagine special forms of slavery which allow of a real and equal risk. Suppose that city-states which previously have not taken prisoners in war but have always put them to death agree by treaty to hold prisoners as slaves instead. Although the concept of justice does not allow justification of the institution of slavery on the grounds that greater gains to some outweigh the losses to others (that is, justice is opposed to the principle of utility), it does allow that an institution may have to be tolerated as necessary or as the best possible advance on previous institutions. In the present special case, assume that these three conditions hold: (1) that the servitude in question is not hereditary, (2) that the citizens of the city-states signing the treaty approved of it, and (3) that the city-states have a roughly similar military force or capacity. Then the form of slavery imagined might even be said not to be unjust. In this case, the slaveholder could say to his slaves that he prefers the present to the previous arrangement and that he does not consider it unjust. He could claim that he has run and continues to run a real and equal risk of becoming a slave himself. As a citizen of his city, he upholds the treaty and has no complaint against it.

This example shows that situations are possible in which there is a real and equal risk of becoming a slave and that in these special cases slavery need not be unjust. (Of course, the historical forms of slavery have not satisfied these conditions, for example, that it not be hereditary. It may therefore be misleading to call the imagined form slavery at all; it might be better to refer to it as a form of contractual servitude.) This is because it satisfies the conditions of the concept of justice, for it is in accordance with what has been mutually acknowledged from an original position of equal liberty. The persons concerned are, by hypothesis, equals as equal citizens of equal city-states, and they have each approved their city joining the treaty. One may, of course, question whether the requisite conditions are ever likely to be satisfied, or whether, if they were satisfied, this form of slavery (or contractual servitude) would not soon be abandoned for a more humane institution, such as the exchange of prisoners. Surely it would be better to have one's loved ones returned than to hold aliens as slaves. But for the moment this is irrelevant. The essential thing is that the equal citizenship of equal city-states permits citizens of these states to do whatever they consent to do as long as they do not infringe on the like liberty of others. If, having this special institution accepted as the best possible advance on previous institutions, they do not abandon it for a more liberal practice, one may think them callous and unfeeling, but one may not think them unjust to one another.

This example is perhaps overly hypothetical, but it illustrates the following point. The correct reply to the natural objection is not to argue that rational individuals, whether or not they know their talents and abilities, would most probably not contract into a caste society. The correct reply is that this objection assumes a real bearing of risk and the possibility of accepting it in connection with our initial position in the social system and that there is no such risk or real possibility. To satisfy the concept of justice, there must then exist in society a position of equal citizenship within which the liberty of the person is secured and which will express in institutions the satisfaction of the first principle. Given this equal liberty, there will exist a position from which the application of the second principle may be discussed and a sense of community maintained.

One can then formulate a further principle as follows. If rational individuals have willingly and knowingly joined a cooperative scheme from an original position of equal liberty (represented by the position of equal citizenship), if they have borne equal risks in doing so, and if they persist in their willing cooperation and have no wish to retract or no complaint to make, then that scheme is fair or at least not unfair (see footnote 3, *supra*). This principle itself would be acknowledged; it is simply an extension of the first principle of justice and permits the establishment of any voluntary scheme which does not interfere with the liberty of those outside it. In view of this principle, which may be referred to as that of free association, an account of the concept of justice need not pass judgment on those forms of cooperation in which rational individuals are willing to engage from a position of equal liberty. In this way, by establishing and preserving a position of original equality and by allowing a liberty to set up cooperative schemes and other associations which may be freely joined, the free decisions of individuals may be left to determine the form of institutions (so far as the concept of justice applies). But, in the case of the basic features of the social system in which each begins (the constitution and the main economic and social forms), the two principles of justice must be satisfied. In the absence of the actual decisions of rational persons under conditions of equal liberty, one must be guided by those principles of which it can be shown that rational persons, when subject to the constraints of morality, would acknowledge them. The principles of hypothetical arrangements which persons might agree to under conditions of real risks are irrelevant.

The discussion of the natural objection may be summarized in the following way. Together with the argument of the analytic construction, this discussion is intended to sketch a proof of the proposition that, when the logical subject is the fundamental structure of the social system in which everyone must begin, the two principles of justice are those which rational persons would acknowledge when subject to the constraints of the concept of morality in circumstances giving rise to questions of justice. But a natural objection to this conjecture is that rational individuals might agree to take a chance on entering a caste system in preference to an open society. They might agree to do this if they each found their expectation of well-being in the caste system sufficiently attractive. Although it is unlikely that they would find it sufficiently attractive, it is not impossible. This objection proposes, in effect, that rational individuals might accept the principle of social utility rather than the two principles as the standard of justice, for, as the measure of expectations was defined, expectations will vary with social utility and will be highest when social utility is maximized.[4]

The refutation of the natural objection is that is presupposes a real risk and the possibility of accepting it in the case of the basic structure of the society in which each must begin, but this presupposition does not hold. Therefore, the natural objection fails as an argument against the two principles as the proper standard of justice in the case of the fundamental form of the social system. Once given a social system satisfying the two principles of justice in its basic structure and so securing an equal liberty of the person, rational individuals may, if they wish, decide which voluntary schemes to engage in by estimating their expectation of well-being. The principle of utility so understood may be used by individuals within the framework of a just society, but it is not the correct principle of justice to apply to the constitution of the social system itself.

Although the natural objection fails as an argument against the two principles of justice, the discussion of its presupposition of the possibility of a real and equal risk has brought out the necessity for a real position of equal liberty in actual institutions. In this way, the concept of justice may be seen to require in the constitution of society liberty of the person and to exclude caste systems and slavery. There is another assumption of the natural objection to which I shall now turn.

---

[4]Recall that the expectation was defined as $\Sigma p_i w_i$, where p_i is the percentage of persons in the ith caste and w_i is the corresponding measure of well-being. Social utility is defined as $\Sigma n_i w_i$, where n_i is the number of persons in the ith caste and w_i the same as before. If $\Sigma n_i = n$ is the total number of persons, the expectation is simply the social utility divided by n. The argument in the text assumes that those outside the society take as welfare indexes those of the groups in the society. Relevant here is Jerome Rothenberg, *The Measurement of Social Welfare* (1961), pp. 267–269. Rothenberg argues that an earlier proposal of Harsanyi's, similar to that of the natural objection, is equivalent to the principle of utility. For this proposal, cf. J.C. Harsanyi, "Cardinal Utility in Welfare Economics and in the Theory of Risk-Taking," *Journal of Political Economy*, LXI (1953), 434–435, and "Cardinal Welfare, Individualistic Ethics, and Interpersonal Comparisons of Utility," *ibid.*, XLIII (1955), 309–321.

The consideration of this assumption will show the manner in which the concept of justice also requires an equal liberty of conscience in the constitution of society.

6.

The second assumption of the natural objection is that the persons who are to acknowledge principles before one another have no obligations, that they are free as individuals to do as they please. If they wish to take a chance on attaining a high place in a caste system, they may do so. But, if the persons in question have obligations as fathers, heads of nations, or of religious sects, the situation changes. Even if a man would, for his part, agree to take a chance on entering a caste system, he cannot and would not be willing to if he is a father and if the position of being lower-caste will be inherited by his children. For a man to face his children, he must insist on the two principles of justice.

The same is true of the heads of religious sects (whether these authorities are represented by a single person, a council, or whatnot). They cannot take chances with the future of their religion. For heads of churches to conduct themselves in any other way would imply, given the concept of religion, that they do not take their religion seriously. If one supposes them to gamble winner take all, as two autocrats might gamble for the rule of certain territories or city-states, they could not be taken as religious persons. They might, perhaps, regard themselves as possessors of certain means of influence to which they had proprietary rights and which they could dispose of as their interests required. Admittedly, the concept of religion might be specified in various ways, but any plausible determination of it would imply that a person under a religious obligation must regard this obligation as binding absolutely in the sense that he cannot qualify his fulfillment of it for the sake of personal advantage. In particular, the obligation to preserve the truth of one's religion and the obligation to live up to its injunctions cannot be compromised for the sake of secular interests.

It might be argued that religious bodies could not acknowledge any principles at all which would limit their pressing their claims on one another. The obligation to religious truth and divine law being absolute, no understanding among persons of different religions is permissible from a religious point of view. Certainly, religious sects have often acted as if they accepted this doctrine. There is no need, however, to argue against it. One may simply observe that, if any principle can be acknowledged, it must be that of equal religious liberty, since the concept of religion is such that each understands that he could not expect another to accept less than an equal liberty. A person may think that another ought to belong to the same faith that he does and that by not doing so the other person is in mortal error. But anyone understanding the concept of religious obligation cannot expect another of a different faith to accept without coercion less than an equal liberty. Much less can it be expected that another will permit him to be the arbiter of the proper interpretation of religious obligations. One may add that, if God wills justice among men (as expressed by the concept of justice as fairness) and if God prefers the worship of men in a free society, then acknowledging an equal liberty is surely permissible, even given the absolute character of religious obligations. In this way, the argument for liberty of conscience from justice may be supported on theological grounds.

These conclusions are further supported by recalling that the relevant acknowledgment is not that which would be made by representatives of religious sects, but that which would be accepted between members of differing sects as citizens. If one supposes that the fundamental position is that of citizenship, then one should ask what rational individuals in the original position could acknowledge as principles to regulate the liberties of the citizen. In this case, it is equally clear that they can acknowledge only an equal liberty of conscience and that this initial position must be final. If each person is thought to regard himself as in general subject to religious obligations (although he may expect that these obligations will change over his life if his religious views change), then he can only acknowledge the principle of equal religious freedom; otherwise he would be violating his interpretation of his religious obligations. A person can accept a less-than-equal religious liberty only if there is a threat of coercion which it seems unwise to resist from the standpoint of these obligations. That is, without resistance, the prospect is that one's religion will be tolerated, but resistance will bring greater repression.

Once each understands that a less-than-equal liberty can be acquiesced in only under these conditions, it will be recognized that equal liberty of conscience is the only principle which can be acknowledged from an original position of equal liberty and thus is the principle which must regulate the liberties of the fundamental office of citizen. It is the only principle which is consistent with a sense of community, for, where there is not equal liberty of conscience, the religious convictions of some citizens are given a priority which those citizens not so privileged cannot acknowledge consistent with their own beliefs. They can only acquiesce in their inferior status under a threat to resist which would put their religion in jeopardy. A sense of community, insofar as it depends upon the concept of justice, is possible only where the rights and privileges of all can be acknowledged by each without anyone's being required to violate what he understands to be his obligations. The principles of justice and in particular equal liberty of conscience (as a special case of the first principle) are the only possible principles in matters of religious toleration which, given the concept of religion, are consistent with a sense of community.

It is now possible to comment on why it is characteristic of the constitutional liberties that they must be equal; why, in respect to these liberties as defined by the structure of the social system in which each begins, no one can be favored. Their role is to mark off and to define a part of the social structure distinct from that part which allows differences in rights and powers and a varied distribution of good things in accordance with the second principle. Roughly, the distinction between these two parts of the social structure is that the first part—the constitutional liberties—expresses in institutions the original position of equal liberty; it represents the position from which the application of the second principle may proceed among persons secure in their fundamental equality. The second part of the social structure contains those distinctions and hierarchies of political, economic, and social forms necessary for the efficient and mutually beneficial arrangement of joint activities; but such distinctions can be acknowledged only in matters of secular and personal interests or, roughly speaking, in matters of welfare.

Given these equal liberties and certain other conditions secured by institutions—in particular, equality of opportunity and a social minimum—any one of a wide range of distributions of good things taking place as a consequence of legitimate inequalities of the second part of the social structure is acceptable to justice. In this way, the social structure provides the latitude necessary in the performance of a well-ordered society.[5] The unifying feature, then, of the constitutional liberties is that they are equal liberties. They are essential features of the position of equal citizenship and as such define the first and primary part of the social structure in a way which is necessary for a sense of community.

7.

Suppose, then, that the concept of justice permits these arguments for an equal liberty of conscience as found in a constitutional democracy. The existence of this liberty means that, according to the constitution, there is freedom of religious belief, worship, and conduct save as limited by the state's interest in public order and security, that the state will favor no particular religion, and that no penalties or disabilities, as expressed in political or legal rights, are attached to any religious affiliation or lack thereof. Particular religious associations may be organized as the members wish and may have their internal discipline, subject to the restriction that members be given the choice of affiliation in the sense that the public order provide the right of sanctuary, that is, that apostasy is not recognized, much less penalized, as a legal offense. In this way, the state secures the original position of equal liberty expressed in institutions by the office of equal citizenship.

Liberty of conscience is limited, everyone agrees, by the state's interest in public order and security. This limitation also is readily derivable from the concept of justice; it does not presuppose the notion that public interests are superior to private (or to ecclesiastical) interests. The acceptance of this limitation does not

---

[5]The essential idea here is that the problem of distributive justice, in the case of the basic structure of the social system, should be viewed as a problem of distributing or assigning rights in the design of the general systems of rules defining and regulating economic activities. It is not a problem of distributing given amounts of income or batches of goods to given individuals with certain patterns of tastes and wants. If one assumes that law and government effectively act to keep markets competitive, resources fully employed, property and wealth widely distributed over time, and maintain a reasonable social minimum, then, if there is equality of opportunity, the resulting distribution will be just or at least not unjust. It will have resulted from the workings of a just system, one against which no one can complain, since it would satisfy principles acknowledged in the original position. For example, since it cannot be supposed that everyone will have sufficient private wealth to tide him over disasters that may befall him, a social minimum is simply a form of rational insurance and prudence. Given a just system, one need not complain or worry about particular outcomes.

imply that the state is prepared to ignore private or religious matters as things indifferent or to claim the right to suppress or curb them when they conflict with its own affairs. Rather, given the concept of justice as here understood, the state is viewed as the association of citizens to regulate their pursuit of their profoundest interests and their fulfillment of their most solemn obligations and to give form to their relations in a manner acceptable to each from an original position of equal liberty.

From this position, each recognizes that an interference with the security of public order is an infringement on the liberty of all. This follows once the maintenance of the public order is understood as a necessary condition for every person's achieving his ends (whatever they are, within certain limits) and for his fulfilling his interpretation of his obligations which all would have a right to do if anyone did. To limit liberty of conscience at the boundary, however inexact, of the state's interest as expressed in the police power is a limit derived from the principle of equal liberty itself; it marks the limit acceptable to those in an original and equal position as being the terms on which persons so placed as the analytic construction supposes would agree and acknowledge before one another. In this conception, then, the state's right to maintain public order is derivative; it is an enabling right, a right which it must have if it is to carry out its duty of impartially supporting the conditions necessary for everyone's pursuing his interests and fulfilling his obligations as he understands them.

Again, liberty of conscience is to be limited only when there is a reasonable expectation that not doing so will interfere with the security of public order; this expectation must be established by evidence and ways of reasoning acceptable to common sense, that is, by observable and provable consequences and by modes of thought which are generally recognized as correct. This reliance on the methods of common sense (and on the methods of rational scientific inquiry generally, where they are not controversial) and this limitation on what can be established and known by all does not imply any particular metaphysical doctrine as to the nature of the world. It does not imply, for example, that what exists is only what can be observed or evidenced by commonsense methods of investigation or that everything is, in some sense, a logical construction of what can be observed or evidenced by rational scientific inquiry. Such a metaphysical view is, one may suppose, sufficient to derive the reasonableness of this restriction to what can be established by common sense; it is not, however, necessary.

Rather, the acceptance of the standard of reasonable expectation as that of common sense is required by the concept of justice, for it is an appeal to what everyone can accept, if any principle can be accepted, in an original position of equal liberty. It is an appeal only to what in fact all have in common in their knowledge and understanding of the world, so that the acceptance of this standard does not infringe on the equal liberty of anyone. A departure from the principles of common sense would involve giving a privileged place to the views of some over others which could not be acknowledged in the original position. Finally, in holding that the consequences for the security of public order should not be merely possible or even probable, but reasonably certain and imminent, there is no implication of any particular philosophical analysis of the concept of knowledge, for this requirement may be understood as an expression of the high place which everyone must accord liberty of conscience and the urgency of religious obligations.

It follows, then, from the concept of justice as applied to the fundamental structure of the social system in which each must begin, that there should be equal liberty of conscience limited only where common sense establishes a reasonably certain interference with the essentials of public order. By this elementary principle alone, many grounds of intolerance given in past ages may be rejected as fallacious. Thus, Aquinas accepted the death penalty for heretics on the ground that it is a far graver matter to corrupt the faith, which is the life of the soul, than to falsify money, which sustains life.[6] So, if it is just to put to death forgers and other criminals, heretics may a fortiori be so dealt with. But the premises on which Aquinas relies cannot be established by the methods of common sense. It is a matter of dogma that faith, as the Roman Church defines it, is the life of the soul and that the suppression of heresy—that is, departures from orthodoxy in defiance of ecclesiastical authority—is necessary for the safety of souls.

Again, the grounds given for limited toleration often run afoul of this elementary principle. Thus, Rousseau thought that people would find it impossible to live in peace with those they regard as damned, for to love them would be to hate God, who punishes them. One who regards another as damned must either reclaim or torment him. Rousseau believed that those who regard others as damned cannot, then, be trusted to preserve civil peace, and he would not tolerate, therefore, those religions which say that outside their church there is no salvation. But the consequences of dogmatic belief which Rousseau conjectures are not borne out by experience; however plausible the a priori psychological argument may be, toleration must not, to accord with the concept of justice, be abandoned on anything but consequences securely established.[7] There is, however, this difference between Rousseau and such others as Bayle and Locke, who advocated a limited toleration, on one side, and Aquinas and the Protestant reformers, on the other, namely, that they limited toleration on the basis of what they supposed were clear and evident consequences for the security of public order. More experience would presumably have convinced them that they were mistaken. With Aquinas and the Protestant reformers, the grounds for intolerance are themselves matters of faith, and this difference is more fundamental than the limits actually drawn to toleration. One view recognizes the priority of principles which can be acknowledged in an original position of equal liberty, whereas the latter does not.

That religious liberty is limited by the necessity of securing public order but that its interference with the public order must be established by the principles of common sense is a principle itself derivable from the concept of justice. In acknowledging this principle, one does not commit oneself either to a particular metaphysical view of the world or to a particular philosophical account of knowledge. One is, rather, committed to it by the requirements of justice.

---

[6]Cf. *Summa Theologica* II–ii. Qu. 11. Art. 3.
[7]Cf. *The Social Contract* iv. 8.

8.

Finally, one may ask whether the concept of justice implies that a religious sect which rejects the principle of equal liberty should itself be tolerated, that is, given that constitutional liberty which it would deny, had it the means, to others. There may certainly be many reasons for toleration; for example, it may be impossible, if the sect is strong in numbers and influence, not to tolerate it without a divisive civil conflict. But I am concerned with reasons of justice alone.

Several questions must be distinguished—first, whether the intolerant sect would have any title to complain if it were not tolerated; second, whether the tolerant sects have a right not to tolerate the intolerant sect; and, finally, whether, having the right, it should be exercised? In considering the first question, it seems that the intolerant sect has no title to complain. This follows if it is assumed that a person has no title to complain of conduct of others toward him which is in accordance with principles which he would, in similar circumstances, follow in his conduct toward them. A person's right to complain is limited to violations of principles which he himself acknowledges. It may be said that members of the intolerant sect profess the principles that God should be obeyed and truth accepted by all. Their complaint, then, is that they but not others act on this principle.

The reply is that, from the standpoint of the original position, no particular sectarian interpretation of religious truth could be acknowledged as binding on citizens. In that position, each person must insist on an equal right to understand what religion requires of him. Thus, the right to complain is further limited to violations of those principles which one accepts and which would be acknowledged in a position of equal liberty. An intolerant sect would not, it seems, have title to complain; its representative member claims, as a citizen, an authority to determine what is true and binding in matters religious which would not be acknowledged and which he would not grant to another in the original position.

Because the intolerant sects do not have a right to complain, it does not, I think, follow that tolerant sects have a right to suppress them. For one thing, others may have a right to complain. To simplify the question, assume that the tolerant sects would have the right not to tolerate the intolerant sects in at least one circumstance, namely, when they sincerely and with reason believe it necessary for their own security. This right follows readily enough from the concept of justice, for, as the circumstances giving rise to questions of justice are defined, no one is required to watch idly while the basis of his existence is destroyed. Therefore, what is in question is the wider restraint, that is, whether there is a right on the part of tolerant sects to curb the intolerant when they are of no danger to the equal liberties of others. This question should be answered from the point of view of the tolerant sects and on the assumption that they each accept the principles constitutive of the concept of justice. It is then clear, I think, that they would not regard themselves as having any such right.

An intolerant sect may be said to authorize others to suppress it in the sense that it cannot complain should it be suppressed. But why should the just act on the authorizations of the unjust? Do the just enjoy, as it were, suppressing the unjust? On the contrary, acceptance of the concept of justice as the basis of a free society requires one to act so far as possible to establish justice throughout society. This means that the fundamental position of equal citizenship, with all its constitutional liberties, should be upheld as far as possible without putting liberty itself in danger. It is from the position of equal citizenship that persons join the various sects, and it is from this position that persons should view one another. However intransigent ecclesiastics and theologians may be, their strength depends in part on the convictions and numbers of the laity. Citizens in a free society should not be held by one another incapable of a sense of justice failing a clear necessity for doing so. Justice and equal liberty of conscience should be upheld to persuade the intolerant (that is, those citizens who belong to the intolerant sect) to justice, this persuasion working on the psychological principle that, other things equal, those whose liberties are secured by a just system will acquire an allegiance to it. The intolerant ecclesiastic is, then, secure through the rights of the citizens whose institutions of faith he administers and whose rights and capacities for justice cannot without the most urgent of reasons be denied.

The conclusion, then, is that an intolerant sect does not itself have title to complain of intolerance and that, although tolerant sects have a right not to tolerate an intolerant sect when they sincerely and with reason believe that their own security and that of the institution of liberty is in danger, they have this right only in this case. What must be the principle of their action is the concept of justice, which requires the establishment for all of the position of equal citizenship with an equal liberty of conscience. The just must be guided by the concept of justice and not by the authorizations of the unjust. They are bound above all else to see that just institutions flourish, and they must not punish the unjust simply because the unjust cannot reproach them.

9.

So much, then, for a brief and all-too-abstract discussion of the arguments derivable from the concept of justice for the two constitutional liberties—liberty of the person and liberty of conscience. What does this discussion suggest is the special sense of the concept of justice, as distinct from other moral concepts? In particular, how does the concept of justice differ from the concept of social utility? I should like to think that the discussion confirms the initial idea that, as applied to social institutions, the sense of the concept of justice is essentially that of the elimination of arbitrary distinctions and the establishment within the structure of an institution of a proper balance, share, or equilibrium between the competing claims of persons prepared to press their rights on one another and that the general characterization of the principles constitutive of the concept is that they are the principles which rational persons, when subject to the constraints of morality, would propose and acknowledge before one another in an original position of equal liberty. This characterization states the just way of defining and limiting people's rights with respect to one another in their claims on institutions, and an institution is just only if it satisfies principles which could be so accepted. If the argument of the analytic construction is correct, it follows that the basic structure of the social system in which everyone begins must satisfy the two principles of justice and therefore that these principles may without impropriety be called the principles of justice.

The peculiar feature of the concept of justice is that it treats each person as an equal sovereign, as it were, and requires a unanimous acknowledgment from a certain original position of equal liberty. This is a strong condition, ostensibly too strong. I have tried to show, by examining the arguments for liberty, that it works out well enough. In contrast to the conception of social utility, the concept of justice excludes the possibility of arguing that the violations of the claims of some is justified (rendered just) by compensating advantages to others. If there is any disadvantage which cannot be acknowledged, an institution is unjust.

The concept of justice is distinct from that of social utility in that justice takes the plurality of persons as fundamental, whereas the notion of social utility does not. The latter seeks to maximize some one thing, it being indifferent in which way it is shared among persons except insofar as it affects this one thing itself. The conception of utility extends the principle of rational choice for one person to the case where there is a plurality of persons, for one person may properly count his advantages now as compensating for his own losses earlier or subsequently, but justice excludes the analogous kind of reasoning between persons. The plurality of persons must construct among themselves the principles in accordance with which they are to decide between institutions, and the general characterization of the circumstances of this construction and the respective positions of persons within it is given by the analytic framework by which the two principles of justice were derived. Moreover, a necessary condition for the moral worth of the people of any society is that they be moved by the principles of such a construction, however hypothetical.

A strong case can be made for the view that the arguments for constitutional liberties founded on the concept of justice are the most fundamental ones and that these arguments ought to be recognized as the surest basis of a free society. It is both unwise and unnecessary to found liberty of conscience and freedom of thought on, say, indifference to religion or philosophical skepticism. These are at best fragile bases for these liberties. They are open to theological and philosophical objection and cannot attain a wide measure of assent in a free society, where diversity of opinion is to be expected. But an examination of the essential parts of the concept of justice as fairness would show, I think, that it is not impossible that a broad understanding might be reached on this concept and on its constitutive principles and thus on the general constraints and forms which the concept requires in the framework of the social structure.

Aristotle thought that it was a peculiarity of man that he had a sense of the just and the unjust and that participation in a common understanding of justice makes a *polis*. [8] Analogously, one might show that participation in the understanding of justice as fairness makes a constitutional democracy.

[8] Cf. *Politics* i. 2. 1253^{a}15.

Rights, Human Rights, and Racial Discrimination[1]

•

Richard Wasserstrom

The subject of natural, or human, rights is one that has recently come to enjoy a new-found intellectual and philosophical respectability. This has come about in part, I think, because of a change in philosophical mood—in philosophical attitudes and opinions toward topics in moral and political theory. And this change in mood has been reflected in a renewed interest in the whole subject of rights and duties. In addition, though, this renaissance has been influenced, I believe, by certain events of recent history—notably the horrors of Nazi Germany and the increasingly obvious injustices of racial discrimination in both the United States and Africa. For in each case one of the things that was or is involved is a denial of certain human rights.

This concern over the subject of natural rights, whatever the causes may be, is, however, in the nature of a reinstatement. Certainly there was, just a relatively few years ago, fairly general agreement that the doctrine of natural rights had been thoroughly and irretrievably discredited. Indeed, this was sometimes looked upon as the paradigm case of the manner in which a moral and political doctrine could be both rhetorically influential and intellectually inadequate and unacceptable. A number of objections, each deemed absolutely disposative, had been put forward: the vagueness of almost every formulation of a set of natural rights, the failure of persons to agree upon what one's natural rights are, the ease with which almost everyone would acknowledge the desirability of overriding or

From *The Journal of Philosophy*, Vol. LXI (October 29, 1964), 628–641. Reprinted with permission of the author and *The Journal of Philosophy*.

[1]Presented in a symposium on "Human Rights" at the sixty-first annual meeting of the American Philosophical Association, Eastern Division, December 27, 1964.

disregarding any proffered natural rights in any one of a variety of readily familiar circumstances, the lack of any ground or argument for any doctrine of natural rights.

Typical is the following statement from J. B. Mabbott's little book, *The State and the Citizen:*[2]

> [T]he niceties of the theory [of natural rights] need not detain us if we can attack it at its roots, and there it is most clearly vulnerable. Natural rights must be self-evident and they must be absolute if they are to be rights at all. For if a right is derivative from a more fundamental right, then it is not natural in the sense intended; and if a right is to be explained or defended by reference to the good of the community or of the individual concerned, then these "goods" are the ultimate values in the case, and their pursuit may obviously infringe or destroy the "rights" in question. Now the only way in which to demonstrate the absurdity of a theory which claims self-evidence for every article of its creed is to make a list of the articles. . . .
>
> Not only are the lists indeterminate and capricious in extent, they are also confused in content. . . . [T]here is no single "natural right" which is, in fact, regarded even by its own supporters as sacrosanct. Every one of them is constantly invaded in the public interest with universal approval (57–58).

Mabbott's approach to the problem is instructive both as an example of the ease with which the subject has been taken up and dismissed, and more importantly, as a reminder of the fact that the theory of natural rights has not been a single coherent doctrine. Instead, it has served, and doubtless may still serve, as a quite indiscriminate collection of a number of logically independent propositions. It is, therefore, at least as necessary here as in many other situations that we achieve considerable precision in defining and describing the specific subject of inquiry.

This paper is an attempt to delineate schematically the form of one set of arguments for natural, or human rights.[3] I do this in the following fashion. First, I consider several important and distinctive features and functions of rights in general. Next, I describe and define certain characteristics of human rights and certain specific functions and attributes that they have. Then, I delineate and evaluate one kind of argument for human rights, as so described and defined. And finally, I analyze one particular case of a denial of human rights—that produced by the system of racial discrimination as it exists in the South today.

---

[2]London: Arrow, 1958.

[3]Because the phrase 'natural rights' is so encrusted with certain special meanings, I shall often use the more neutral phrase 'human rights'. For my purposes there are no differences in meaning between the two expressions.

I

If there are any such things as human rights, they have certain important characteristics and functions just because rights themselves are valuable and distinctive moral "commodities." This is, I think, a point that is all too often overlooked whenever the concept of a right is treated as a largely uninteresting, derivative notion—one that can be taken into account in wholly satisfactory fashion through an explication of the concepts of duty and obligation.[4]

Now, it is not my intention to argue that there can be rights for which there are no correlative duties, nor that there can be duties for which there are no correlative rights—although I think that there are, e.g., the duty to be kind to animals or the duty to be charitable. Instead, what I want to show is that there are important differences between rights and duties, and, in particular, that rights fulfill certain functions that neither duties (even correlative duties) nor any other moral or legal concepts can fulfill.

Perhaps the most obvious thing to be said about rights is that they are constitutive of the domain of entitlements. They help to define and serve to protect those things concerning which one can make a very special kind of claim—a claim of right. To claim or to acquire anything as a matter of right is crucially different from seeking or obtaining it as through the grant of a privilege, the receipt of a favor, or the presence of a permission. To have a right to something is, typically, to be entitled to receive or possess or enjoy it now,[5] and to do so without securing the consent of another. As long as one has a right to anything, it is beyond the reach of another properly to withhold or deny it. In addition, to have a right is to be absolved from the obligation to weigh a variety of what would in other contexts be relevant considerations; it is to be entitled to the object of the right—at least *prima facie*—without any more ado. To have a right to anything is, in short, to have a very strong moral or legal claim upon it. It is the strongest kind of claim that there is.

Because this is so, it is apparent, as well, that the things to which one is entitled as a matter of right are not usually trivial or insignificant. The objects of rights are things that matter.

Another way to make what are perhaps some of the same points is to observe that rights provide special kinds of grounds or reasons for making moral judgments of at least two kinds. First, if a person has a right to something, he can properly cite that right as the *justification* for having acted in accordance with or in the exercise of that right. If a person has acted so as to exercise his right, he has, without more ado, acted rightly—at least *prima facie*. To exercise one's right is to

---

[4]See, for example, S. I. Benn and R. S. Peters, *Social Principles and the Democratic State*, p. 89: "Right and duty are different names for the same normative relation, according to the point of view from which it is regarded."

[5]There are some rights as to which the possession of the object of the right can be claimed only at a future time, e.g., the right (founded upon a promise) to be repaid next week.

act in a way that gives appreciable assurance of immunity from criticism. Such immunity is far less assured when one leaves the areas of rights and goes, say, to the realm of the permitted or the nonprohibited.

And second, just as exercising or standing upon one's rights by itself needs no defense, so invading or interfering with or denying another's rights is by itself appropriate ground for serious censure and rebuke. Here there is a difference in emphasis and import between the breach or neglect of a duty and the invasion of or interference with a right. For to focus upon duties and their breaches is to concentrate necessarily upon the person who has the duty; it is to invoke criteria by which to make moral assessments of his conduct. Rights, on the other hand, call attention to the injury inflicted; to the fact that the possessor of the right was adversely affected by the action. Furthermore, the invasion of a right constitutes, as such, a special and independent injury, whereas this is not the case with less stringent claims.

Finally, just because rights are those moral commodities which delineate the areas of entitlement, they have an additional important function: that of defining the respects in which one can reasonably entertain certain kinds of expectations. To live in a society in which there are rights and in which rights are generally respected is to live in a society in which the social environment has been made appreciably more predictable and secure. It is to be able to count on receiving and enjoying objects of value. Rights have, therefore, an obvious psychological, as well as moral, dimension and significance.

II

If the above are some of the characteristics and characteristic functions of rights in general, what then can we say about human rights? More specifically, what is it for a right to be a human right, and what special role might human rights play?

Probably the simplest thing that might be said of a human right is that it is a right possessed by human beings. To talk about human rights would be to distinguish those rights which humans have from those which nonhuman entities, e.g., animals or corporations, might have.

It is certain that this is not what is generally meant by human rights. Rather than constituting the genus of all particular rights that humans have, human rights have almost always been deemed to be one species of these rights. If nothing else about the subject is clear, it is evident that one's particular legal rights, as well as some of one's moral rights, are not among one's human rights. If any right is a *human* right, it must, I believe, have at least four very general characteristics. First, it must be possessed by all human beings, as well as only by human beings. Second, because it is the same right that all human beings possess, it must be possessed equally by all human beings. Third, because human rights are possessed by all human beings, we can rule out as possible candidates any of those rights which one might have in virtue of occupying any particular status or relationship, such as that of parent, president, or promisee. And fourth, if there are any human rights, they have the additional characteristic of being assertable, in a manner of speaking, "against the whole world." That is to say, because they are rights that are not possessed in virtue of any contingent status or relationship, they are rights that can be claimed equally against any and every other human being.

Furthermore, to repeat, if there are any human *rights,* they also have certain characteristics as rights. Thus, if there are any human rights, these constitute the strongest of all moral claims that all men can assert. They serve to define and protect those things which all men are entitled to have and enjoy. They indicate those objects toward which and those areas within which every human being is entitled to act without securing further permission or assent. They function so as to put certain matters beyond the power of anyone else to grant or to deny. They provide every human being with a ready justification for acting in certain ways, and they provide each person with ready grounds upon which to condemn any interference or invasion. And they operate, as well, to induce well-founded confidence that the values or objects protected by them will be readily and predictably obtainable. If there are any human rights, they are powerful moral commodities.

Finally, it is, perhaps, desirable to observe that there are certain characteristics I have not ascribed to these rights. In particular, I have not said that human rights need have either of two features: absoluteness and self-evidence, which Mabbott found to be most suspect. I have not said that human rights are absolute in the sense that there are no conditions under which they can properly be overridden, although I have asserted—what is quite different—that they are absolute in the sense that they are possessed equally without any special, additional qualification by all human beings.[6]

Neither have I said (nor do I want to assert) that human rights are self-evident in any sense. Indeed, I want explicitly to deny that a special manner of knowing or a specific epistemology is needed for the development of a theory of human rights. I want to assert that there is much that can be said in defense or support of the claim that a particular right is a human right. And I want to insist, as well, that to adduce reasons for human rights is consistent with their character as human, or natural, rights. Nothing that I have said about human rights entails a contrary conclusion.

III

To ask whether there are any human, or natural rights is to pose a potentially misleading question. Rights of any kind, and particularly natural rights,

---

[6]For the purposes of this paper and the points I wish here to make, I am not concerned with whether human rights are *prima facie* or absolute. I do not think that anything I say depends significantly upon this distinction. Without analyzing the notion, I will assume, though, that they are *prima facie* rights in the sense that there may be cases in which overriding a human right would be less undesirable than protecting it.

are not like chairs or trees. One cannot simply look and see whether they are there. There are, though, at least two senses in which rights of all kinds can be said to exist. There is first the sense in which we can ask and answer the empirical question of whether in a given society there is intellectual or conceptual acknowledgment of the fact that persons or other entities have rights at all. We can ask, that is, whether the persons in that society "have" the concept of a right (or a human right), and whether they regard that concept as meaningfully applicable to persons or other entities in that society. And there is, secondly, the sense in which we can ask the question, to what extent, in a society that acknowledges the existence of rights, is there general respect for, protection of, or noninterference with the exercise of those rights.[7]

These are not, though, the only two questions that can be asked. For we can also seek to establish whether any rights, and particularly human rights, ought to be both acknowledged and respected. I want now to begin to do this by considering the way in which an argument for human rights might be developed.

It is evident, I think, that almost any argument for the acknowledgment of any rights as human rights starts with the factual assertion that there are certain respects in which all persons are alike or equal. The argument moves typically from that assertion to the conclusion that there are certain human rights. What often remains unclear, however, is the precise way in which the truth of any proposition about the respects in which persons are alike advances an argument for the acknowledgment of human rights. And what must be supplied, therefore, are the plausible intermediate premises that connect the initial premise with the conclusion.

One of the most careful and complete illustrations of an argument that does indicate some of these intermediate steps is that provided by Gregory Vlastos in an article entitled, "Justice and Equality."[8] Our morality, he says, puts an equal intrinsic value on each person's well-being and freedom. In detail, the argument goes like this:

There is, Vlastos asserts, a wide variety of cases in which all persons are capable of experiencing the same values.

> *Thus, to take a perfectly clear case, no matter how A and B might differ in taste and style of life, they would both crave relief from acute physical pain. In that case we would put the same value on giving this to either of them, regardless of the fact that A might be a talented, brilliantly successful person, B "a mere nobody". . . . [I]n all cases where human beings are capable of enjoying the same goods, we feel that the intrinsic value of their enjoyment is the same. In just this sense we hold that (1) one man's well-being is as valuable as any other's. . . .*

[7]This is an important distinction. Incontinence in respect to rights is a fairly common occurrence. In the South, for example, many persons might acknowledge that Negroes have certain rights while at the same time neglecting or refusing (out of timidity, cowardice, or general self-interest) to do what is necessary to permit these rights to be exercised.

[8]In Richard B. Brandt, ed., *Social Justice* (Englewood Cliffs, N.J.: Prentice-Hall, 1962), pp. 31–72.

> [*Similarly*] *we feel that choosing for oneself what one will do, believe,*
> *approve, say, read, worship, has its own intrinsic value, the same for*
> *all persons, and quite independently of the value of the things they hap-*
> *pen to choose. Naturally we hope that all of them will make the best*
> *possible use of their freedom of choice. But we value their exercise of the*
> *freedom, regardless of the outcome; and we value it equally for all. For*
> *us (2) one man's freedom is as valuable as any other's. . . . [Thus],*
> *since we do believe in equal value as to human well-being and freedom,*
> *we should also believe in the* prima facie *equality of men's right to well-*
> *being and to freedom (51–52).*

As it is stated, I am not certain that this argument answers certain kinds of attack. In particular, there are three questions that merit further attention. First, why should anyone have a right to the enjoyment of any goods at all, and, more specifically, well-being and freedom? Second, for what reasons might we be warranted in believing that the intrinsic value of the enjoyment of such goods is the same for all persons? And third, even if someone ought to have a right to well-being and freedom and even if the intrinsic value of each person's enjoyment of these things is equal, why should all men have the equal right—and hence the human right—to secure, obtain, or enjoy these goods?

I think that the third question is the simplest of the three to answer. If anyone has a right to well-being and freedom and if the intrinsic value of any person's enjoyment of these goods is equal to that of any other's, then all men do have an equal right—and hence a human right—to secure, obtain, or enjoy these goods, just because it would be irrational to distinguish among persons as to the possession of these rights. That is to say, the principle that no person should be treated differently from any or all other persons unless there is some general and relevant reason that justifies this difference in treatment is a fundamental principle of morality, if not of rationality itself. Indeed, although I am not certain how one might argue for this, I think it could well be said that all men do have a "second-order" human right—that is, an absolute right—to expect all persons to adhere to this principle.

This principle, or this right, does not by itself establish that there are any specific human rights. But either the principle or the right does seem to establish that well-being and freedom are human rights if they are rights at all and if the intrinsic value of each person's enjoyment is the same. For, given these premises, it does appear to follow that there is no relevant and general reason to differentiate among persons as to the possession of this right.

I say "seem to" and "appear to" because this general principle of morality may not be strong enough. What has been said so far does not in any obvious fashion rule out the possibility that there is some general and relevant principle of differentiation. It only, apparently, rules out possible variations in intrinsic value as a reason for making differentiations.

The requirement of *relevance* does, I think, seem to make the argument secure. For, if *the reason* for acknowledging in a person a right to freedom and well-being is the intrinsic value of his enjoyment of these goods, then the nature of the intrinsic value of any other person's enjoyment is the only relevant reason for making exceptions or for differentiating among persons as to the possession of these rights.[9]

As to the first question, that of whether a person has a right to well-being and freedom, I am not certain what kind of answer is most satisfactory. If Vlastos is correct in asserting that these enjoyments are *values*, then that is, perhaps, answer enough. That is to say, if enjoying well-being is something *valuable*—and especially if it is intrinsically valuable—then it seems to follow that this is the kind of thing to which one ought to have a right. For if anything ought to be given the kind of protection afforded by a right, it ought surely be that which is valuable. Perhaps, too, there is nothing more that need be said other than to point out that we simply do properly value well-being and freedom.

I think that another, more general answer is also possible. Here I would revert more specifically to my earlier discussion of some of the characteristics and functions of rights. There are two points to be made. First, if we are asked, why ought anyone have a right to anything? or why not have a system in which there are not rights at all? the answer is that such a system would be a morally impoverished one. It would prevent persons from asserting those kinds of claims, it would preclude persons from having those types of expectations, and it would prohibit persons from making those kinds of judgments which a system of rights makes possible.

Thus, if we can answer the question of why have rights at all, we can then ask and answer the question of what things—among others—ought to be protected by *rights*. And the answer, I take it, is that one ought to be able to claim as entitlements those minimal things without which it is impossible to develop one's capabilities and to live a life as a human being. Hence, to take one thing that is a precondition of well-being, the relief from acute physical pain, this is the kind of enjoyment that ought to be protected as a right of some kind just because without such relief there is precious little that one can effectively do or become. And similarly for the opportunity to make choices, examine beliefs, and the like.

To recapitulate. The discussion so far has indicated two things: (1) the conditions under which any specific right would be a human right, and (2) some possible grounds for arguing that certain values or enjoyments ought to be regarded as matters of right. The final question that remains is whether there are any specific rights that satisfy the conditions necessary to make them human rights. Or, more specifically, whether it is plausible to believe that there are no general and relevant principles that justify making distinctions among persons in respect to their rights to well-being and freedom.

[9]See, e.g., Bernard Williams, "The Idea of Equality," in P. Laslett and W. G. Runciman, eds., *Philosophy, Politics and Society*, II (Oxford: Basil Blackwell, 1962), pp. 111–113.
Professor Vlastos imposes a somewhat different requirement which, I think, comes to about the same thing: "An equalitarian concept of justice may admit just inequalities without inconsistency if, and only if, it provides grounds for equal human rights *which are also grounds for unequal rights of other sorts*" (Vlastos, *op. cit.*, p. 40; italics in text).

Vlastos has it that the rights to well-being and freedom do satisfy these conditions, since he asserts that we, at least, do regard each person's well-being and freedom as having equal intrinsic value. If this is correct, if each person's well-being and freedom do have *equal* intrinsic value, then there is no general and relevant principle for differentiating among persons as to these values and, hence, as to their rights to secure these values. But this does not seem wholly satisfactory. It does not give us any reason for supposing that it is plausible to ascribe equal intrinsic value to each person's well-being and freedom.

The crucial question, then, is the plausibility of ascribing equal intrinsic value to each person's well-being and freedom. There are, I think, at least three different answers that might be given.

First, it might be asserted that this ascription simply constitutes another feature of our morality. The only things that can be done are to point out that this is an assumption that we do make and to ask persons whether they would not prefer to live in a society in which such an assumption is made.

While perhaps correct and persuasive, this does not seem to me to be all that can be done. In particular, there are, I think, two further arguments that may be made.

The first is that there are cases in which all human beings *equally* are capable of enjoying the same goods, e.g., relief from acute physical pain,[10] or that they are capable of deriving equal enjoyment from the same goods. If this is true, then if anyone has a right to this enjoyment, that right is a human right just because there is no rational ground for preferring one man's enjoyment to another's. For, if all persons do have equal capacities of these sorts and if the existence of these capacities is the reason for ascribing these rights to anyone, then all persons ought to have the right to claim equality of treatment in respect to the possession and exercise of these rights.

The difficulty inherent in this argument is at the same time the strength of the next one. The difficulty is simply that it does seem extraordinarily difficult to know how one would show that all men are equally capable of enjoying any of the same goods, or even how one might attempt to gather or evaluate relevant evidence in this matter. In a real sense, interpersonal comparisons of such a thing as the ability to bear pain seem to be logically as well as empirically unobtainable. Even more unobtainable, no doubt, is a measure of the comparative enjoyments derivable from choosing for oneself.[11] These are simply enjoyments the comparative worths of which, as possessed by different persons, there is no way to assess. If this is so, then this fact gives rise to an alternative argument.

---

[10]See Williams, *op. cit.*, p. 112: "These respects [in which men are alike] are notably the capacity to feel pain, both from immediate physical causes and from various situations represented in perception and in thought; and the capacity to feel affection for others, and the consequences of this, connected with the frustration of this affection, loss of its objects, etc."

[11]At times, Vlastos seems to adopt this view as well as the preceding one. See, e.g., Vlastos, *op. cit.*, p. 49: "So understood a person's well-being and freedom are aspects of his individual existence as unique and unrepeatable as is that existence itself. . . ."

We do know, through inspection of human history as well as of our own lives, that the denial of the opportunity to experience the enjoyment of these goods makes it impossible to live either a full or a satisfying life. In a real sense, the enjoyment of these goods differentiates human from nonhuman entities. And therefore, even if we have no meaningful or reliable criteria for comparing and weighing capabilities for enjoyment or for measuring their quantity or quality, we probably know all we need to know to justify our refusal to attempt to grade the value of the enjoyment of these goods. Hence, the dual grounds for treating their intrinsic values as equal for all persons: either these values are equal for all persons, or, if there are differences, they are not in principle discoverable or measurable. Hence, the argument, or an argument, for the human rights to well-being and freedom.

Because the foregoing discussion has been quite general and abstract, I want finally to consider briefly one illustration of a denial of human rights and to delineate both the several ways in which such a denial can occur and some of the different consequences of that denial. My example is that of the way in which Negro persons are regarded and treated by many whites in the South.

The first thing that is obvious is that many white Southerners would or might be willing to accept all that has been said so far and yet seek to justify their attitudes and behavior toward Negroes.

They might agree, for example, that all persons do have a right to be accorded equal treatment unless there is a general and relevant principle of differentiation. They would also surely acknowledge that some persons do have rights to many different things, including most certainly well-being and freedom. But they would insist, nonetheless, that there exists a general and relevant principle of differentiation, namely, that some persons are Negroes and others are not.

Now, those who do bother to concern themselves with arguments and with the need to give reasons would not, typically, assert that the mere fact of color difference does constitute a general and relevant reason. Rather, they would argue that this color difference is correlated with certain other characteristics and attitudes that are relevant.[12] In so doing, they invariably commit certain logical and moral mistakes.

First, the purported differentiating characteristic is usually not relevant to the differentiation sought to be made; e.g., none of the characteristics that supposedly differentiate Negroes from whites has any relevance to the capacity to bear acute physical pain or to the strength of the desire to be free from it. Indeed, almost all arguments neglect the fact that the capacities to enjoy those things which are constitutive of well-being and freedom are either incommensurable among persons or alike in all persons.

Second, the invocation of these differentiating characteristics always violates the requirement of relevance in another sense. For, given the typical definition of a Negro (in Alabama the legal definition is any person with "a drop of Negro blood"), it is apparent that there could not—under any plausible scientific

[12]See Williams, *op. cit.*, p. 113.

theory—be good grounds for making any differentiations between Negroes and whites.[13]

Third, and related to the above, any argument that makes distinctions as to the possession of human rights in virtue of the truth of certain empirical generalizations invariably produces some unjust denials of those rights. That is to say, even if some of the generalizations about Negroes are correct, they are correct only in the sense that the distinguishing characteristics ascribed to Negroes are possessed by some or many Negroes but not by all Negroes. Yet, before any reason for differentiating among persons as to the possession of human rights can be a relevant reason, that reason must be relevant in respect to *each person* so affected or distinguished. To argue otherwise is to neglect the fact, among other things, that human rights are personal and of at least *prima facie* equal importance to each possessor of those rights.

A different reaction or argument of white Southerners in respect to recent events in the South is bewilderment. Rather than (or in addition to) arguing for the existence of principles of differentiation, the white Southerner will say that he simply cannot understand the Negro's dissatisfaction with his lot. This is so because he, the white Southerner, has always treated his Negroes very well. With appreciable sincerity, he will assert that he has real affection for many Negroes. He would never needlessly inflict pain or suffering upon them. Indeed, he has often assumed special obligations to make certain that their lives were free from hunger, pain, and disease.

Now of course, this description of the facts is seldom accurate at all. Negroes have almost always been made to endure needless and extremely severe suffering in all too many obvious ways for all too many obviously wrong reasons. But I want to assume for my purposes the accuracy of the white Southerner's assertions. For these assertions are instructive just because they reveal some of the less obvious effects of a denial of human rights.

What is wholly missing from this description of the situation is the ability and inclination to conceptualize the Negro—any Negro—as the possible possessor of rights of any kind, and *a fortiori* of any human rights. And this has certain especially obnoxious consequences.

In the first place, the white Southerner's moral universe illustrates both the fact that it is possible to conceive of duties without conceiving of their correlative rights and the fact that the mistakes thereby committed are not chiefly mistakes of logic and definition. The mistakes matter morally. For what this way of conceiving most denies to any Negro is the opportunity to assert claims as a matter of right. It denies him the standing to protest against the way he is treated. If the white Southerner fails to do his duty, that is simply a matter between him and his conscience.

[13]This is to say nothing, of course, of the speciousness of any principle of differentiation that builds upon inequalities that are themselves produced by the unequal and unjust distribution of *opportunities*.

In the second place, it requires of any Negro that *he* make out his case for the enjoyment of any goods. It reduces all of *his* claims to the level of requests, privileges, and favors. But there are simply certain things, certain goods, that nobody ought to have to request of another. There are certain things that no one else ought to have the power to decide to refuse or to grant. To observe what happens to any person who is required to adopt habits of obsequious, deferential behavior in order to minimize the likelihood of physical abuse, arbitrary treatment, or economic destitution is to see most graphically how important human rights are and what their denial can mean. To witness what happens to a person's own attitudes, aspirations, and conceptions of himself[14] when he must request or petition for the opportunity to voice an opinion, to consult with a public official, or to secure the protection of the law is to be given dramatic and convincing assurance of the moral necessity of a conception of human rights.

And there is one final point. In a real sense, a society that simply lacks any conception of human rights is less offensive than one which has such a conception but denies that some persons have these rights. This is so not just because of the inequality and unfairness involved in differentiating for the wrong reasons among persons. Rather, a society based on such denial is especially offensive because it implicitly, if not explicitly, entails that there are some persons who do not and would not desire or need or enjoy those minimal goods which all men do need and desire and enjoy. It is to read certain persons, all of whom are most certainly human beings, out of the human race. This is surely among the greatest of all moral wrongs.

I know of no better example of the magnitude of this evil than that provided by a lengthy account in a Southern newspaper about the high school band program in a certain city. The article described fully the magnificence of the program and emphasized especially the fact that it was a program in which *all high school students* in the city participated.

Negro children neither were nor could be participants in the program. The article, however, saw no need to point this out. I submit that it neglected to do so not because everyone knew the fact, but because in a real sense the writer and the newspaper do not regard Negro high school students as children—persons, human beings—at all.

What is the Negro parent who reads this article to say to his children? What are his children supposed to think? How does a Negro parent even begin to demonstrate to the world that his children are really children, too? These are burdens no civilized society ought ever to impose. These are among the burdens that an established and acknowledged system of human rights helps to eliminate.

---

[14]Vlastos puts what I take to be the same point this way: "Any practice which tends to so weaken and confuse the personal esteem of a group of persons—slavery, serfdom or, in our own time racial segregation—may be morally condemned on this one ground, even if there were no other for indicting it" (Vlastos, *op. cit.*, p. 71).

Rights, Claimants, and Beneficiaries

•

David Lyons

To have a right, Bentham held, is to be the *beneficiary* of another's duty or obligation.[1] This theory, one of the more attractive and plausible suggestions about the nature of rights, appears supported by innumerable cases. It is reflected in the notion common to laymen, lawyers, and philosophers that someone with a right is on the advantageous side of a legal or moral relation. It promises to explain why rights are such valuable and important commodities. And it seems bolstered by a variety of facts, for example that compensation or reparation is often required, and might always be required, when one's rights are violated or infringed.

But Bentham's theory has been criticized, most notably by H. L. A. Hart, and it is not now, I think, very widely or seriously entertained. This is unfortunate, since none of the received arguments appears decisive against the beneficiary theory as such. In this paper I shall attempt to show that Hart's objections are weaker than they must at first appear because their force is largely dispelled against but

From the *American Philosophical Quarterly*, Vol. 6 (July 1969), 173–185. Reprinted with permission of the *American Philosophical Quarterly*.

[1]This is my formulation, not Bentham's. It is designed to encompass the two interpretations of Bentham's theory discussed in this paper. Bentham's relevant views about rights are expressed in various ways and are spread virtually throughout his *Works* (ed. by J. Bowring, Edinburgh, 1843), which include most but not all of his published writings. I give some references below; others may be found in H. L. A. Hart, "Bentham," *British Academy Proceedings*, vol. 48 (1962), pp. 297–320. See also C. K. Ogden (ed.), *Bentham's Theory of Fictions* (London, 1932; Patterson, 1959).

Note that Bentham's theory concerns what it is *to have* a right, not what "a right" itself is; it should not be confused with theories like those of Jhering and Salmond, who hold that a right is an interest. (See *Salmond on Jurisprudence*, 11th edn., by G. Williams [London, 1957], ch. 10.)

one form of beneficiary theory. Another, "qualified," beneficiary theory is much less vulnerable to Hart's objections and still worthy of our consideration.

In the first section I develop and explain the beneficiary theory and distinguish two versions that might be attributed to Bentham. In the second section I argue that being a beneficiary, in a certain qualified sense, is sufficient for having a right. In the third section I chiefly discuss some difficulties surrounding the claim that being a beneficiary is a necessary condition as well.

In this paper I shall assume that straightforward statements about moral rights can be analyzed in terms of moral obligations in the same way that statements about legal rights can be analyzed in terms of legal obligations. I shall take the beneficiary theory to apply to moral as well as legal rights.[2]

I

Many writers have held that the notion of a right must be analyzed in terms of duty or obligation—or, more generally, in terms of requirements or prohibitions on someone's behavior.[3] This is Bentham's view.

> It is by imposing obligations, or by abstaining from imposing them, that rights are established or granted. . . . How can a right of property in land be conferred on me? It is by imposing upon everybody else the obligation of not touching its productions, &c. &c. How can I possess the right of going into all the streets of a city? It is because there exists no obligation which hinders me, and because everybody is bound by an obligation not to hinder me.[4]

So the idea of obligation is central to that of a right, though these ideas may be related in different ways, according to the type of right in question. Property rights, as Bentham suggests, involve others' obligations to forbear from using the property without permission. Some rights imply others' obligations even more obviously, e.g., a right to be paid ten dollars by Jones, a right to be cared for by one's parents, a right to be given equal consideration, a right not to be killed, and in such cases the statement of the right may be held to be equivalent to the statement of the corresponding obligation. But a right to *do* (or to refrain from doing) something has as its core the *absence* of an obligation to do otherwise.[5] Even here, however—as

[2]Bentham restricted his theory to legal rights, and in his attack on natural rights implied that there could not be any extralegal rights. His reasons for holding the latter view seem largely independent of his analysis of rights in terms of beneficial obligations.

[3]The differences between duties or obligations, on the one hand, and mere prohibitions or requirements, on the other, are touched on below. I assume in this paper that the differences between duties and obligations can be ignored.

[4]*Works,* vol. III, p. 181; see also pp. 159ff., 217ff.

[5]Or perhaps a sphere of activity in which one is free to do as one pleases. It should be observed that we are ignoring here those species of rights that lawyers call "powers" or "ca-

Bentham's second example and his general remarks suggest, and as others have agreed—one's right also seems to involve others' obligations, i.e., obligations to refrain from interfering.

Bentham held, then, that rights can be "reduced" to duties or obligations. But he did not hold the closely associated view, that rights and duties are necessarily "correlatives." That is, he did not hold that duties always imply rights. This is important to Bentham's analysis of rights. To see why, let us consider the notion of correlativity briefly.

When Bernard owes Alvin ten dollars we have equal reason to ascribe a right to Alvin (to be paid ten dollars by Bernard) and an obligation to Bernard (to pay Alvin ten dollars), and whatever would falsify one ascription would likewise falsify the other. Neither the right nor the obligation can arise without the other, and if one is discharged, waived, canceled, voided, forfeited, or otherwise extinguished the other must be extinguished as well. For the ground of the obligation— the debt—is the title of the right. Alvin's right and Bernard's obligation *necessarily coexist*, and a full statement of one logically implies a full statement of the other.

This pattern of correlations is extremely common. It obtains not only when debts are owed but also when certain other relations exist between two (or possibly more) particular individuals—as a consequence, for example, of promises and contracts, wrongful injuries that require reparation, good turns that require reciprocation, relationships such as parent to child and teacher to student. In such cases it is natural to speak of *A*'s having certain rights *against B* and of *B*'s having (or *owing*) corresponding obligations *to A*.[6] And it is important that, when obligations are so grounded on such special relations or transactions and consequently can be said to be "owed" to particular persons, we can infer that the person to whom the obligation is owed has a corresponding right and that he holds it against the person with the obligation.

It is important to note what these words will be taken to signify. When *A*, in particular, holds a certain right *against B*, *A* is a *claimant* against *B*. A "claimant" is one empowered to press or waive a claim against someone with a corresponding duty or obligation. He can, if he wishes, release the other from his obligation and cancel it, or he can insist upon its performance. A creditor, for example, is a claimant against his debtor. A promisee is a claimant against one who makes a valid and binding promise to him. So too is a person to whom a debt of reparation is owed because of wrongful injury done. A claimant is thus one to whom the performance of a duty or obligation is *owed*—he is the one who holds the claim against the other and who is entitled to administer the claim as he chooses. There are obviously moral as well as legal claimants in this sense.

The pattern of relations between rights and obligations I have just described does not seem to be universal. When behavior is simply required or pro-

---

pacities" on the one hand and "immunities" on the other. I assume that these are rights in a different sense, or senses, of the term.

[6]See Joel Feinberg's very helpful discussion in "Duties, Rights, and Claims," *American Philosophical Quarterly*, vol. 3 (1966), pp. 137–142.

hibited by law or morals, without presupposing such special relations or transactions between particular individuals as I have mentioned, we often say that "duties" or "obligations" are imposed. But since these duties or obligations are *not* "owed" to anyone in particular, we cannot determine who, if anyone, has corresponding rights by noting to whom they are "owed." Indeed, although rights sometimes do correlate with such duties or obligations, we cannot infer *that there are* such rights merely from the fact *that there are* such duties or obligations. This point is essential to a theory like Bentham's.

Consider the following contrast. When children who have reached their majority are required by (criminal) law to support their aged and indigent parents it seems plausible to say that their parents have a legal right to such support from their children, even though legally the parents may not be "claimants" against their children, they cannot release them from their obligations, and thus the children legally do not "owe" support *to* their parents in the full sense given above. But if children are required by law to inform the authorities of their parents' seditious remarks and activities (for which the punishment is death) we may have some hesitancy in saying that their parents have corresponding rights to be informed upon by their children. (We would be inclined to ascribe such rights only in very special circumstances.) This contrast is meant to suggest that from the fact that the law requires that A be treated in a certain way it does not follow, without any further assumptions, that A may be said to have a right to be treated in that way. That is, rights do not follow from duties or obligations, or from requirements or prohibitions, alone. Other conditions must be satisfied.

Bentham held that rights are conferred only by beneficial obligations. "To assure to individuals the possession of a certain good, is to confer *a right* upon them."[7] Goods are assured by imposing duties or obligations, by requiring acts or forbearances of others. Obligations do not correspond to rights unless they protect or serve rather than harm or threaten those they directly concern. So Bentham held that rights "correlate" with duties or obligations in the following way, by virtue of the very notion of a right: rights imply duties, but only beneficial ones. And thus duties do not necessarily correspond to rights; they do so only when they "assure goods."

It will be useful to characterize Bentham's theory as follows: to have a right is, essentially, to be the *beneficiary* of another's duty or obligation (or of some requirement or prohibition upon another's behavior). But this needs certain qualifications before it can properly be evaluated.

Two qualifications can safely be made before considering alternative interpretations of Bentham's theory. We may note, first, that obligations are not necessarily performed. They can be breached or not fulfilled, and then the benefits or goods their performances would confer cannot be conferred in that way. Thus, a "beneficiary" in the relevant sense is not one who actually benefits but rather one who would benefit from the performance of the obligation. Secondly, a person with a right need not positively gain even when the obligation is met or discharged.

[7]*Works,* vol. III, p. 159.

For there may be indirect and irrelevant consequences resulting from (or following) the performance of an obligation. (Alvin might spend on drink the ten dollars he receives from Bernard in payment of the debt, wreck his car, and suffer serious injury—none of which would happen if Bernard fails to perform as required.) Most important, obligations may require "negative" rather than "positive" services, as Bentham says, e.g., *not* robbing, assaulting, or killing.[8] One may "benefit" in the sense of *not losing* rather than in the sense of gaining; what may be "assured" is not so much a good as the avoidance of an evil. The term "beneficiary" can be misleading, therefore, but we shall continue to use it with these implicit qualifications.

Beyond this point, however, Bentham's precise position is difficult to determine. Two main currents run through Bentham's discussions of rights, from which one can construct two significantly different versions of beneficiary theory.

The Unqualified Beneficiary Theory. On the one hand Bentham seems to hold that rights are conferred whenever (and only when) rules that impose duties are justified according to the utilitarian test, that is, when the rules and the duties they impose are useful.[9] Good laws serve the interests of individuals, and these laws confer rights. But bad laws impose duties from which no one (or hardly anyone) stands to benefit and therefore fail to confer rights. Various passages suggest that Bentham held the unqualified beneficiary theory, as attributed to him by Hart: that someone with a right is simply one "likely to benefit" or "capable of benefiting" or one who "stands to benefit" by the performance of a duty.[10]

This is the theory attacked by Hart. We shall examine his objections, but we need not share his alternative view in order to see that such a theory, straightforwardly understood, could not be correct. It is open to innumerable counter-examples. Suppose that Bernard owed Alvin ten dollars and also that Alvin has privately decided to give Charles a present if and only if the debt is repaid. Let us suppose further that Alvin is in no way indebted to Charles and that he has made no promises—not even tacit promises—to give Charles anything. It would seem then that Alvin has the right that corresponds to Bernard's obligation (the right to be paid ten dollars by Bernard) and that Charles has no relevant right (save the right to accept a gift from Alvin, which is clearly *independent* of Bernard's obligation). But the unqualified beneficiary theory does not differentiate between the positions of Alvin and Charles with respect to Bernard's obligation, and seems to imply that each has a right, since each "stands to benefit" from the performance of Bernard's obligation. (Indeed, Charles "stands to benefit" more than Alvin.) But it is absurd to suppose that Charles has a relevant right.

[8]*Ibid.*, pp. 159, 181.
[9]*Ibid.*, pp. 181, 220f.
[10]See "Bentham," *op. cit.*, pp. 313–315, and also Hart's "Are There Any Natural Rights?", *The Philosophical Review*, vol. 64 (1955), pp. 180ff. [reprinted in this volume, pp. 14–25—*Ed.*], where Hart criticizes the beneficiary theory without, however, attributing it to anyone.

The Qualified Beneficiary Theory. If the theory is to be rendered more plausible, the notion of a "beneficiary" must be refined. Two considerations seem fairly obvious. (1) Alvin's benefiting is *relevant* to Bernard's obligation in a way that Charles's benefiting is not. For Bernard's obligation directly *concerns* Alvin, that is, it requires treating *him* or behaving toward him in a certain way. But it does not similarly concern Charles, for Bernard's behavior toward Charles is not relevant to the question whether or not Bernard has met or breached his obligation. But the fact that an obligation *concerns* Alvin does not suffice to show either that he is a beneficiary in any recognizable sense or that he has a corresponding right. Brown's duty as executioner concerns the condemned Green, who (failing special circumstances) would not be called a beneficiary of the performance of Brown's duty, and who (failing certain theories of punishment) would not be said to have a corresponding right. But (2) both Alvin's benefiting and Charles's benefiting are related *contingently* to Bernard's obligation. Alvin's benefiting, or the fact that Bernard's obligation "assures" to him a certain good, *does not follow* from the obvious and literal specification of Bernard's obligation, which is simply *to pay Alvin ten dollars*. So, if the connection between Alvin's benefiting and Bernard's obligation is not *merely* accidental, and if this connection is supposed to be essential to the very notion of Alvin's right, how might it be defined?

Some remarks by Bentham suggest the view that a person with a right is a "beneficiary" in a narrower and more appropriate sense: he is *supposed* to benefit by or from the performance of another's obligation. He is the direct, intended beneficiary of that duty or obligation.[11]

If we consider the obligations we have, and in particular those that do correspond to the rights of others, we shall find this suggestion not implausible. Viewed in an obvious and literal but, I think, somewhat superficial way, obligations do not generally require the conferring of goods *as such*; like Bernard's obligation to pay Alvin they simply require certain acts or forbearances or patterns of behavior. But we would fail to *understand* the obligations we have—we would be unable to determine what we ought to do on the basis of them—unless we could also say whether or not those they directly concern are supposed to benefit from them. And it seems plausible to suggest that, when we fully understand the obligations we have that *do* correspond to others' *rights*, we also see that those they directly concern *are* supposed to benefit from them. This is patently true in some cases; obligations of indebtedness, reparation, and reciprocation, for example, essentially involve and require the returning or restoring of goods to particular persons. Other cases are more difficult, particularly obligations imposed by the criminal law and analogous rules of morality, on the one hand, and promissory or contractual obligations on the other. I shall deal with these separately and in some detail.

According to the qualified beneficiary theory, then, a person with a right is not one who merely "stands to benefit" from the performance of another's obligation. He is one for whom a good is "assured," or an evil obstructed, by re-

[11]See, e.g., *Works*, vol. III, p. 159.

quirements or prohibitions upon others' behavior, in the sense that some other person or persons are required to act or forbear in ways designed or intended to serve, secure, promote, or protect his interests or an interest of his. He is a beneficiary in what I shall call the "qualified" sense of the term; he is "the party to be benefited."[12] This is not to say that the conferring of certain benefits or the avoidance of specific losses or injuries is strictly *guaranteed* to him. For, aside from the fact that obligations can be breached, the specific performance of the relevant obligations might actually fail, for various reasons, to serve his interests. But I am suggesting that, on the basis of our understanding of the relation or transaction or rule that grounds the obligation, we can say in some cases that someone's interests are to be served. And, according to the qualified beneficiary theory, such persons and only such persons have rights.

II

Hart maintains, against Bentham, that:

> *According to the strict usage of most modern English jurists following Austin . . . the person who has a right is something more than a possible beneficiary of duty; he is the person who may, at his option, demand the execution of the duty or waive it . . . and it is neither necessary nor sufficient (though it is usually true) that he will also benefit from the performance of it.*[13]

In this section I shall argue, with regard to Hart's criminal law examples, that the qualified beneficiary theory gives a sufficient condition for having a right (although the unqualified theory fails to do so). In the next section I extend the argument to promissory rights and counter Hart's claim that the theory fails to provide a necessary condition as well.

Hart agrees with Bentham that rights imply duties or obligations but that the latter do not always imply the former. But Hart's reasons for saying that not all duties imply rights are different from Bentham's. Bentham, as we have seen, holds that the law can and unfortunately often does impose "barren" duties or "ascetic" obligations, that is, duties or obligations without beneficiaries, which have no corresponding rights. But Hart holds that duties without claimants have no corresponding rights. And these positions are different because being a claimant

---

[12]As Bentham defines "beneficiary" in his discussion of trusts: *Works*, vol. I, p. 106. But it should be emphasized that Bentham does not argue explicitly that such beneficiaries, and only such persons, have rights in the relevant sense.

[13]"Bentham," *op. cit.*, p. 315. For criticisms of other kinds see Hart's *Definition and Theory in Jurisprudence* (Oxford, 1953). Here I deal only with Bentham's *beneficiary* theory (the first stage of Bentham's analysis of rights) and am unconcerned with, e.g., Bentham's naturalism, manifested in his further analysis of legal duty or obligation.

is not a necessary condition for being a beneficiary of another's duty. This is shown by the fact that there are obligations with beneficiaries but without private claimants in the sense discussed above. Under the civil (as distinct from the criminal) law, private individuals are empowered to enforce their own rights; they alone can initiate proceedings against others who violate or threaten their rights. But there are no private claimants under the criminal law—only *complainants*. For the substantive rules of the criminal law impose duties or obligations that cannot be canceled by a private party; they can be "canceled" only by a change in the rules. A private individual, such as the victim of a criminal offense, can impede or aid a prosecution, but he lacks the analogous legal "power" his counterpart has under the civil law to sue. Public officials have both the legal power and the responsibility of enforcing the criminal law. Moreover, civil law obligations typically arise from special relations or transactions between the parties, whereby such obligations are incurred or assumed, but criminal law obligations are simply laid down or imposed and thus it is less natural to speak of them as being "owed" to particular individuals, and they are not "owed" in the full sense discussed above.

A similar distinction can be drawn within the class of moral duties and obligations. Some can be incurred or assumed, by promising for example, and these can be canceled by the one to whom the promise is made and to whom its performance is owed. But some moral principles simply forbid or require, they lay down what one may not or must do, and while these may be said to impose "duties" or "obligations" they cannot always be waived or canceled.

Accordingly, Hart claims that, strictly speaking, there are no rights under the criminal law or in the analogous part of morality, because such duties or obligations are not administered by private claimants. Hart observes that jurists generally prefer not to speak of "rights" under the criminal law, for reasons akin to his. But he *also* concedes that usage differs on this point:

> that a somewhat wider usage of the expression "a right" is common among non-lawyers and especially among writers on political theory who might not hesitate to say, for example, that when the criminal law forbids murder and assault it thereby secures to individuals a right to security of the person, even though he is in no position to waive a duty imposed by the criminal law. [14]

The so-called "wider" usage lacks the requirement that the person with the right (or anyone else) be a claimant. Hart goes on to suggest that such a wider use of "right" can be tolerated if it retains a central feature of the allegedly strict sense explicated by his claimant theory. We might continue to speak of rights under the criminal law provided we recognize that laws which confer rights as well as impose duties "also provide, in a distinctively distributive way, for the individual who has the right." This part of Hart's argument is somewhat difficult to interpret, but his position seems roughly the following. When the term "right" is used strictly, a

[14]"Bentham," *op. cit.*, p. 315.

person with a right has *his own* special powers as a claimant, his "limited sovereignty over the person who has the duty." This is, presumably, the "distributive" feature Hart refers to. Under a tolerable wider use, a distributive feature would be retained when talk of rights under the criminal law is confined to cases in which the law protects the security *of the individual*—as opposed to, say, the security of the community as a whole—that is, where a breach of such a duty "necessarily involves the infliction of harm upon a specific or (in Bentham's language) 'assignable' individual." But Hart claims that Bentham's analysis contains no such distributive feature, because on Bentham's theory one can qualify as having a right if he is merely "a member of a class who as a class may be indiscriminately benefited by the performance of a duty." For Bentham's theory would allegedly accord rights not only to persons protected by rules such as those forbidding murder and assault—who might be said to have "rights" under a tolerably extended usage of the term—but also to those who *might possibly* benefit by the performance of *any* useful duties, even though they do not serve the interests of individuals directly. The breach of such legal duties as income tax and military service (Hart's examples) does not necessarily involve the infliction of harm upon a specific individual, "but at the most merely makes it likely that the community as a whole will be less secure."[15]

Now Hart seems correct when he says that certain *ascriptions* of rights (e.g., under the criminal law) are "wider" than others (e.g., under the civil law) in the sense that the former lack implications which the latter have that the person with the right is a claimant. For rights under the civil law arise from special relations or transactions between the persons concerned and they, unlike rights under the criminal law, may be ascribed as rights "against" those having the corresponding duties, which are reciprocally "owed." (Similar remarks apply to classes of moral rights and their ascriptions.) But from this it does not follow that ascribing rights where there are no claimants involves a wider *sense of the term* "right" or uses an extended concept. For the differences between the ascriptions *as a whole* might be accounted for by the fact that some are qualified as rights "against" particular persons while others are not, depending on the sorts of conditions that warrant the ascription of the right. That is, unless we assume that being a claimant is essential to having a right in the "strict" sense of the term, we have as yet no reason to suppose that the concept of a right itself is extended when it happens not to be instantiated as a right "against" another.

Straightforward talk about rights is not generally confined to contexts in which there are private claimants. Rights may be ascribed, for example, in the context of the criminal law for the purpose of noting that some act or omission is not unlawful, e.g., when one is challenged, when interference is threatened, or to draw certain contrasts. For example, a motorist has a right to make a right turn on a red light in California which he lacks in New York because of differences between the respective traffic laws. Such a right is not held against or with respect to any par-

---

[15]*Ibid.*

ticular person, but this does not seem to make it any less of a right or a right in only an extended or loose sense of the term.

A right not to be killed may be analogous. Is it clear that we speak loosely or that we stretch our ordinary notion of a right when we ascribe, in the context of the criminal law or on the basis of general moral prohibitions, the right not to be killed? One way of finding out is by determining whether there is a single acceptable account of rights within both sorts of context, i.e., with and without private claimants. This is what the beneficiary theory purports to give.

Now let us consider more directly the force of Hart's objection against the beneficiary theory concerning rights without claimants under the criminal law. Hart maintains that rules such as those forbidding murder and assault may be said to confer rights, as the beneficiary theory implies, but only in a wider sense of the term; while rules requiring payment of income tax and military service, even when useful, cannot be said to confer rights, even in such a wider sense, although the beneficiary theory implies they do. Hart says that rights can be ascribed in the former cases because such a usage retains a certain "distributive" feature of the notion of a right, since the breach of such a duty "necessarily involves the infliction of harm upon a specific . . . individual."

But there is another and I think more obvious and plausible way of understanding why rights are and can be ascribed when murder and assault are prohibited. Such rules "assure goods" or obstruct evils to those they are supposed to protect. The qualified beneficiary theory can account for such rights without implying that every useful duty has a corresponding right. Hart's objection is directed against the unqualified beneficiary theory and, as I shall try to show, it has no force against the qualified theory.

Any rule that has a utilitarian justification and is in that sense "useful" ultimately serves (or can reasonably be expected to serve) the interest of individuals, but rules can do so in different ways. The rules that serve individuals most directly do so by imposing *beneficial* duties, in a qualified sense, which implies that there are beneficiaries in the sense employed by the qualified beneficiary theory. Rules such as those forbidding murder and assault are of this type; they can only be understood as requiring that we not harm or injure others in certain ways. The duties they impose patently require treating others in ways designed or intended to serve, secure, promote, or protect their interests. The rules define the classes of persons protected, and any member of such a class is a beneficiary in the qualified sense. He does not merely "stand to benefit" by the performance of such a duty, nor does he merely "stand to suffer" if the duty is breached, for his loss at the hands of the person with the duty would be directly relevant to the question whether the duty is breached. From the point of view of the rules and the duties they impose, such a person is neither a lucky bystander in one case nor an unlucky one in the other. He is one who, according to the rules, is not to be harmed in such a way. And thus, despite the fact that such a person cannot be said to have a right "against" anyone in particular—since he cannot waive or cancel the corresponding obligation and it does not rest upon any *special* relation between him and those bound by the rules—and despite the fact that the duty is not "owed" to him in particular—since he is not a claimant—nevertheless, it does seem plausible to say that he is *entitled* to be treated in a certain way, e.g., not to be assaulted or killed, and that saying this is not speaking loosely. For others are duty-bound so to treat him, and his *right* does correspond to and correlate with their duties.

But other rules that can be justified on utilitarian grounds serve individuals much less directly. If there is a good utilitarian reason for requiring payment of income tax, for example, benefits to individuals must be expected ultimately to accrue. (As Bentham held, the interest or good of the community cannot be understood except in terms of the interests or good of its members.) But the possible, intended, or desired benefits that might ultimately accrue to individuals do not flow directly from the performance of such duties, and no harm results directly, if at all, from their breach. Duties imposed by such rules I shall call (merely) "useful." Such duties have no beneficiaries in the qualified sense. Money collected from income tax payments can be used to serve the community, and therefore its members, in various ways. But these ways are not determined by the act of payment itself. Most important, the content of the duty to pay income tax concerns payment and payment only. It does not concern the uses to which the revenue might be put. And one who might possibly benefit from the use of such revenues, and accordingly may "stand to benefit" from the performance of the duty to pay income tax, is not a beneficiary in the qualified sense. His benefit or loss is not directly relevant to the question whether or not the duty is discharged.

There is not even a traceable connection, normally, between someone's gain or loss as a result of payment or nonpayment and another person's discharge or breach of his duty to pay income tax. The payment marks the beginning of a long, complex chain that may, but does not necessarily, lead to benefits to individuals. Generally speaking, a particular person's payment or nonpayment is neither necessary nor sufficient for bringing about or preventing another person's ultimate benefits or losses. Usually, benefits cannot accrue in the long run unless observance of such duties is widespread. Even if it is widespread, the actual result depends on how the money is used. Suppose, however, that individuals ultimately do receive benefits that are partly traceable to income tax revenues. It remains extremely unlikely, if not impossible, that we should be able to ascribe anyone's benefits to particular performances of the duty to pay income tax. And if harm results or benefits do not accrue because payments are commonly withheld, it is again extremely unlikely, if not impossible, that particular losses could be ascribed to particular breaches. Moreover, no loss will be caused by nonpayment unless breaches are common. So it is neither necessarily the case nor even likely that anyone will suffer or lose as a consequence of one breach (or several breaches) of a merely useful duty.

Hart's objection is, then, that the unqualified beneficiary theory implies that merely useful as well as beneficial duties give rise to rights. This is because such a weak condition as "Someone stands to benefit by the performance of another's duty" *must* be satisfied whenever useful duties are imposed. But this objection has no force against the qualified beneficiary theory, since merely useful duties have no beneficiaries in the qualified sense. So, while it may be implausible to say that a merely useful duty gives rise to a corresponding right, it is also difficult to construe the qualified beneficiary theory as implying it. Hart's objection has therefore been met. Rights correspond to obligations under the criminal law in just the way Hart claims, according to the qualified beneficiary theory. Rights correlate with beneficial duties and not with merely useful ones.

Before closing this section it may be illuminating to note that the qualified beneficiary theory accounts for rights that are related, indirectly, to such duties as military service and payment of income tax. Consider, for example, those persons who supposedly "stand to benefit" from income tax payments. More precisely, consider those who *qualify by law* as recipients of governmental services and expenditures, e.g., public education, unemployment compensation, garbage collection, and so on. The rules that govern such expenditures also provide criteria for qualification. And if one qualifies by law it would seem that he is legally *entitled* to the benefits or services and thus has a legal right to them. These rights can readily be accounted for by the qualified beneficiary theory. For *corresponding* duties—not duties to pay income tax, but duties to distribute the benefits and administer the services—fall upon those whose job it is to do such things. So, the qualified beneficiary theory seems also to account for rights that Hart does not consider. And it does so by using one purported sense of "right," which is applied in other contexts as well.[16]

III

Hart's more formidable objection to the beneficiary theory concerns the case of the "third-party beneficiary."[17] Promises—when they are valid and binding—engender rights to promisees and obligations to promisors. A promisee often stands to benefit from the promised performance, but when a promise is meant to benefit a "third party" (i.e., one who is not a party to the agreement) then, according to Hart, the promisee as usual acquires a right even though he is not a beneficiary, while the third party, who is supposed to benefit, acquires no right. This shows that being a beneficiary is neither necessary nor sufficient for having a right.

In Hart's example, a son extracts a promise from another (let us say a friend) to care for his aged mother in his absence. Hart argues that the son has the right. The promise is made *to* him and he, therefore, has the claim against the friend. The friend's performance is *owed* to or *due* him. He alone can press or waive the claim, can insist upon its performance or release his friend from the promise.

[16]Hart's claimant theory might be extended to accommodate rights where provision of services or benefits is conditional upon application; but it cannot accommodate cases in which there is no choice or option to exercise, e.g., where free public education is also compulsory.

[17]Although Hart mentions this case in "Bentham," *op. cit.*, p. 314, his discussion of it is found in "Are There Any Natural Rights?", *op. cit.*, pp. 180ff. [this volume, pp. 14–25—Ed.].

If the promise is not kept, Hart argues, the son is *wronged* even if he is not harmed. But the mother (a third-party beneficiary) has no right. She might be harmed if the promise is not kept, but she cannot be wronged. For the promise is not made *to her*, and thus the performance is not owed to or due her. One with a right admittedly may be, and usually is, a beneficiary of a duty. But this is not what it is to have a right. The promisee alone has a moral claim upon the promisor. He is

> *morally in a position to determine by his choice how [the promisor] shall act and in this way to limit [the promisor's] freedom of choice; and it is this fact, not the fact that he stands to benefit, that makes it appropriate to say that he has* a right.[18]

I shall try to show the limits of this objection to the qualified beneficiary theory. First, I shall argue that Hart's objection rests in part upon a misconstrual of the third-party beneficiary's position with respect to another's obligation. Because Hart considers only the unqualified beneficiary theory with its inadequate notion of a beneficiary, he assimilates the mother's position in his example to that of persons who merely "stand to benefit" by the performance of a duty and have no relevant rights. The alternative suggestion, offered by the qualified beneficiary theory, is that the mother, like those in other contexts who may properly be said to have rights although they are not claimants, can be accorded a right precisely because she is a beneficiary in the qualified sense. Then I shall examine the question whether claimants, who seem clearly to have rights, are necessarily beneficiaries—in other words, whether being a beneficiary is a necessary condition for having a right.

In Hart's discussion of the third-party beneficiary case, he concedes (as we saw he does also with regard to the criminal law) that "common usage" may sanction the ascription of rights to beneficiaries—to animals and infants for example, who are said to have rights to proper treatment because we have duties not to ill-treat them. But Hart maintains that this way of speaking employs only "the philosopher's generalized sense of 'duty' " and that it makes "an idle use of the expression 'a right'." He contends that "the moral situation can be simply and adequately described here by saying that it is wrong or that we ought not to ill-treat" babies or animals. But "right" and "duty" have a "specific force" in other contexts that cannot be captured by such uses of "wrong" and "ought."[19] When "right" and "duty" are used strictly, and not merely in a "generalized" sense, the person with the duty may be said to be "bound to" the person with the right. The right-holder is a claimant, who controls the duty. Thus the friend has a duty "to" the son, to whom he *owes* the promised performance. But the friend has a duty "to" the mother only in the sense that his duty concerns her. The friend does not

---

[18]"Are There Any Natural Rights?", *ibid.*, p. 180 [this volume, p. 18—*Ed.*].

[19]*Ibid.*, p. 181 [this volume, p. 18—*Ed.*]. On related points see also Hart's "Legal and Moral Obligation" in A. I. Melden (ed.), *Essays in Moral Philosophy* (Seattle, 1958), esp. pp. 82–84, 100–105.

"owe" the performance to the mother, and thus she has no right to the promised services, for she has no right "against" the friend.

Hart's avowed purpose here is to draw our attention to special features of our discourse about rights, features that set it off from talk about what ought to be done or what it would be wrong to do or about "duties" that are not "owed" to claimants. He suggests that the beneficiary theory obscures the differences between these sectors of moral and legal discourse. Hart's view involves a threefold distinction, between (a) contexts in which rights in the "strict" sense can be ascribed; (b) contexts in which rights can be ascribed only in a wider sense; and (c) contexts in which "duties" may be ascribed, but not rights. The qualified beneficiary theory does not, however, eliminate any of these distinctions (although it draws the lines somewhat differently). Corresponding to Hart's contexts (a) and (b) are those in which ascriptions of rights can be made in a single sense of the term, although the ascriptions are warranted by different sorts of conditions (depending on whether or not the duty or obligation is "owed" to the person with the right). Corresponding to Hart's context (c) is that in which duties or obligations are not beneficial and rights cannot be ascribed, even if the duties are useful. Since such distinctions between sectors of moral and legal discourse are not obscured by the qualified beneficiary theory (although they may be obscured by the unqualified theory), we need not dwell upon them.

We may consider instead what may be *common* to the various plausible ascriptions of rights to see whether being a beneficiary is both common and essential. Hart seems to suggest here that what is common when rights are ascribed in both the strict and the wider sense of the term is that the behavior of others that is required or prohibited *concerns* the person with the right. But this condition is surely not peculiar to requirements that might be held to correspond to rights. For as we have noted, Green's duty as executioner concerns the condemned Brown, while it is doubtful that Brown acquires a corresponding right. And it concerns Brown differently than the restrictions regarding babies and animals concern them. For our duties regarding babies and animals assure goods or obstruct evils to them.

The cases of babies and animals raise complications we need not examine here, e.g., whether legal or moral personality or agency is required for the possession of rights. But it should be observed, nonetheless, that the position of the third-party beneficiary in Hart's example is different from that of babies and animals. The friend's obligation to serve the mother is not merely an instance of a general duty to refrain from harming the helpless. The friend's obligation arises from a specific agreement, and it is one he otherwise would not have. He has agreed to care for the mother. The mother is the one the promised services are intended to benefit. She is a direct, intended beneficiary.

Joel Feinberg suggests that Hart has overstated his point. Third-party beneficiaries are *sometimes* accorded rights in both morals and law. But, he says:

> it does not follow necessarily *from the fact that a person is an intended beneficiary of a promised service that he has a right to it; whereas it*

always follows necessarily from the fact that a person is a promisee that
he has a right to what is promised. [20]

Third-party beneficiaries can have rights, but "only in virtue of moral or judicial policies and rules." A third-party beneficiary's right seems to follow from his position as beneficiary only when, for example, it is also plausible "to say that the promisor made a *tacit promise* to the beneficiary in addition to the express promise to his promisee." The parties to the agreement let the beneficiary know of it and he thereupon "acts in reliance on its performance." [21]

Here again, however, there is evidence that the objection hinges on a misconstrual of the mother's position. Feinberg's unwillingness to allow that third-party beneficiaries *necessarily* have rights seems based on a weak sense he (as well as Hart) attaches to "third-party beneficiary." When this expression is so used that it can apply even to those who, as he says, merely "stand to gain, if only indirectly" or "who will profit in merely picayune and remote ways" from the promised performance, [22] a third-party beneficiary does *not* necessarily have a right. But if it is used in the qualified sense, the expression better characterizes the mother in Hart's example and it seems to *follow* that she has a right. The mother's interest is directly relevant to the friend's obligation. A complete specification of the friend's obligation includes *essential* reference to the mother, who is supposed to benefit by its performance. Her loss in case the promise is broken would not be a remote, accidental consequence of the friend's behavior; it would be the predictable and relevant consequence of a dereliction. The fact that she was not cared for would be the chief ground for saying that the friend had failed to discharge his obligation. Her receipt of the services would be the chief reason for saying that he had discharged his obligation. The friend's obligation is beneficial, and the mother is the beneficiary. The mother is *entitled* to the services required by the friend's obligation as one entitled to be treated in a certain way when another has an obligation specifically so to behave. Does she not *have a right* to be cared for by him?

Of course, in such a case the mother may not be aware of the friend's promise and thus may not know that she is entitled to his services. But knowledge of the relevant facts is surely not a necessary condition for having a right. If ignorant of the agreement, she would be in no position to complain in case the friend broke his promise. But if she became aware of the relevant facts it would seem that she could legitimately complain and "press" her right (whether or not she was *further* inconvenienced because she relied upon the friend's help). Indeed, she might also refuse the services and thus effectively "release" the friend from his obligation, especially if she could care for herself and did not need the help arranged for her by her son. But this does not mean that she has a right *because* she

[20]"Duties, Rights, and Claims," *op. cit.*, p. 138. Assuming the promise is valid and binding, presumably.
[21]*Ibid.*
[22]*Ibid.*, p. 137; see also p. 138, including note 3.

is a *claimant*; it means, rather, that she *may act as* a claimant (if she is in a position to do so) precisely *because she has a right* to be cared for by the friend.

These considerations suggest once more that being a beneficiary is sufficient for having a right. But they do not show that being a beneficiary is a necessary condition, and thus the more serious threat posed by Hart's objection has not been met. For the son, as promisee, would seem to have a right against the friend. But the son does not appear to be a *beneficiary* in any straightforward sense. The promise is meant to benefit the mother, not the son, and she alone will benefit directly from the friend's care. Moreover, it is the friend's treatment of the mother, not his treatment of the son, that is relevant to the obligation, that determines whether or not it is discharged. This seems to indicate that being a beneficiary of a beneficial obligation is not a necessary condition of having a right.

If this part of Hart's objection is allowed, a defender of the beneficiary theory might be content with the following observations. The argument has tended to show that being a beneficiary of a beneficial obligation is, first of all, a sufficient condition for having a right. Hart's objection shows at best that being a beneficiary is not a necessary condition for having a right. But it does not show that rights are conferred even when there are no such beneficiaries. And this may not be an insignificant point. For it would seem that outside the contexts of promises (contracts, agreements) counter-examples to the qualified beneficiary theory are not easy to find. In other contexts in both law and morals it would seem that rights are ascribed when and only when obligations or restrictions upon others' behavior assure goods or obstruct evils to individuals and thus when breaches of the corresponding obligations would involve loss or harm to those with the rights. The apparent possibility of counter-examples arises because it does not seem to be a condition of a valid and binding promise that its performance serve the interests of the *promisee*. But in such cases there is at least a *third-party* beneficiary. It is difficult to imagine promises—or, generally, obligations that correspond to rights—which are valid and binding and yet serve no one's interests. On the contrary, our understanding of the nature of binding promises is shown by the fact that, when their fulfillment threatens unexpected disadvantages to those they are meant to serve, it would be wrong to keep them.

But if we pursue this line of argument and attempt to clarify the respects in which promises may be said to "serve someone's interests," then it would also appear that a promisee, even in a third-party beneficiary case, is a "beneficiary" in the qualified sense.

Suppose that Jones extracts a promise from Brown. The promise is not intended to benefit a third party, and there is no one who could plausibly be regarded as a "third-party beneficiary" in the appropriate sense. Brown makes the promise because he is led by Jones to believe that he, Jones, wants the promised act performed. But suppose that Jones is, in fact, unconcerned whether or not the promise is kept. He extracts the promise on the merest whim or out of malice. It seems clear that the conditions of a valid and binding promise are not satisfied (whether or not Brown knows this), and thus that Jones does not acquire *a right* to what was promised and that Brown incurs no *obligation* (although he may *think* that he is obligated). But if Jones had really wanted what was promised and Brown had freely agreed to do it, then—barring immoral purposes—a valid and binding promise would have been made.

What does this show? One of the conditions of a valid and binding promise, and thus a condition of a right accruing to the promisee, is that he really wants what is promised.[23] Now this does not imply that there must be *benefits* in any straightforward sense. But it does, I think, imply that the obligation "assures a good" to the promisee. For it is the promisee's very want, wish, or desire *to have what is promised done* that the promise is *meant* to satisfy. And it is not implausible to suggest that the satisfaction of someone's (morally permissible) want, wish, or desire amounts to the conferring on him of a certain good.

If we try to imagine cases in which this claim is not satisfied, we shall find the ascription of a right and of a corresponding promissory obligation moot. Suppose, for example, that the promisee asks another to do him an injury or to kill him. We can imagine cases where, to avoid greater evil or unbearable pain, for example, such a promise might be reasonably requested and made and consequently binding. But in such cases there is also as much reason to say that the promise "assures a certain good" to the promisee. If there is no such good reason for the promise but only, say, a desire for self-destruction or mutilation, it is not at all clear that one would be morally free to make such a promise or that once made the promise could be regarded as morally binding.

Let us return now to Hart's example. If a son extracts a promise from his friend to care for his aged mother in his absence, we might reasonably suppose that he does so because, say, he is concerned, as an affectionate son, about his mother's well-being; or, perhaps, because he thinks he is serving his own interests in providing for her care; or even because he wants to discharge what is to him a totally disagreeable filial obligation. That is, we might reasonably suppose that, for one reason or another, the son really wants his mother cared for in his absence, that he has *some* interest in her being cared for, and that he extracts the promise accordingly. But let us not assume any such thing. Let us suppose instead that the son merely wants his friend to make such a promise, but that it is not part of his intention to provide for her care and that he has no interest in doing do.

Now, on the one hand, it might transpire that the friend acquires an obligation to care for the mother and that the mother acquires a right to the promised services—that the promise is binding to this degree, despite the son's secret indifference. For the mother has an interest that needs to be served and the friend freely agrees to serve it. But on the other hand, it would not seem that the son is truly entitled to complain if the friend fails to keep his promise. And that is because he has not satisfied the conditions necessary for acquiring such a right. If there is an obligation, it is not owed to the son (whether or not the friend knows it). If

[23]For a similar point concerning promissory obligations, see Jerome Schneewind, "A Note on Promising," *Philosophical Studies*, vol. 17 (1966), pp. 33–35.

there is a legitimate claim it is not the son's claim but the mother's; and if there is a right it is not his either.

If there is such a difference between the son's moral status in this case and in Hart's original example, so that it is more plausible to ascribe a right to him in the latter than in the former, that difference has to do with the son's reasons for and his sincerity in extracting the promise. What is true of Hart's example that is not true here? The son wants his mother cared for, and for that reason asks his friend to do so. The reason he gives his friend is the same in both cases; but only in Hart's example is that really his reason. So, in both cases at least part of the point of the promise is to satisfy such a desire or wish on the part of the son—to provide for his mother's care—but only in Hart's case will the keeping of the promise actually satisfy such a wish or desire.

This is not to say that the difference between the two cases, which may account for the fact that the son acquires a right in one but not the other, is the fact that in one but not the other the son "stands to *benefit*" from the promised performance. Nevertheless, the fact that the son has an interest in his mother's care and wants her cared for, coupled with the fact that it is *this* wish or desire of the son's that the friend's promise is designed to satisfy, shows that the friend's obligation "assures a good" to the son.

I do not mean to claim that this defense of the beneficiary theory is conclusive. I hope to have shown, rather, that the theory cannot be *dismissed* without further consideration. It is less vulnerable than its critics have supposed, largely because of the differences between its qualified and unqualified versions.

I shall conclude by considering an example that may indicate serious difficulties for the beneficiary theory. The example is suggested (in another connection) by Hart, who maintains that a certain class of moral rights correlates with "political obligations"—obligations to conform to certain social rules. These rights and obligations arise, Hart says, in the following circumstances:

> *when a number of persons conduct any joint enterprise according to rules and thus restrict their liberty, those who have submitted to these restrictions when required have a right to a similar submission from those who have benefited by their submission. The rules may provide that officials should have authority to enforce obedience and make further rules, and this will create a structure of legal rights and duties, but the moral obligation to obey the rules in such circumstances is due to the co-operating members of the society, and they have the correlative moral rights to obedience.* [24]

As I have argued elsewhere,[25] certain qualifications should be added, at least to make the character of the present argument clear. These include (a) actual con-

[24]"Are There Any Natural Rights?", *op. cit.*, p. 185 [this volume, p. 21—*Ed.*].
[25]*Forms and Limits of Utilitarianism* (Oxford, 1965), ch. 5, Sect. A.

formity to the rules is sufficiently widespread to produce some shareable good or to prevent some common evil; (b) this desirable result could not be achieved without such cooperation; (c) the benefits and burdens are fairly distributed; (d) the total benefits outweigh the burdens imposed; (e) *universal* cooperation by those who stand to benefit is *not* required to achieve the desirable end. The last condition is most important, because it explains how it is possible for a "freeloader" to take advantage of others' cooperation without himself performing as the rules require. The conditions also show that the duties imposed by the rules and the moral obligations to conform to them are not beneficial in the qualified sense employed above. For a single breach of such a rule is not sufficient for anyone's loss, and the performances required by these duties and obligations do not consist in directly serving the interests of someone with a correlative right.

The sort of social rule that might satisfy such conditions as I have outlined is the legal rule requiring payment of income tax. This rule imposes a legal duty to pay income tax and, if the conditions are satisfied, then, according to the argument given, one has a moral obligation to conform to such a rule and others have a right to one's conformity or cooperation. Consequently, the qualified beneficiary theory cannot account for such rights, since the legal duties in question are merely useful and the same holds for the moral obligation to obey such a law.

What are the connections between goods and rights in this case? On the one hand, there cannot be such an obligation unless the law, or system of law, is useful (as conditions (a), (b), and (d) require), and unless everyone stands to benefit (as conditions (c) would I think require). So goods *are* essentially involved; but they are involved indirectly, as in the case of merely useful duties. For (as condition (e) seems to guarantee), the obligation to obey the law is *not* contingent on universal obedience being needed for the usefulness of the general practice. The idea that underlies such an obligation and its correlative right is that it would be *unfair* or *unjust* for someone who benefits from others' burdensome cooperation or conformity to fail to perform when his turn came. The idea is not that his failure to conform or cooperate would detract from the usefulness of the general practice or would decrease in any way the benefits that accrue to individuals. For according to the conditions of the argument, even, say, the secret and harmless breaking of necessary rationing restrictions would be wrong and would involve the violation of such a right and the breach of such an obligation.

If this is correct, then it would seem that the only good that can be assured by such an obligation to obey the law in *each* of its instances is the *abstract* or *impersonal* good of justice. It is not a personal good, not a good *to* or *for* a person with a corresponding right. And this does not satisfy the conditions of the qualified beneficiary theory.

Utilitarians would, of course, deny that there is such an obligation, or would insist that it rests on the fact that nonconformity or noncooperation can reasonably be expected to have bad results, by setting a bad example which may lead others to disobey, thus tending eventually to decrease the usefulness of the law. This suggests that the good assured to individuals is simply the confidence that their burdensome cooperation will not be in vain. Alternatively, utilitarians may seek to argue that the abstract or impersonal good of justice reduces, ultimately, to personal goods.[26]

[26]Earlier versions of this paper were read at Cornell University and the Universities of Waterloo, Massachusetts, Pittsburgh, Michigan, and Texas, where I received helpful comments and criticisms. I have also benefited greatly from discussions with Norman Malcolm and Michael Stocker and from the suggestions of Ellen Coleman, Robert Monk, William Nelson, and John Turner.

The Nature and Value
of Rights[1]
•
Joel Feinberg

1

I would like to begin by conducting a thought experiment. Try to imagine Nowheresville—a world very much like our own except that no one, or hardly anyone (the qualification is not important), has *rights*. If this flaw makes No-wheresville too ugly to hold very long in contemplation, we can make it as pretty as we wish in other moral respects. We can, for example, make the human beings in it as attractive and virtuous as possible without taxing our conceptions of the limits of human nature. In particular, let the virtues of moral sensibility flourish. Fill this imagined world with as much benevolence, compassion, sympathy, and pity as it will conveniently hold without strain. Now we can imagine men helping one another from compassionate motives merely, quite as much or even more than they do in our actual world from a variety of more complicated motives.

This picture, pleasant as it is in some respects, would hardly have satisfied Immanuel Kant. Benevolently motivated actions do good, Kant admitted, and therefore are better, *ceteris paribus*, than malevolently motivated actions; but no action can have supreme kind of worth—what Kant called "moral worth"—unless its whole motivating power derives from the thought that it is *required by duty*. Accordingly, let us try to make Nowheresville more appealing to Kant by intro-

From *The Journal of Value Inquiry*, Vol. 4 (Winter 1970), 243–257. Reprinted with permission of the author and *The Journal of Value Inquiry*.

[1]This article was first given as an Isenberg Memorial Lecture at Michigan State University, Winter Series, 1969. Presented to the Conference on Political and Moral Philosophy held at Ripon College, Wisconsin, Sept. 18 and 19, 1969, and to AMINATAPHIL, Nov. 1969.

ducing the idea of duty into it, and letting the sense of duty be a sufficient motive for many beneficent and honorable actions. But doesn't this bring our original thought experiment to an abortive conclusion? If duties are permitted entry into Nowheresville, are not rights necessarily smuggled in along with them?

The question is well-asked, and requires here a brief digression so that we might consider the so-called "doctrine of the logical correlativity of rights and duties." This is the doctrine that (i) all duties entail other people's rights and (ii) all rights entail other people's duties. Only the first part of the doctrine, the alleged entailment from duties to rights, need concern us here. Is this part of the doctrine correct? It should not be surprising that my answer is: "In a sense yes and in a sense no." Etymologically, the word "duty" is associated with actions that are *due* someone else, the payments of debts *to* creditors, the keeping of agreements with promisees, the payment of club dues, or legal fees, or tariff levies to appropriate authorities or their representatives. In this original sense of "duty," all duties are correlated with the rights of those *to* whom the duty is owed. On the other hand, there seem to be numerous classes of duties, both of a legal and non-legal kind, that are *not* logically correlated with the rights of other persons. This seems to be a consequence of the fact that the word "duty" has come to be used for *any* action understood to be *required,* whether by the rights of others, or by law, or by higher authority, or by conscience, or whatever. When the notion of requirement is in clear focus it is likely to seem the only element in the idea of duty that is essential, and the other component notion—that a duty is something *due* someone else— drops off. Thus, in this widespread but derivative usage, "duty" tends to be used for any action we feel we *must* (for whatever reason) do. It comes, in short, to be a term of moral modality merely; and it is no wonder that the first thesis of the logical correlativity doctrine often fails.

Let us then introduce duties into Nowheresville; but only in the sense of actions that are, or are believed to be, morally mandatory, but not in the older sense of actions that are due others and can be claimed by others as their right. Nowheresville now can have duties of the sort imposed by positive law. A legal duty is not something we are implored or advised to do merely; it is something the law, or an authority under the law, *requires* us to do whether we want to or not, under pain of penalty. When traffic lights turn red, however, there is no determinate person who can plausibly be said to claim our stopping as his due, so that the motorist owes it to *him* to stop, in the way a debtor owes it to his creditor to pay. In our own actual world, of course, we sometimes owe it to our *fellow motorists* to stop; but that kind of right-correlated duty does not exist in Nowheresville. There, motorists "owe" obedience to the Law, but they owe nothing to one another. When they collide, no matter who is at fault, no one is morally accountable to anyone else, and no one has any sound grievance or "right to complain."

When we leave legal contexts to consider moral obligations and other extra-legal duties, a greater variety of duties-without-correlative-rights present themselves. Duties of charity, for example, require us to contribute to one or another of a large number of eligible recipients, no one of whom can claim our contribution from us as his due. Charitable contributions are more like gratuitous services, favors, and gifts than like repayments of debts or reparations; and yet we do have duties to be charitable. Many persons, moreover, in our actual world believe that they are required by their own consciences to do more than that "duty" that *can* be demanded of them by their prospective beneficiaries. I have quoted elsewhere the citation from H. B. Acton of a character in a Malraux novel who "gave all his supply of poison to his fellow prisoners to enable them by suicide to escape the burning alive which was to be their fate and his." This man, Acton adds, "probably did not think that [the others] had more of a right to the poison than he had, though he thought it his duty to give it to them."[2] I am sure that there are many actual examples, less dramatically heroic than this fictitious one, of persons who believe, rightly or wrongly, that they *must do* something (hence the word "duty") for another person in excess of what that person can appropriately demand of him (hence the absence of "right").

Now the digression is over and we can return to Nowheresville and summarize what we have put in it thus far. We now find spontaneous benevolence in somewhat larger degree than in our actual world, and also the acknowledged existence of duties of obedience, duties of charity, and duties imposed by exacting private consciences, and also, let us suppose, a degree of conscientiousness in respect to those duties somewhat in excess of what is to be found in our actual world. I doubt that Kant would be fully satisfied with Nowheresville even now that duty and respect for law and authority have been added to it; but I feel certain that he would regard their addition at least as an improvement. I will now introduce two further moral practices into Nowheresville that will make that world very little more appealing to Kant, but will make it appear more familiar to us. These are the practices connected with the notions of *personal desert* and what I call a *sovereign monopoly of rights*.

When a person is said to deserve something good from us what is meant in part is that there would be a certain propriety in our giving that good thing to him in virtue of the kind of person he is, perhaps, or more likely, in virtue of some specific thing he has done. The propriety involved here is a much weaker kind than that which derives from our having promised him the good thing or from his having qualified for it by satisfying the well-advertised conditions of some public rule. In the latter case he could be said not merely to deserve the good thing but also to have a *right* to it, that is to be in a position to demand it as his due; and of course we will not have that sort of thing in Nowheresville. That weaker kind of propriety which is mere desert is simply a kind of *fittingness* between one party's character or action and another party's favorable response, much like that between humor and laughter, or good performance and applause.

The following seems to be the origin of the idea of deserving good or bad treatment from others: A master or lord was under no obligation to reward his servant for especially good service; still a master might naturally feel that there would be a special fittingness in giving a gratuitous reward as a grateful response

[2]H. B. Acton, "Symposium on 'Rights'," *Proceedings of the Aristotelian Society,* Supplementary Volume 24 (1950), pp. 107–8.

to the good service (or conversely imposing a penalty for bad service). Such an act while surely fitting and proper was entirely supererogatory. The fitting response in turn from the rewarded servant should be gratitude. If the deserved reward had not been given him he should have had no complaint, since he only *deserved* the reward, as opposed to having a *right* to it, or a ground for claiming it as his due.

The idea of desert has evolved a good bit away from its beginnings by now, but nevertheless, it seems clearly to be one of those words J. L. Austin said "never entirely forget their pasts."[3] Today servants qualify for their wages by doing their agreed upon chores, no more and no less. If their wages are not forthcoming, their contractual rights have been violated and they can make legal claim to the money that is their due. If they do less than they agreed to do, however, their employers may "dock" them, by paying them proportionately less than the agreed upon fee. This is all a matter of right. But if the servant does a splendid job, above and beyond his minimal contractual duties, the employer is under no further obligation to reward him, for this was not agreed upon, even tacitly, in advance. The additional service was all the servant's idea and done entirely on his own. Nevertheless, the morally sensitive employer may feel that it would be exceptionally appropriate for him to respond, freely on *his* own, to the servant's meritorious service, with a reward. The employee cannot demand it as his due, but he will happily accept it, with gratitude, as a fitting response to his desert.

In our age of organized labor, even this picture is now archaic; for almost every kind of exchange of service is governed by hard bargained contracts so that even bonuses can sometimes be demanded as a matter of right, and nothing is given for nothing on either side of the bargaining table. And perhaps that is a good thing; for consider an anachronistic instance of the earlier kind of practice that survives, at least as a matter of form, in the quaint old practice of "tipping." The tip was originally conceived as a reward that has to be earned by "zealous service." It is not something to be taken for granted as a standard response to *any* service. That is to say that its payment is a *"gratuity,"* not a discharge of obligation, but something given apart from, or in addition to, anything the recipient can expect as a matter of right. That is what tipping originally meant at any rate, and tips are still referred to as "gratuities" in the tax forms. But try to explain all that to a New York cab driver! If he has *earned* his gratuity, by God, he has it coming, and there had better be sufficient acknowledgement of his desert or he'll give you a piece of his mind! I'm not generally prone to defend New York cab drivers, but they do have a point here. There is the making of a paradox in the queerly unstable concept of an "earned gratuity." One can understand how "desert" in the weak sense of "propriety" or "mere fittingness" tends to generate a stronger sense in which desert is itself the ground for a claim of right.

In Nowheresville, nevertheless, we will have only the original weak kind of desert. Indeed, it will be impossible to keep this idea out if we allow such practices as teachers grading students, judges awarding prizes, and servants serving benevolent but class-conscious masters. Nowheresville is a reasonably good world

[3]J. L. Austin, "A Plea for Excuses," *Proceedings of the Aristotelian Society*, Vol. 57 (1956–57).

in many ways, and its teachers, judges, and masters will generally try to give students, contestants, and servants the grades, prizes, and rewards they deserve. For this the recipients will be grateful; but they will never think to complain, or even feel aggrieved, when expected responses to desert fail. The masters, judges, and teachers don't *have* to do good things, after all, for *anyone*. One should be happy that they *ever* treat us well, and not grumble over their occasional lapses. Their hoped for responses, after all, are *gratuities*, and there is no wrong in the omission of what is merely gratuitous. Such is the response of persons who have no concept of *rights*, even persons who are proud of their own deserts.[4]

Surely, one might ask, rights have to come in somewhere, if we are to have even moderately complex forms of social organization. Without rules that confer rights and impose obligations, how can we have ownership of property, bargains and deals, promises and contracts, appointments and loans, marriages and partnerships? Very well, let us introduce all of these social and economic practices into Nowheresville, but *with one big twist*. With them I should like to introduce the curious notion of a "sovereign right-monopoly." You will recall that the subjects in Hobbes's *Leviathan* had no rights whatever against their sovereign. He could do as he liked with them, even gratuitously harm them, but this gave them no valid grievance against him. The sovereign, to be sure, had a certain duty to treat his subjects well, but this duty was owed not to the subjects directly, but to God, just as we might have a duty to a person to treat his property well, but of course no duty to the property itself but only to its owner. Thus, while the sovereign was quite capable of *harming* his subjects, he could commit no wrong against them that they could complain about, since they had no prior claims against his conduct. The only party *wronged* by the sovereign's mistreatment of his subjects was God, the supreme lawmaker. Thus, in repenting cruelty to his subjects, the sovereign might say to God, as David did after killing Uriah, "to Thee only have I sinned."[5]

Even in the *Leviathan*, however, ordinary people had ordinary rights *against one another*. They played roles, occupied offices, made agreements, and signed contracts. In a genuine "sovereign right-monopoly," as I shall be using that phrase, they will do all those things too, and thus incur genuine obligations toward one another; but the obligations (here is the twist) will not be owed directly *to* promisees, creditors, parents, and the like, but rather to God alone, or to the members of some elite, or to a single sovereign under God. Hence, the rights correlative to the obligations that derive from these transactions are all owned by some "outside" authority.

As far as I know, no philosopher has ever suggested that even our role and contract obligations (in this, our actual world) are all owed directly to a divine intermediary; but some theologians have approached such extreme moral occa-

[4]For a fuller discussion of the concept of personal desert see my "Justice and Personal Desert," *Nomos VI, Justice*, ed. by C. J. Friedrich and J. Chapman (New York: Atherton Press, 1963), pp. 69–97.

[5]II Sam. 11. Cited with approval by Thomas Hobbes in *The Leviathan*, Part II, Chap. 21.

sionalism. I have in mind the familiar phrase in certain widely distributed religious tracts that "it takes three to marry," which suggests that marital vows are not made between bride and groom directly but between each spouse and God, so that if one breaks his vow, the other cannot rightly complain of being wronged, since only God could have claimed performance of the marital duties as his *own* due; and hence God alone had a claim-right violated by nonperformance. If John breaks his vow to God, he might then properly repent in the words of David: "To Thee only have I sinned."

In our actual world, very few spouses conceive of their mutual obligations in this way; but their small children, at a certain stage in their moral upbringing, are likely to feel precisely this way toward *their* mutual obligations. If Billy kicks Bobby and is punished by Daddy, he may come to feel contrition for his naughtiness induced by his painful estrangement from the loved parent. He may then be happy to make amends and sincere apology *to Daddy*; but when Daddy insists that he apologize to his wronged brother, that is another story. A direct apology to Billy would be a tacit recognition of Billy's status as a right-holder against him, someone he can wrong as well as harm, and someone to whom he is directly accountable for his wrongs. This is a status Bobby will happily accord Daddy; but it would imply a respect for Billy that he does not presently feel, so he bitterly resents according it to him. On the "three-to-marry" model, the relations between each spouse and God would be like those between Bobby and Daddy: respect for the other spouse as an independent claimant would not even be necessary; and where present, of course, never sufficient.

The advocates of the "three to marry" model who conceive it either as a description of our actual institution of marriage or a recommendation of what marriage ought to be, may wish to escape this embarrassment by granting rights to spouses in capacities other than as promisees. They may wish to say, for example, that when John promises God that he will be faithful to Mary, a right is thus conferred not only on God as promisee but also on Mary herself as third-party beneficiary, just as when John contracts with an insurance company and names Mary as his intended beneficiary, she has a right to the accumulated funds after John's death, even though the insurance company made no promise to her. But this seems to be an unnecessarily cumbersome complication contributing nothing to our understanding of the marriage bond. The life insurance transaction is necessarily a three-party relation, involving occupants of three distinct offices, no two of whom alone could do the whole job. The transaction, after all, is defined as the purchase by the customer (first office) from the vendor (second office) of protection for a beneficiary (third office) against the customer's untimely death. Marriage, on the other hand, in this our actual world, appears to be a binary relation between a husband and wife, and even though third parties such as children, neighbors, psychiatrists, and priests may sometimes be helpful and even causally necessary for the survival of the relation, they are not logically necessary to our *conception* of the relation, and indeed many married couples do quite well without them. Still, I am not now purporting to describe our actual world, but rather trying to contrast it with a counterpart world of the imagination. In *that* world, it takes three to make almost *any* moral relation and all rights are owned by God or some sovereign under God.

There will, of course, be delegated authorities in the imaginary world, empowered to give commands to their underlings and to punish them for their disobedience. But the commands are all given in the name of the right-monopoly who in turn are the only persons to whom obligations are owed. Hence, even intermediate superiors do not have claim-rights against their subordinates but only legal *powers* to create obligations in the subordinates *to* the monopolistic right-holders, and also the legal *privilege* to impose penalties in the name of that monopoly.

2

So much for the imaginary "world without rights." If some of the moral concepts and practices I have allowed into that world do not sit well with one another, no matter. Imagine Nowheresville with all of these practices if you can, or with any harmonious subset of them, if you prefer. The important thing is not what I've let into it, but what I have kept out. The remainder of this paper will be devoted to an analysis of what precisely a world is missing when it does not contain rights and why that absence is morally important.

The most conspicuous difference, I think, between the Nowheresvillians and ourselves has something to do with the activity of *claiming*. Nowheresvillians, even when they are discriminated against invidiously, or left without the things they need, or otherwise badly treated, do not think to leap to their feet and make righteous demands against one another, though they may not hesitate to resort to force and trickery to get what they want. They have no notion of rights, so they do not have a notion of what is their due: hence they do not claim before they take. The conceptual linkage between personal rights and claiming has long been noticed by legal writers and is reflected in the standard usage in which "claim-rights" are distinguished from the mere liberties, immunities, and powers, also sometimes called "rights," with which they are easily confused. When a person has a legal claim-right to X, it must be the case (i) that he is at liberty in respect to X, i.e., that he has no duty to refrain from or relinquish X, and also (ii) that his liberty is the ground of other people's *duties* to grant him X or not to interfere with him in respect to X. Thus, in the sense of claim-rights, it is true by definition that rights logically entail other people's duties. The paradigmatic examples of such rights are the creditor's right to be paid a debt by his debtor, and the landowner's right not to be interfered with by anyone in the exclusive occupancy of his land. The creditor's right against his debtor, for example, and the debtor's duty to his creditor, are precisely the same relation seen from two different vantage points, as inextricably linked as the two sides of the same coin.

And yet, this is not quite an accurate account of the matter, for it fails to do justice to the way claim-rights are somehow prior to, or more basic than, the duties with which they are necessarily correlated. If Nip has a claim-right against

Tuck, it is because of this fact that Tuck has a duty to Nip. It is only because some-thing from Tuck is *due* Nip (directional element) that there is something Tuck *must do* (modal element). This is a relation, moreover, in which Tuck is bound and Nip is free. Nip not only *has* a right, but he can choose whether or not to exercise it, whether to claim it, whether to register complaints upon its infringement, even whether to release Tuck from his duty, and forget the whole thing. If the personal claim-right is also backed up by criminal sanctions, however, Tuck may yet have a duty of obedience to the law from which no one, not even Nip, may release him. He would even have such duties if he lived in Nowheresville; but duties subject to acts of claiming, duties derivative from and contingent upon the personal rights of others, are unknown and undreamed of in Nowheresville.

Many philosophical writers have simply identified rights with claims. The dictionaries tend to define "claims," in turn, as "assertions of right," a dizzying piece of circularity that led one philosopher to complain—"We go in search of rights and are directed to claims, and then back again to rights in bureaucratic futility."[6] What then is the relation between a claim and a right?

As we shall see, a right *is* a kind of claim, and a claim is "an assertion of right," so that a formal definition of either notion in terms of the other will not get us very far. Thus if a "formal definition" of the usual philosophical sort is what we are after, the game is over before it has begun, and we can say that the concept of a right is a "simple, undefinable, unanalysable primitive." Here as elsewhere in philosophy this will have the effect of making the commonplace seem unnec-essarily mysterious. We would be better advised, I think, not to attempt a formal definition of either "right" or "claim," but rather to use the idea of a claim in in-formal elucidation of the idea of a right. This is made possible by the fact that *claiming* is an elaborate sort of rule-governed *activity*. A claim is that which is claimed, the object of the act of claiming. There is, after all, a verb "to claim," but no verb "to right." If we concentrate on the whole activity of claiming, which is public, familiar, and open to our observation, rather than on its upshot alone, we may learn more about the generic nature of rights than we could ever hope to learn from a formal definition, even if one were possible. Moreover, certain facts about rights more easily, if not solely, expressible in the language of claims and claiming are essential to a full understanding not only of what rights are, but also why they are so vitally important.

Let us begin then by distinguishing between: (i) making claim to. . . . , (ii) claiming that. . . . , and (iii) having a claim. One sort of thing we may be doing when we claim is to *make claim to something*. This is "to petition or seek by virtue of supposed right; to demand as due." Sometimes this is done by an acknowledged right-holder when he serves notice that he now wants turned over to him that which has already been acknowledged to be his, something borrowed, say, or im-properly taken from him. This is often done by turning in a chit, a receipt, an I.O.U., a check, an insurance policy, or a deed, that is, a *title* to something currently in the possession of someone else. On other occasions, making claim is making

[6]H. B. Acton. *Op. cit.*

application for titles or rights themselves, as when a mining prospector stakes a claim to mineral rights, or a householder to a tract of land in the public domain, or an inventor to his patent rights. In the one kind of case, to make claim is to exercise rights one already has by presenting title; in the other kind of case it is to apply for the title itself, by showing that one has satisfied the conditions specified by a rule for the ownership of title and therefore that one can demand it as one's due.

Generally speaking, only the person who has a title or who has qualified for it, or someone speaking in his name, can make claim to something as a matter of right. It is an important fact about rights (or claims), then, that they can be claimed only by those who have them. Anyone can claim, of course, *that* this umbrella is yours, but only you or your representative can actually claim the umbrella. If Smith owes Jones five dollars, only Jones can claim the five dollars as his own, though any bystander can *claim that* it belongs to Jones. One important difference then between *making legal claim to* and *claiming that* is that the former is a legal performance with direct legal consequences whereas the latter is often a mere piece of descriptive commentary with no legal force. Legally speaking, *making claim to* can itself make things happen. This sense of "claiming," then, might well be called "the performative sense." The legal power to claim (performatively) one's right or the things to which one has a right seems to be essential to the very notion of a right. A right to which one could not make claim (i.e., not even for recognition) would be a very "imperfect" right indeed!

Claiming that one has a right (what we can call "propositional claiming" as opposed to "performative claiming") is another sort of thing one can do with language, but it is not the sort of doing that characteristically has legal consequences. To claim that one has rights is to make an assertion that one has them, and to make it in such a manner as to demand or insist that they be recognized. In this sense of "claim" many things in addition to rights can be claimed, that is, many other kinds of proposition can be asserted in the claiming way. I can claim, for example, that you, he, or she has certain rights, or that Julius Caesar once had certain rights; or I can claim that certain statements are true, or that I have certain skills, or accomplishments, or virtually anything at all. I can claim that the earth is flat. What is essential to *claiming that* is the manner of assertion. One can assert without even caring very much whether anyone is listening, but part of the point of propositional claiming is to *make sure* people listen. When I claim to others that I know something, for example, I am not merely asserting it, but rather "obtruding my putative knowledge upon their attention, demanding that it be recognized, that appropriate notice be taken of it by those concerned. . . ."[7] Not every truth is properly assertable, much less claimable, in every context. To claim that something is the case in circumstances that justify no more than calm assertion is to behave like a boor. (This kind of boorishness, I might add, is probably less common in No-

[7]G. J. Warnock, "Claims to Knowledge," *Proceedings of the Aristotelian Society,* Supplementary Volume 36 (1962), p. 21.

wheresville.) But not to claim in the appropriate circumstances that one has a right is to be spiritless or foolish. A list of "appropriate circumstances" would include occasions when one is challenged, when one's possession is denied, or seems insufficiently acknowledged or appreciated; and of course even in these circumstances, the claiming should be done only with an appropriate degree of vehemence.

Even if there are conceivable circumstances in which one would admit rights diffidently, there is no doubt that their characteristic use and that for which they are distinctively well suited, is to be claimed, demanded, affirmed, insisted upon. They are especially sturdy objects to "stand upon," a most useful sort of moral furniture. Having rights, of course, makes claiming possible; but it is claiming that gives rights their special moral significance. This feature of rights is connected in a way with the customary rhetoric about what it is to be a human being. Having rights enables us to "stand up like men," to look others in the eye, and to feel in some fundamental way the equal of anyone. To think of oneself as the holder of rights is not to be unduly but properly proud, to have that minimal self-respect that is necessary to be worthy of the love and esteem of others. Indeed, respect for persons (this is an intriguing idea) may simply be respect for their rights, so that there cannot be the one without the other; and what is called "human dignity" may simply be the recognizable capacity to assert claims. To respect a person then, or to think of him as possessed of human dignity, simply *is* to think of him as a potential maker of claims. Not all of this can be packed into a definition of "rights"; but these are *facts* about the possession of rights that argue well their supreme moral importance. More than anything else I am going to say, these facts explain what is wrong with Nowheresville.

We come now to the third interesting employment of the claiming vocabulary, that involving not the verb "to claim" but the substantive "a claim." What is it to *have a claim* and how is this related to rights? I would like to suggest that *having a claim consists in being in a position to claim, that is, to make claim to* or *claim that.* If this suggestion is correct it shows the primacy of the verbal over the nominative forms. It links claims to a kind of activity and obviates the temptation to think of claims as *things,* on the model of coins, pencils, and other material possessions which we can carry in our hip pockets. To be sure, we often make or establish our claims by presenting titles, and these typically have the form of receipts, tickets, certificates, and other pieces of paper or parchment. The title, however, is not the same thing as the claim; rather it is the evidence that establishes the claim as valid. On this analysis, one might have a claim without ever claiming that to which one is entitled, or without even knowing that one has the claim; for one might simply be ignorant of the fact that one is in a position to claim; or one might be unwilling to exploit that position for one reason or another, including fear that the legal machinery is broken down or corrupt and will not enforce one's claim despite its validity.

Nearly all writers maintain that there is some intimate connection between having a claim and having a right. Some identify right and claim without qualification; some define "right" as justified or justifiable claim, others as recognized claim, still others as valid claim. My own preference is for the latter definition. Some writers, however, reject the identification of rights with valid claims on the ground that all claims as such are valid, so that the expression "valid claim" is redundant. These writers, therefore, would identify rights with claims *simpliciter*. But this is a very simple confusion. All claims, to be sure, are *put forward* as justified, whether they are justified in fact or not. A claim conceded even by its maker to have no validity is not a claim at all, but a mere demand. The highwayman, for example, *demands* his victim's money; but he hardly makes claim to it as rightfully his own.

But it does not follow from this sound point that it is redundant to qualify claims as justified (or as I prefer, valid) in the definition of a right; for it remains true that not all claims put forward as valid really are valid; and only the valid ones can be acknowledged as rights.

If having a valid claim is not redundant, i.e., if it is not redundant to pronounce *another's* claim valid, there must be such a thing as having a claim that is not valid. What would this be like? One might accumulate just enough evidence to argue with relevance and cogency that one has a right (or ought to be granted a right), although one's case might not be overwhelmingly conclusive. In such a case, one might have strong enough argument to be entitled to a hearing and given fair consideration. When one is in this position, it might be said that one "has a claim" that deserves to be weighed carefully. Nevertheless, the balance of reasons may turn out to militate against recognition of the claim, so that the claim, which one admittedly had, and perhaps still does, is not a valid claim or right. "Having a claim" in this sense is an expression very much like the legal phrase "having a *prima facie* case." A plaintiff establishes a *prima facie* case for the defendant's liability when he establishes grounds that will be sufficient for liability unless outweighed by reasons of a different sort that may be offered by the defendant. Similarly, in the criminal law, a grand jury returns an indictment when it thinks that the prosecution has sufficient evidence to be taken seriously and given a fair hearing, whatever countervailing reasons may eventually be offered on the other side. That initial evidence, serious but not conclusive, is also sometimes called a *prima facie* case. In a parallel *"prima facie* sense" of "claim," having a claim to X is not (yet) the same as having a right to X, but is rather having a case of at least minimal plausibility that one has a right to X, a case that does establish a right, not to X, but to a fair hearing and consideration. Claims, so conceived, differ in degree: some are stronger than others. Rights, on the other hand, do not differ in degree; no one right is more of a right than another.[8]

---

[8]This is the important difference between rights and mere claims. It is analogous to the difference between *evidence* of guilt (subject to degrees of cogency) and conviction of guilt (which is all or nothing). One can "have evidence" that is not conclusive just as one can "have a claim" that is not valid. "Prima-facieness" is built into the sense of "claim," but the notion of a "prima-facie right" makes little sense. On the latter point see A. I. Melden, *Rights and Right Conduct* (Oxford: Basil Blackwell, 1959), pp. 18–20, and Herbert Morris, "Persons and Punishment," *The Monist*, Vol. 52 (1968), pp. 498–9.

Another reason for not identifying rights with claims *simply* is that there is a well-established usage in international law that makes a theoretically interesting distinction between claims and rights. Statesmen are sometimes led to speak of "claims" when they are concerned with the natural needs of deprived human beings in conditions of scarcity. Young orphans *need* good upbringings, balanced diets, education, and technical training everywhere in the world; but unfortunately there are many places where these goods are in such short supply that it is impossible to provision all who need them. If we persist, nevertheless, in speaking of these needs as constituting rights and not merely claims, we are committed to the conception of a right which is an entitlement *to* some good, but not a valid claim *against* any particular individual; for in conditions of scarcity there may be no determinate individuals who can plausibly be said to have a duty to provide the missing goods to those in need. J. E. S. Fawcett therefore prefers to keep the distinction between claims and rights firmly in mind. "Claims," he writes, "are needs and demands in movement, and there is a continuous transformation, as a society advances [toward greater abundance] of economic and social claims into civil and political rights . . . and not all countries or all claims are by any means at the same stage in the process."[9] The manifesto writers on the other side who seem to identify needs, or at least basic needs, with what they call "human rights," are more properly described, I think, as urging upon the world community the moral principle that *all* basic human needs ought to be recognized as *claims* (in the customary *prima facie* sense) worthy of sympathy and serious consideration right now, even though, in many cases, they cannot yet plausibly be treated as *valid* claims, that is, as grounds of any other people's duties. This way of talking avoids the anomaly of ascribing to all human beings now, even those in pre-industrial societies, such "economic and social rights" as "periodic holidays with pay."[10]

Still, for all of that, I have a certain sympathy with the manifesto writers, and I am even willing to speak of a special "manifesto sense" of "right," in which a right need not be correlated with another's duty. Natural needs are real claims if only upon hypothetical future beings not yet in existence. I accept the moral principle that to have an unfulfilled need is to have a kind of claim against the world, even if against no one in particular. A natural need for some good as such, like a natural desert, is always a reason in support of a claim to that good. A person in need, then, is always "in a position" to make a claim, even when there is no one in the corresponding position to do anything about it. Such claims, based on need alone, are "permanent possibilities of rights," the natural seed from which rights grow. When manifesto writers speak of them as if already actual rights, they are easily forgiven, for this is but a powerful way of expressing the conviction that they ought to be recognized by states here and now as potential rights and con-

[9] J. E. S. Fawcett. "The International Protection of Human Rights," in *Political Theory and the Rights of Man*, ed. by D. D. Raphael (Bloomington: Indiana University Press, 1967), pp. 125 and 128.

[10] As declared in Article 24 of *The Universal Declaration of Human Rights* adopted on December 10, 1948, by the General Assembly of the United Nations.

sequently as determinants of *present* aspirations and guides to *present* policies. That usage, I think, is a valid exercise of rhetorical licence.

I prefer to characterize rights as valid claims rather than justified ones, because I suspect that justification is rather too broad a qualification. "Validity," as I understand it, is justification of a peculiar and narrow kind, namely justification within a system of rules. A man has a legal right when the official recognition of his claim (as valid) is called for by the governing rules. This definition, of course, hardly applies to moral rights, but that is not because the genus of which moral rights are a species is something other than *claims*. A man has a moral right when he has a claim the recognition of which is called for—not (necessarily) by legal rules—but by moral principles, or the principles of an enlightened conscience.

There is one final kind of attack on the generic identification of rights with claims, and it has been launched with great spirit in a recent article by H. J. McCloskey, who holds that rights are not essentially claims at all, but rather entitlements. The springboard of his argument is his insistence that rights in their essential character are always *rights to*, not *rights against*:

> My right to life is not a right against anyone. It is my right and by virtue of it, it is normally permissible for me to sustain my life in the face of obstacles. It does give rise to rights against others in the sense that others have or may come to have duties to refrain from killing me, but it is essentially a right of mine, not an infinite list of claims, hypothetical and actual, against an infinite number of actual, potential, and as yet nonexistent human beings. . . . Similarly, the right of the tennis club member to play on the club courts is a right to play, not a right against some vague group of potential or possible obstructors.[11]

The argument seems to be that since rights are essentially rights *to*, whereas claims are essentially claims *against*, rights cannot be claims, though they can be grounds for claims. The argument is doubly defective though. First of all, contrary to McCloskey, rights (at least legal claim-rights) *are* held *against* others. McCloskey admits this in the case of *in personam* rights (what he calls "special rights") but denies it in the case of *in rem* rights (which he calls "general rights"):

> Special rights are sometimes against specific individuals or institutions—e.g. rights created by promises, contracts, etc. . . . but these differ from . . . characteristic . . . general rights where the right is simply a right to. . . .[12]

As far as I can tell, the only reason McCloskey gives for denying that *in rem* rights are against others is that those against whom they would have to hold make up an enormously multitudinous and "vague" group, including hypothetical people

[11]H. J. McCloskey, "Rights," *Philosophical Quarterly*, Vol. 15 (1965), p. 118.
[12]*Loc. cit.*

not yet even in existence. Many others have found this a paradoxical consequence of the notion of *in rem* rights, but I see nothing troublesome in it. If a general rule gives me a right of noninterference in a certain respect against everybody, then there are literally hundreds of millions of people who have a duty toward me in that respect; and if the same general rule gives the same right to everyone else, then it imposes on me literally hundreds of millions of duties—or duties towards hundreds of millions of people. I see nothing paradoxical about this, however. The duties, after all, are negative; and I can discharge all of them at a stroke simply by minding my own business. And if all human beings make up one moral community and there are hundreds of millions of human beings, we should expect there to be hundreds of millions of moral relations holding between them.

McCloskey's other premise is even more obviously defective. There is no good reason to think that all *claims* are "essentially" *against,* rather than *to.* Indeed most of the discussion of claims above has been of claims *to,* and as we have seen, the law finds it useful to recognize claims *to* (or "mere claims") that are not yet qualified to be claims *against,* or rights (except in a "manifesto sense" of "rights").

Whether we are speaking of claims or rights, however, we must notice that they seem to have two dimensions, as indicated by the prepositions "to" and "against," and it is quite natural to wonder whether either of these dimensions is somehow more fundamental or essential than the other. All rights seem to merge *entitlements to* do, have, omit, or be something with *claims against* others to act or refrain from acting in certain ways. In some statements of rights the entitlement is perfectly determinate (e.g., *to* play tennis) and the claim vague (e.g., *against* "some vague group of potential or possible obstructors"); but in other cases the object of the claim is clear and determinate (e.g., *against* one's parents), and the entitlement general and indeterminate (e.g., to be given a proper upbringing). If we mean by "entitlement" that *to* which one has a right and by "claim" something directed at those *against* whom the right holds (as McCloskey apparently does), then we can say that all claim-rights necessarily involve both, though in individual cases the one element or the other may be in sharper focus.

In brief conclusion: To have a right is to have a claim against someone whose recognition as valid is called for by some set of governing rules or moral principles. To have a *claim* in turn, is to have a case meriting consideration, that is, to have reasons or grounds that put one in a position to engage in performative and propositional claiming. The activity of claiming, finally, as much as any other thing, makes for self-respect and respect for others, gives a sense to the notion of personal dignity, and distinguishes this otherwise morally flawed world from the even worse world of Nowheresville.

Taking Rights Seriously
•
Ronald Dworkin

1. The Rights of Citizens

The language of rights now dominates political debate in the United States. Does the Government respect the moral and political rights of its citizens? Or does the Government's foreign policy, or its race policy, fly in the face of these rights? Do the minorities whose rights have been violated have the right to violate the law in return? Or does the silent majority itself have rights, including the right that those who break the law be punished? It is not surprising that these questions are now prominent. The concept of rights, and particularly the concept of rights against the Government, has its most natural use when a political society is divided, and appeals to co-operation or a common goal are pointless.

The debate does not include the issue of whether citizens have *some* moral rights against their Government. It seems accepted on all sides that they do. Conventional lawyers and politicians take it as a point of pride that our legal system recognizes, for example, individual rights of free speech, equality, and due process. They base their claim that our law deserves respect, at least in part, on that fact, for they would not claim that totalitarian systems deserve the same loyalty.

From *Taking Rights Seriously* by Ronald Dworkin (Cambridge: Harvard University Press, 1977), pp. 184–205. Originally published in the *New York Review of Books,* December 17, 1970. Copyright © 1970 by NYREV, Inc. and 1977 by Ronald Dworkin. Reprinted by permission of the author and the publishers.

Some philosophers, of course, reject the idea that citizens have rights apart from what the law happens to give them. Bentham thought that the idea of moral rights was 'nonsense on stilts'. But that view has never been part of our orthodox political theory, and politicians of both parties appeal to the rights of the people to justify a great part of what they want to do. I shall not be concerned, in this essay, to defend the thesis that citizens have moral rights against their governments; I want instead to explore the implications of that thesis for those, including the present United States Government, who profess to accept it.

It is much in dispute, of course, what *particular* rights citizens have. Does the acknowledged right to free speech, for example, include the right to participate in nuisance demonstrations? In practice the Government will have the last word on what an individual's rights are, because its police will do what its officials and courts say. But that does not mean that the Government's view is necessarily the correct view; anyone who thinks it does must believe that men and women have only such moral rights as Government chooses to grant, which means that they have no moral rights at all.

All this is sometimes obscured in the United States by the constitutional system. The American Constitution provides a set of individual *legal* rights in the First Amendment, and in the due process, equal protection, and similar clauses. Under present legal practice the Supreme Court has the power to declare an act of Congress or of a state legislature void if the Court finds that the act offends these provisions. This practice has led some commentators to suppose that individual moral rights are fully protected by this system, but that is hardly so, nor could it be so.

The Constitution fuses legal and moral issues, by making the validity of a law depend on the answer to complex moral problems, like the problem of whether a particular statute respects the inherent equality of all men. This fusion has important consequences for the debates about civil disobedience; I have described these elsewhere[1] and I shall refer to them later. But it leaves open two prominent questions. It does not tell us whether the Constitution, even properly interpreted, recognizes all the moral rights that citizens have, and it does not tell us whether, as many suppose, citizens would have a duty to obey the law even if it did invade their moral rights.

Both questions become crucial when some minority claims moral rights which the law denies, like the right to run its local school system, and which lawyers agree are not protected by the Constitution. The second question becomes crucial when, as now, the majority is sufficiently aroused so that Constitutional amendments to eliminate rights, like the right against self-incrimination, are seriously proposed. It is also crucial in nations, like the United Kingdom, that have no constitution of a comparable nature.

Even if the Constitution were perfect, of course, and the majority left it alone, it would not follow that the Supreme Court could guarantee the individual rights of citizens. A Supreme Court decision is still a legal decision, and it must

[1]See Chapter 8 [of *Taking Rights Seriously*—Ed.].

take into account precedent and institutional considerations like relations between the Court and Congress, as well as morality. And no judicial decision is necessarily the right decision. Judges stand for different positions on controversial issues of law and morals and, as the fights over Nixon's Supreme Court nominations showed, a President is entitled to appoint judges of his own persuasion, provided that they are honest and capable.

So, though the Constitutional system adds something to the protection of moral rights against the Government, it falls far short of guaranteeing these rights, or even establishing what they are. It means that, on some occasions, a department other than the legislature has the last word on these issues, which can hardly satisfy someone who thinks such a department profoundly wrong.

It is of course inevitable that some department of government will have the final say on what law will be enforced. When men disagree about moral rights, there will be no way for either side to prove its case, and some decision must stand if there is not to be anarchy. But that piece of orthodox wisdom must be the beginning and not the end of a philosophy of legislation and enforcement. If we cannot insist that the Government reach the right answers about the rights of its citizens, we can insist at least that it try. We can insist that it take rights seriously, follow a coherent theory of what these rights are, and act consistently with its own professions. I shall try to show what that means, and how it bears on the present political debates.

2. Rights and the Right to Break the Law

I shall start with the most violently argued issue. Does an American ever have the moral right to break a law? Suppose someone admits a law is valid; does he therefore have a duty to obey it? Those who try to give an answer seem to fall into two camps. The conservatives, as I shall call them, seem to disapprove of any act of disobedience; they appear satisfied when such acts are prosecuted, and disappointed when convictions are reversed. The other group, the liberals, are much more sympathetic to at least some cases of disobedience; they sometimes disapprove of prosecutions and celebrate acquittals. If we look beyond these emotional reactions, however, and pay attention to the arguments the two parties use, we discover an astounding fact. Both groups give essentially the same answer to the question of principle that supposedly divides them.

The answer that both parties give is this. In a democracy, or at least a democracy that in principle respects individual rights, each citizen has a general moral duty to obey all the laws, even though he would like some of them changed. He owes that duty to his fellow citizens, who obey laws that they do not like, to his benefit. But this general duty cannot be an absolute duty, because even a society that is in principle just may produce unjust laws and policies, and a man has duties other than his duties to the State. A man must honour his duties to his God and to his conscience, and if these conflict with his duty to the State, then he is entitled, in the end, to do what he judges to be right. If he decides that he must break the law, however, then he must submit to the judgment and punishment that the State imposes, in recognition of the fact that his duty to his fellow citizens was overwhelmed but not extinguished by his religious or moral obligation.

Of course this common answer can be elaborated in very different ways. Some would describe the duty to the State as fundamental, and picture the dissenter as a religious or moral fanatic. Others would describe the duty to the State in grudging terms, and picture those who oppose it as moral heroes. But these are differences in tone, and the position I described represents, I think, the view of most of those who find themselves arguing either for or against civil disobedience in particular cases.

I do not claim that it is everyone's view. There must be some who put the duty to the State so high that they do not grant that it can ever be overcome. There are certainly some who would deny that a man ever has a moral duty to obey the law, at least in the United States today. But these two extreme positions are the slender tails of a bell curve, and all those who fall in between hold the orthodox position I described—that men have a duty to obey the law but have the right to follow their consciences when it conflicts with that duty.

But if that is so, then we have a paradox in the fact that men who give the same answer to a question of principle should seem to disagree so much, and to divide so fiercely, in particular cases. The paradox goes even deeper, for each party, in at least some cases, takes a position that seems flatly inconsistent with the theoretical position they both accept. This position was tested, for example, when someone evaded the draft on grounds of conscience, or encouraged others to commit this crime. Conservatives argued that such men must be prosecuted, even though they are sincere. Why must they be prosecuted? Because society cannot tolerate the decline in respect for the law that their act constitutes and encourages. They must be prosecuted, in short, to discourage them and others like them from doing what they have done.

But there seems to be a monstrous contradiction here. If a man has a right to do what his conscience tells him he must, then how can the State be justified in discouraging him from doing it? Is it not wicked for a state to forbid and punish what it acknowledges that men have a right to do?

Moreover, it is not just conservatives who argue that those who break the law out of moral conviction should be prosecuted. The liberal is notoriously opposed to allowing racist school officials to go slow on desegregation, even though he acknowledges that these school officials think they have a moral right to do what the law forbids. The liberal does not often argue, it is true, that the desegregation laws must be enforced to encourage general respect for law. He argues instead that the desegregation laws must be enforced because they are right. But his position also seems inconsistent: can it be right to prosecute men for doing what their conscience requires, when we acknowledge their right to follow their conscience?

We are therefore left with two puzzles. How can two parties to an issue of principle, each of which thinks it is in profound disagreement with the other, embrace the same position on that issue? How can it be that each side urges solutions to particular problems which seem flatly to contradict the position of principle that both accept? One possible answer is that some or all of those who accept the common position are hypocrites, paying lip service to rights of conscience which in fact they do not grant.

There is some plausibility in this charge. A sort of hypocrisy must have been involved when public officials who claim to respect conscience denied Muhammad Ali the right to box in their states. If Ali, in spite of his religious scruples, had joined the Army, he would have been allowed to box even though, on the principles these officials say they honour, he would have been a worse human being for having done so. But there are few cases that seem so straightforward as this one, and even here the officials did not seem to recognize the contradiction between their acts and their principles. So we must search for some explanation beyond the truth that men often do not mean what they say.

The deeper explanation lies in a set of confusions that often embarrass arguments about rights. These confusions have clouded all the issues I mentioned at the outset and have crippled attempts to develop a coherent theory of how a government that respects rights must behave.

In order to explain this, I must call attention to the fact, familiar to philosophers, but often ignored in political debate, that the word 'right' has different force in different contexts. In most cases when we say that someone has a 'right' to do something, we imply that it would be wrong to interfere with his doing it, or at least that some special grounds are needed for justifying any interference. I use this strong sense of right when I say that you have the right to spend your money gambling, if you wish, though you ought to spend it in a more worthwhile way. I mean that it would be wrong for anyone to interfere with you even though you propose to spend your money in a way that I think is wrong.

There is a clear difference between saying that someone has a right to do something in this sense and saying that it is the 'right' thing for him to do, or that he does no 'wrong' in doing it. Someone may have the right to do something that is the wrong thing for him to do, as might be the case with gambling. Conversely, something may be the right thing for him to do and yet he may have no right to do it, in the sense that it would not be wrong for someone to interfere with his trying. If our army captures an enemy soldier, we might say that the right thing for him to do is to try to escape, but it would not follow that it is wrong for us to try to stop him. We might admire him for trying to escape, and perhaps even think less of him if he did not. But there is no suggestion here that it is wrong of us to stand in his way; on the contrary, if we think our cause is just, we think it right for us to do all we can to stop him.

Ordinarily this distinction, between the issues of whether a man has a right to do something and whether it is the right thing for him to do, causes no trouble. But sometimes it does, because sometimes we say that a man has a right to do something when we mean only to deny that it is the wrong thing for him to do. Thus we say that the captured soldier has a 'right' to try to escape when we mean, not that we do wrong to stop him, but that he has no duty not to make the attempt. We use 'right' this way when we speak of someone having the 'right' to act on his own principles, or the 'right' to follow his own conscience. We mean that he does no wrong to proceed on his honest convictions, even though we disagree with these convictions, and even though, for policy or other reasons, we must force him to act contrary to them.

Suppose a man believes that welfare payments to the poor are profoundly wrong, because they sap enterprise, and so declares his full income-tax each year but declines to pay half of it. We might say that he has a right to refuse to pay, if he wishes, but that the Government has a right to proceed against him for the full tax, and to fine or jail him for late payment if that is necessary to keep the collection system working efficiently. We do not take this line in most cases; we do not say that the ordinary thief has a right to steal, if he wishes, so long as he pays the penalty. We say a man has the right to break the law, even though the State has a right to punish him, only when we think that, because of his convictions, he does no wrong in doing so.[2]

These distinctions enable us to see an ambiguity in the orthodox question: Does a man ever have a right to break the law? Does that question mean to ask whether he ever has a right to break the law in the strong sense, so that the Government would do wrong to stop him, by arresting and prosecuting him? Or does it mean to ask whether he ever does the right thing to break the law, so that we should all respect him even though the Government should jail him?

If we take the orthodox position to be an answer to the first—and most important—question, then the paradoxes I described arise. But if we take it as an answer to the second, they do not. Conservatives and liberals do agree that sometimes a man does not do the wrong thing to break a law, when his conscience so requires. They disagree, when they do, over the different issue of what the State's response should be. Both parties do think that sometimes the State should prosecute. But this is not inconsistent with the proposition that the man prosecuted did the right thing in breaking the law.

The paradoxes seem genuine because the two questions are not usually distinguished, and the orthodox position is presented as a general solution to the problem of civil disobedience. But once the distinction is made, it is apparent that the position has been so widely accepted only because, when it is applied, it is treated as an answer to the second question but not the first. The crucial distinction is obscured by the troublesome idea of a right to conscience; this idea has been at the centre of most recent discussions of political obligation, but it is a red herring drawing us away from the crucial political questions. The state of a man's conscience may be decisive, or central, when the issue is whether he does something

---

[2]It is not surprising that we sometimes use the concept of having a right to say that others must not interfere with an act and sometimes to say that the act is not the wrong thing to do. Often, when someone has *no* right to do something, like attacking another man physically, it is true *both* that it is the wrong thing to do and that others are entitled to stop it, by demand, if not by force. It is therefore natural to say that someone has a right when we mean to deny *either* of these consequences, as well as when we mean to deny both.

morally wrong in breaking the law; but it need not be decisive or even central when the issue is whether he has a right, in the strong sense of that term, to do so. A man does not have the right, in that sense, to do whatever his conscience demands, but he may have the right, in that sense, to do something even though his conscience does not demand it.

If that is true, then there has been almost no serious attempt to answer the questions that almost everyone means to ask. We can make a fresh start by stating these questions more clearly. Does an American ever have the right, in a strong sense, to do something which is against the law? If so, when? In order to answer these questions put in that way, we must try to become clearer about the implications of the idea, mentioned earlier, that citizens have at least some rights against their government.

I said that in the United States citizens are supposed to have certain fundamental rights against their Government, certain moral rights made into legal rights by the Constitution. If this idea is significant, and worth bragging about, then these rights must be rights in the strong sense I just described. The claim that citizens have a right to free speech must imply that it would be wrong for the Government to stop them from speaking, even when the Government believes that what they will say will cause more harm than good. The claim cannot mean, on the prisoner-of-war analogy, only that citizens do no wrong in speaking their minds, though the Government reserves the right to prevent them from doing so.

This is a crucial point, and I want to labour it. Of course a responsible government must be ready to justify anything it does, particularly when it limits the liberty of its citizens. But normally it is a sufficient justification, even for an act that limits liberty, that the act is calculated to increase what the philosophers call general utility—that it is calculated to produce more over-all benefit than harm. So, though the New York City Government needs a justification for forbidding motorists to drive up Lexington Avenue, it is sufficient justification if the proper officials believe, on sound evidence, that the gain to the many will outweigh the inconvenience to the few. When individual citizens are said to have rights against the Government, however, like the right of free speech, that must mean that this sort of justification is not enough. Otherwise the claim would not argue that individuals have special protection against the law when their rights are in play, and that is just the point of the claim.

Not all legal rights, or even Constitutional rights, represent moral rights against the Government. I now have the legal right to drive either way on Fifty-seventh Street, but the Government would do no wrong to make that street one-way if it thought it in the general interest to do so. I have a Constitutional right to vote for a congressman every two years, but the national and state governments would do no wrong if, following the amendment procedure, they made a congressman's term four years instead of two, again on the basis of a judgment that this would be for the general good.

But those Constitutional rights that we call fundamental, like the right of free speech, are supposed to represent rights against the Government in the strong sense; that is the point of the boast that our legal system respects the fundamental rights of the citizen. If citizens have a moral right of free speech, then governments would do wrong to repeal the First Amendment that guarantees it, even if they were persuaded that the majority would be better off if speech were curtailed.

I must not overstate the point. Someone who claims that citizens have a right against the Government need not go so far as to say that the State is *never* justified in overriding that right. He might say, for example, that although citizens have a right to free speech, the Government may override that right when necessary to protect the rights of others, or to prevent a catastrophe, or even to obtain a clear and major public benefit (though if he acknowledged this last as a possible justification he would be treating the right in question as not among the most important or fundamental). What he cannot do is to say that the Government is justified in overriding a right on the minimal grounds that would be sufficient if no such right existed. He cannot say that the Government is entitled to act on no more than a judgment that its act is likely to produce, overall, a benefit to the community. That admission would make his claim of a right pointless, and would show him to be using some sense of 'right' other than the strong sense necessary to give his claim the political importance it is normally taken to have.

But then the answers to our two questions about disobedience seem plain, if unorthodox. In our society a man does sometimes have the right, in the strong sense, to disobey a law. He has that right whenever that law wrongly invades his rights against the Government. If he has a moral right to free speech, that is, then he has a moral right to break any law that the Government, by virtue of his right, had no right to adopt. The right to disobey the law is not a separate right, having something to do with conscience, additional to other rights against the Government. It is simply a feature of these rights against the Government, and it cannot be denied in principle without denying that any such rights exist.

These answers seem obvious once we take rights against the Government to be rights in the strong sense I described. If I have a right to speak my mind on political issues, then the Government does wrong to make it illegal for me to do so, even if it thinks this is in the general interest. If, nevertheless, the Government does make my act illegal, then it does a further wrong to enforce that law against me. My right against the Government means that it is wrong for the Government to stop me from speaking; the Government cannot make it right to stop me just by taking the first step.

This does not, of course, tell us exactly what rights men do have against the Government. It does not tell us whether the right of free speech includes the right of demonstration. But it does mean that passing a law cannot affect such rights as men do have, and that is of crucial importance, because it dictates the attitude that an individual is entitled to take toward his personal decision when civil disobedience is in question.

Both conservatives and liberals suppose that in a society which is generally decent everyone has a duty to obey the law, whatever it is. That is the source of the 'general duty' clause in the orthodox position, and though liberals believe that this duty can sometimes be 'overridden', even they suppose, as the orthodox position maintains, that the duty of obedience remains in some submerged form, so that a man does well to accept punishment in recognition of that duty. But this general duty is almost incoherent in a society that recognizes rights. If a man believes he has a right to demonstrate, then he must believe that it would be wrong for the Government to stop him, with or without benefit of a law. If he is entitled to believe that, then it is silly to speak of a duty to obey the law as such, or of a duty to accept the punishment that the State has no right to give.

Conservatives will object to the short work I have made of their point. They will argue that even if the Government was wrong to adopt some law, like a law limiting speech, there are independent reasons why the Government is justified in enforcing the law once adopted. When the law forbids demonstration, then, so they argue, some principle more important than the individual's right to speak is brought into play, namely the principle of respect for law. If a law, even a bad law, is left unenforced, then respect for law is weakened, and society as a whole suffers. So an individual loses his moral right to speak when speech is made criminal, and the Government must, for the common good and for the general benefit, enforce the law against him.

But this argument, though popular, is plausible only if we forget what it means to say that an individual has a right against the State. It is far from plain that civil disobedience lowers respect for law, but even if we suppose that it does, this fact is irrelevant. The prospect of utilitarian gains cannot justify preventing a man from doing what he has a right to do, and the supposed gains in respect for law are simply utilitarian gains. There would be no point in the boast that we respect individual rights unless that involved some sacrifice, and the sacrifice in question must be that we give up whatever marginal benefits our country would receive from overriding these rights when they prove inconvenient. So the general benefit cannot be a good ground for abridging rights, even when the benefit in question is a heightened respect for law.

But perhaps I do wrong to assume that the argument about respect for law is only an appeal to general utility. I said that a state may be justified in overriding or limiting rights on other grounds, and we must ask, before rejecting the conservative position, whether any of these apply. The most important—and least well understood—of these other grounds invokes the notion of *competing rights* that would be jeopardized if the right in question were not limited. Citizens have personal rights to the State's protection as well as personal rights to be free from the State's interference, and it may be necessary for the Government to choose between these two sorts of rights. The law of defamation, for example, limits the personal right of any man to say what he thinks, because it requires him to have good grounds for what he says. But this law is justified, even for those who think that it does invade a personal right, by the fact that it protects the right of others not to have their reputations ruined by a careless statement.

The individual rights that our society acknowledges often conflict in this way, and when they do it is the job of government to discriminate. If the Government makes the right choice, and protects the more important at the cost of the less, then it has not weakened or cheapened the notion of a right; on the contrary it would have done so had it failed to protect the more important of the two. So we must acknowledge that the Government has a reason for limiting rights if it plausibly believes that a competing right is more important.

May the conservative seize on this fact? He might argue that I did wrong to characterize his argument as one that appeals to the general benefit, because it appeals instead to competing rights, namely the moral right of the majority to have its laws enforced, or the right of society to maintain the degree of order and security it wishes. These are the rights, he would say, that must be weighed against the individual's right to do what the wrongful law prohibits.

But this new argument is confused, because it depends on yet another ambiguity in the language of rights. It is true that we speak of the 'right' of society to do what it wants, but this cannot be a 'competing right' of the sort that may justify the invasion of a right against the Government. The existence of rights against the Government would be jeopardized if the Government were able to defeat such a right by appealing to the right of a democratic majority to work its will. A right against the Government must be a right to do something even when the majority thinks it would be wrong to do it, and even when the majority would be worse off for having it done. If we now say that society has a right to do whatever is in the general benefit, or the right to preserve whatever sort of environment the majority wishes to live in, and we mean that these are the sort of rights that provide justification for overruling any rights against the Government that may conflict, then we have annihilated the latter rights.

In order to save them, we must recognize as competing rights only the rights of other members of the society as individuals. We must distinguish the 'rights' of the majority as such, which cannot count as a justification for overruling individual rights, and the personal rights of members of a majority, which might well count. The test we must use is this. Someone has a competing right to protection, which must be weighed against an individual right to act, if that person would be entitled to demand that protection from his government on his own title, as an individual, without regard to whether a majority of his fellow citizens joined in the demand.

It cannot be true, on this test, that anyone has a right to have all the laws of the nation enforced. He has a right to have enforced only those criminal laws, for example, that he would have a right to have enacted if they were not already law. The laws against personal assault may well fall into that class. If the physically vulnerable members of the community—those who need police protection against personal violence—were only a small minority, it would still seem plausible to say that they were entitled to that protection. But the laws that provide a certain level of quiet in public places, or that authorize and finance a foreign war, cannot be thought to rest on individual rights. The timid lady on the streets of Chicago is not entitled to just the degree of quiet that now obtains, nor is she entitled to have boys drafted to fight in wars she approves. There are laws—perhaps desirable laws—that provide these advantages for her, but the justification for these laws, if they can be justified at all, is the common desire of a large majority, not her personal right. If, therefore, these laws do abridge someone else's moral right to protest, or his right to personal security, she cannot urge a competing right to justify the abridgement. She has no personal right to have such laws passed, and she has no competing right to have them enforced either.

So the conservative cannot advance his argument much on the ground of competing rights, but he may want to use another ground. A government, he may argue, may be justified in abridging the personal rights of its citizens in an emergency, or when a very great loss may be prevented, or perhaps, when some major benefit can clearly be secured. If the nation is at war, a policy of censorship may be justified even though it invades the right to say what one thinks on matters of political controversy. But the emergency must be genuine. There must be what Oliver Wendell Holmes described as a clear and present danger, and the danger must be one of magnitude.

Can the conservative argue that when any law is passed, even a wrongful law, this sort of justification is available for enforcing it? His argument might be something of this sort. If the Government once acknowledges that it may be wrong—that the legislature might have adopted, the executive approved, and the courts left standing, a law that in fact abridges important rights—then this admission will lead not simply to a marginal decline in respect for law, but to a crisis of order. Citizens may decide to obey only those laws they personally approve, and that is anarchy. So the Government must insist that whatever a citizen's rights may be before a law is passed and upheld by the courts, his rights thereafter are determined by that law.

But this argument ignores the primitive distinction between what may happen and what will happen. If we allow speculation to support the justification of emergency or decisive benefit, then, again, we have annihilated rights. We must, as Learned Hand said, discount the gravity of the evil threatened by the likelihood of reaching that evil. I know of no genuine evidence to the effect that tolerating some civil disobedience, out of respect for the moral position of its authors, will increase such disobedience, let alone crime in general. The case that it will must be based on vague assumptions about the contagion of ordinary crimes, assumptions that are themselves unproved, and that are in any event largely irrelevant. It seems at least as plausible to argue that tolerance will increase respect for officials and for the bulk of the laws they promulgate, or at least retard the rate of growing disrespect.

If the issue were simply the question whether the community would be marginally better off under strict law enforcement, then the Government would have to decide on the evidence we have, and it might not be unreasonable to decide, on balance, that it would. But since rights are at stake, the issue is the very different one of whether tolerance would destroy the community or threaten it with great harm, and it seems to me simply mindless to suppose that the evidence makes that probable or even conceivable.

The argument from emergency is confused in another way as well. It assumes that the Government must take the position either that a man never has the right to break the law, or that he always does. I said that any society that claims to recognize rights at all must abandon the notion of a general duty to obey the law that holds in all cases. This is important, because it shows that there are no short cuts to meeting a citizen's claim to right. If a citizen argues that he has a moral right not to serve in the Army, or to protest in a way he finds effective, then an official who wants to answer him, and not simply bludgeon him into obedience, must respond to the particular point he makes, and cannot point to the draft law or a Supreme Court decision as having even special, let alone decisive, weight. Sometimes an official who considers the citizen's moral arguments in good faith will be persuaded that the citizen's claim is plausible, or even right. It does not follow, however, that he will always be persuaded or that he always should be.

I must emphasize that all these propositions concern the strong sense of right, and they therefore leave open important questions about the right thing to do. If a man believes he has the right to break the law, he must then ask whether he does the right thing to exercise that right. He must remember that reasonable men can differ about whether he has a right against the Government, and therefore the right to break the law, that he thinks he has; and therefore that reasonable men can oppose him in good faith. He must take into account the various consequences his acts will have, whether they involve violence, and such other considerations as the context makes relevant; he must not go beyond the rights he can in good faith claim, to acts that violate the rights of others.

On the other hand, if some official, like a prosecutor, believes that the citizen does *not* have the right to break the law, then *he* must ask whether he does the right thing to enforce it. In Chapter 8 [of *Taking Rights Seriously*—Ed.] I argue that certain features of our legal system, and in particular the fusion of legal and moral issues in our Constitution, mean that citizens often do the right thing in exercising what they take to be moral rights to break the law, and that prosecutors often do the right thing in failing to prosecute them for it. I will not anticipate those arguments here; instead I want to ask whether the requirement that Government take its citizens' rights seriously has anything to do with the crucial question of what these rights are.

3. Controversial Rights

The argument so far has been hypothetical: if a man has a particular moral right against the Government, that right survives contrary legislation or adjudication. But this does not tell us what rights he has, and it is notorious that reasonable men disagree about that. There is wide agreement on certain clearcut cases; almost everyone who believes in rights at all would admit, for example, that a man has a moral right to speak his mind in a non-provocative way on matters of political concern, and that this is an important right that the State must go to great pains to protect. But there is great controversy as to the limits of such paradigm rights, and the so-called 'anti-riot' law involved in the famous Chicago Seven trial of the last decade is a case in point.

The defendants were accused of conspiring to cross state lines with the intention of causing a riot. This charge is vague—perhaps unconstitutionally vague—but the law apparently defines as criminal emotional speeches which argue that violence is justified in order to secure political equality. Does the right of free speech protect this sort of speech? That, of course, is a legal issue, because it invokes the free-speech clause of the First Amendment of the Constitution. But it is also a moral issue, because, as I said, we must treat the First Amendment as an attempt to protect a moral right. It is part of the job of governing to 'define' moral rights through statutes and judicial decisions, that is, to declare officially the extent that moral rights will be taken to have in law. Congress faced this task in voting on the anti-riot bill, and the Supreme Court has faced it in countless cases. How should the different departments of government go about defining moral rights?

They should begin with a sense that whatever they decide might be wrong. History and their descendants may judge that they acted unjustly when they thought they were right. If they take their duty seriously, they must try to limit their mistakes, and they must therefore try to discover where the dangers of mistake lie.

They might choose one of two very different models for this purpose. The first model recommends striking a balance between the rights of the individual and the demands of society at large. If the Government *infringes* on a moral right (for example, by defining the right of free speech more narrowly than justice requires), then it has done the individual a wrong. On the other hand, if the Government *inflates* a right (by defining it more broadly than justice requires) then it cheats society of some general benefit, like safe streets, that there is no reason it should not have. So a mistake on one side is as serious as a mistake on the other. The course of government is to steer to the middle, to balance the general good and personal rights, giving to each its due.

When the Government, or any of its branches, defines a right, it must bear in mind, according to the first model, the social cost of different proposals and make the necessary adjustments. It must not grant the same freedom to noisy demonstrations as it grants to calm political discussion, for example, because the former causes much more trouble than the latter. Once it decides how much of a right to recognize, it must enforce its decision to the full. That means permitting an individual to act within his rights, as the Government has defined them, but not beyond, so that if anyone breaks the law, even on grounds of conscience, he must be punished. No doubt any government will make mistakes, and will regret decisions once taken. That is inevitable. But this middle policy will ensure that errors on one side will balance out errors on the other over the long run.

The first model, described in this way, has great plausibility, and most laymen and lawyers, I think, would respond to it warmly. The metaphor of balancing the public interest against personal claims is established in our political and judicial rhetoric, and this metaphor gives the model both familiarity and appeal. Nevertheless, the first model is a false one, certainly in the case of rights generally regarded as important, and the metaphor is the heart of its error.

The institution of rights against the Government is not a gift of God, or an ancient ritual, or a national sport. It is a complex and troublesome practice that makes the Government's job of securing the general benefit more difficult and more expensive, and it would be a frivolous and wrongful practice unless it served some point. Anyone who professes to take rights seriously, and who praises our Government for respecting them, must have some sense of what that point is. He must accept, at the minimum, one or both of two important ideas. The first is the vague but powerful idea of human dignity. This idea, associated with Kant, but defended by philosophers of different schools, supposes that there are ways of treating a man that are inconsistent with recognizing him as a full member of the human community, and holds that such treatment is profoundly unjust.

The second is the more familiar idea of political equality. This supposes that the weaker members of a political community are entitled to the same concern and respect of their government as the more powerful members have secured for themselves, so that if some men have freedom of decision whatever the effect on the general good, then all men must have the same freedom. I do not want to defend or elaborate these ideas here, but only to insist that anyone who claims that citizens have rights must accept ideas very close to these.[3]

It makes sense to say that a man has a fundamental right against the Government, in the strong sense, like free speech, if that right is necessary to protect his dignity, or his standing as equally entitled to concern and respect, or some other personal value of like consequence. It does not make sense otherwise.

So if rights make sense at all, then the invasion of a relatively important right must be a very serious matter. It means treating a man as less than a man, or as less worthy of concern than other men. The institution of rights rests on the conviction that this is a grave injustice, and that it is worth paying the incremental cost in social policy or efficiency that is necessary to prevent it. But then it must be wrong to say that inflating rights is as serious as invading them. If the Government errs on the side of the individual, then it simply pays a little more in social efficiency than it has to pay; it pays a little more, that is, of the same coin that it has already decided must be spent. But if it errs against the individual it inflicts an insult upon him that, on its own reckoning, it is worth a great deal of that coin to avoid.

So the first model is indefensible. It rests, in fact, on a mistake I discussed earlier, namely the confusion of society's rights with the rights of members of society. 'Balancing' is appropriate when the Government must choose between competing claims of right—between the Southerner's claim to freedom of association, for example, and the black man's claim to an equal education. Then the Government can do nothing but estimate the merits of the competing claims, and act on its estimate. The first model assumes that the 'right' of the majority is a competing right that must be balanced in this way; but that, as I argued before, is a confusion

---

[3]He need not consider these ideas to be axiomatic. He may, that is, have reasons for insisting that dignity or equality are important values, and these reasons may be utilitarian. He may believe, for example, that the general good will be advanced, *in the long run,* only if we treat indignity or inequality as very great injustices, and never allow our *opinions* about the general good to justify them. I do not know of any good arguments for or against this sort of 'institutional' utilitarianism, but it is consistent with my point, because it argues that we must treat violations of dignity and equality as special moral crimes, beyond the reach of ordinary utilitarian justification.

that threatens to destroy the concept of individual rights. It is worth noticing that the community rejects the first model in that area where the stakes for the individual are highest, the criminal process. We say that it is better that a great many guilty men go free than that one innocent man be punished, and that homily rests on the choice of the second model for government.

The second model treats abridging a right as much more serious than inflating one, and its recommendations follow from that judgment. It stipulates that once a right is recognized in clear-cut cases, then the Government should act to cut off that right only when some compelling reason is presented, some reason that is consistent with the suppositions on which the original right must be based. It cannot be an argument for curtailing a right, once granted, simply that society would pay a further price for extending it. There must be something special about that further cost, or there must be some other feature of the case, that makes it sensible to say that although great social cost is warranted to protect the original right, this particular cost is not necessary. Otherwise, the Government's failure to extend the right will show that its recognition of the right in the original case is a sham, a promise that it intends to keep only until that becomes inconvenient.

How can we show that a particular cost is not worth paying without taking back the initial recognition of a right? I can think of only three sorts of grounds that can consistently be used to limit the definition of a particular right. First, the Government might show that the values protected by the original right are not really at stake in the marginal case, or are at stake only in some attenuated form. Second, it might show that if the right is defined to include the marginal case, then some competing right, in the strong sense I described earlier, would be abridged. Third, it might show that if the right were so defined, then the cost to society would not be simply incremental, but would be of a degree far beyond the cost paid to grant the original right, a degree great enough to justify whatever assault on dignity or equality might be involved.

It is fairly easy to apply these grounds to one group of problems the Supreme Court faced, imbedded in constitutional issues. The draft law provided an exemption for conscientious objectors, but this exemption, as interpreted by the draft boards, has been limited to those who object to *all* wars on *religious* grounds. If we suppose that the exemption is justified on the ground that an individual has a moral right not to kill in violation of his own principles, then the question is raised whether it is proper to exclude those whose morality is not based on religion, or whose morality is sufficiently complex to distinguish among wars. The Court held, as a matter of Constitutional law, that the draft boards were wrong to exclude the former, but competent to exclude the latter.

None of the three grounds I listed can justify either of these exclusions as a matter of political morality. The invasion of personality in forcing men to kill when they believe killing immoral is just as great when these beliefs are based on secular grounds, or take account of the fact that wars differ in morally relevant ways, and there is no pertinent difference in competing rights or in national emergency. There are differences among the cases, of course, but they are insufficient to justify the distinction. A government that is secular on principle cannot prefer a religious to a non-religious morality as such. There are utilitarian arguments in favour of limiting the exception to religious or universal grounds—an exemption so limited may be less expensive to administer, and may allow easier discrimination between sincere and insincere applicants. But these utilitarian reasons are irrelevant, because they cannot count as grounds for limiting a right.

What about the anti-riot law, as applied in the Chicago trial? Does the law represent an improper limitation of the right to free speech, supposedly protected by the First Amendment? If we were to apply the first model for government to this issue, the argument for the anti-riot law would look strong. But if we set aside talk of balancing as inappropriate, and turn to the proper grounds for limiting a right, then the argument becomes a great deal weaker. The original right of free speech must suppose that it is an assault on human personality to stop a man from expressing what he honestly believes, particularly on issues affecting how he is governed. Surely the assault is greater, and not less, when he is stopped from expressing those principles of political morality that he holds most passionately, in the face of what he takes to be outrageous violations of these principles.

It may be said that the anti-riot law leaves him free to express these principles in a non-provocative way. But that misses the point of the connection between expression and dignity. A man cannot express himself freely when he cannot match his rhetoric to his outrage, or when he must trim his sails to protect values he counts as nothing next to those he is trying to vindicate. It is true that some political dissenters speak in ways that shock the majority, but it is arrogant for the majority to suppose that the orthodox methods of expression are the proper ways to speak, for this is a denial of equal concern and respect. If the point of the right is to protect the dignity of dissenters, then we must make judgments about appropriate speech with the personalities of the dissenters in mind, not the personality of the 'silent' majority for whom the anti-riot law is no restraint at all.

So the argument fails, that the personal values protected by the original right are less at stake in this marginal case. We must consider whether competing rights, or some grave threat to society, nevertheless justify the anti-riot law. We can consider these two grounds together, because the only plausible competing rights are rights to be free from violence, and violence is the only plausible threat to society that the context provides.

I have no right to burn your house, or stone you or your car, or swing a bicycle chain against your skull, even if I find these to be natural means of expression. But the defendants in the Chicago trial were not accused of direct violence; the argument runs that the acts of speech they planned made it likely that others would do acts of violence, either in support of or out of hostility to what they said. Does this provide a justification?

The question would be different if we could say with any confidence how much and what sort of violence the anti-riot law might be expected to prevent. Will it save two lives a year, or two hundred, or two thousand? Two thousand dollars of property, or two hundred thousand, or two million? No one can say, not simply because prediction is next to impossible, but because we have no firm understanding of the process by which demonstration disintegrates into riot, and in particular of the part played by inflammatory speech, as distinct from poverty, police brutality, blood lust, and all the rest of human and economic failure. The Government must try, of course, to reduce the violent waste of lives and property, but it must recognize that any attempt to locate and remove a cause of riot, short of a reorganization of society, must be an exercise in speculation, trial, and error. It must make its decisions under conditions of high uncertainty, and the institution of rights, taken seriously, limits its freedom to experiment under such conditions.

If forces the Government to bear in mind that preventing a man from speaking or demonstrating offers him a certain and profound insult, in return for a speculative benefit that may in any event be achieved in other if more expensive ways. When lawyers say that rights may be limited to protect other rights, or to prevent catastrophe, they have in mind cases in which cause and effect are relatively clear, like the familiar example of a man falsely crying 'Fire!' in a crowded theater.

But the Chicago story shows how obscure the causal connections can become. Were the speeches of Hoffman or Rubin necessary conditions of the riot? Or had thousands of people come to Chicago for the purposes of rioting anyway, as the Government also argues? Were they in any case sufficient conditions? Or could the police have contained the violence if they had not been so busy contributing to it, as the staff of the President's Commission on Violence said they were?

These are not easy questions, but if rights mean anything, then the Government cannot simply assume answers that justify its conduct. If a man has a right to speak, if the reasons that support that right extend to provocative political speech, and if the effects of such speech on violence are unclear, then the Government is not entitled to make its first attack on that problem by denying that right. It may be that abridging the right to speak is the least expensive course, or the least damaging to police morale, or the most popular politically. But these are utilitarian arguments in favor of starting one place rather than another, and such arguments are ruled out by the concept of rights.

This point may be obscured by the popular belief that political activists look forward to violence and 'ask for trouble' in what they say. They can hardly complain, in the general view, if they are taken to be the authors of the violence they expect, and treated accordingly. But this repeats the confusion I tried to explain earlier between having a right and doing the right thing. The speaker's motives may be relevant in deciding whether he does the right thing in speaking passionately about issues that may inflame or enrage the audience. But if he has a right to speak, because the danger in allowing him to speak is speculative, his motives cannot count as independent evidence in the argument that justifies stopping him.

But what of the individual rights of those who will be destroyed by a riot, of the passer-by who will be killed by a sniper's bullet or the shopkeeper who will be ruined by looting? To put the issue in this way, as a question of competing rights, suggests a principle that would undercut the effect of uncertainty. Shall we say that some rights to protection are so important that the Government is justified in doing all it can to maintain them? Shall we therefore say that the Government may abridge the rights of others to act when their acts might simply increase the risk, by however slight or speculative a margin, that some person's right to life or property will be violated?

Some such principle is relied on by those who oppose the Supreme Court's recent liberal rulings on police procedure. These rulings increase the chance that a guilty man will go free, and therefore marginally increase the risk that any particular member of the community will be murdered, raped, or robbed. Some critics believe that the Court's decisions must therefore be wrong.

But no society that purports to recognize a variety of rights, on the ground that a man's dignity or equality may be invaded in a variety of ways, can accept such a principle. If forcing a man to testify against himself, or forbidding him to speak, does the damage that the rights against self-incrimination and the right of free speech assume, then it would be contemptuous for the State to tell a man that he must suffer this damage against the possibility that other men's risk of loss may be marginally reduced. If rights make sense, then the degrees of their importance cannot be so different that some count not at all when others are mentioned.

Of course the Government may discriminate and may stop a man from exercising his right to speak when there is a clear and substantial risk that his speech will do great damage to the person or property of others, and no other means of preventing this are at hand, as in the case of the man shouting 'Fire!' in a theater. But we must reject the suggested principle that the Government can simply ignore rights to speak when life and property are in question. So long as the impact of speech on these other rights remains speculative and marginal, it must look elsewhere for levers to pull.

4. Why Take Rights Seriously?

I said at the beginning of this essay that I wanted to show what a government must do that professes to recognize individual rights. It must dispense with the claim that citizens never have a right to break its law, and it must not define citizens' rights so that these are cut off for supposed reasons of the general good. Any Government's harsh treatment of civil disobedience, or campaign against vocal protest, may therefore be thought to count against its sincerity.

One might well ask, however, whether it is wise to take rights all that seriously after all. America's genius, at least in her own legend, lies in not taking any abstract doctrine to its logical extreme. It may be time to ignore abstractions, and concentrate instead on giving the majority of our citizens a new sense of their Government's concern for their welfare, and of their title to rule.

That, in any event, is what former Vice-President Agnew seemed to believe. In a policy statement on the issue of 'weirdos' and social misfits, he said that the liberals' concern for individual rights was a headwind blowing in the face of the ship of state. That is a poor metaphor, but the philosophical point it expresses is very well taken. He recognized, as many liberals do not, that the majority cannot travel as fast or as far as it would like if it recognizes the rights of individuals to do what, in the majority's terms, is the wrong thing to do.

Spiro Agnew supposed that rights are divisive, and that national unity and a new respect for law may be developed by taking them more skeptically. But he is wrong. America will continue to be divided by its social and foreign policy, and if the economy grows weaker again the divisions will become more bitter. If we want our laws and our legal institutions to provide the ground rules within which these issues will be contested, then these ground rules must not be the conqueror's law that the dominant class imposes on the weaker, as Marx supposed the law of a capitalist society must be. The bulk of the law—that part which defines and implements social, economic, and foreign policy—cannot be neutral. It must state, in its greatest part, the majority's view of the common good. The institution of rights is therefore crucial, because it represents the majority's promise to the minorities that their dignity and equality will be respected. When the divisions among the groups are most violent, then this gesture, if law is to work, must be most sincere.

The institution requires an act of faith on the part of the minorities, because the scope of their rights will be controversial whenever they are important, and because the officers of the majority will act on their own notions of what these rights really are. Of course these officials will disagree with many of the claims that a minority makes. That makes it all the more important that they take their decisions gravely. They must show that they understand what rights are, and they must not cheat on the full implications of the doctrine. The Government will not re-establish respect for law without giving the law some claim to respect. It cannot do that if it neglects the one feature that distinguishes law from ordered brutality. If the Government does not take rights seriously, then it does not take law seriously either.

Servility and Self-Respect

•

Thomas E. Hill, Jr.

Several motives underlie this paper.[1] In the first place, I am curious to see if there is a legitimate source for the increasingly common feeling that servility can be as much a vice as arrogance. There seems to be something morally defective about the Uncle Tom and the submissive housewife; and yet, on the other hand, if the only interests they sacrifice are their own, it seems that we should have no right to complain. Secondly, I have some sympathy for the now unfashionable view that each person has duties to himself as well as to others. It does seem absurd to say that a person could literally violate his own rights or owe himself a debt of gratitude, but I suspect that the classic defenders of duties to oneself had something different in mind. If there are duties to oneself, it is natural to expect that a duty to avoid being servile would have a prominent place among them. Thirdly, I am interested in making sense of Kant's puzzling, but suggestive, remarks about respect for persons and respect for the moral law. On the usual reading, these remarks seem unduly moralistic; but, viewed in another way, they suggest an argument for a kind of self-respect which is incompatible with a servile attitude.

My procedure will not be to explicate Kant directly. Instead I shall try to isolate the defect of servility and sketch an argument to show why it is objectionable, noting only in passing how this relates to Kant and the controversy about

From *The Monist*, Vol. 57, no. 1 (January 1973), 87–104. Reprinted by permission of the author and the publisher.

[1]An earlier version of this paper was presented at the meetings of the American Philosophical Association, Pacific Division. A number of revisions have been made as a result of the helpful comments of others, especially Norman Dahl, Sharon Hill, Herbert Morris, and Mary Mothersill.

duties to oneself. What I say about self-respect is far from the whole story. In particular, it is not concerned with esteem for one's special abilities and achievements or with the self-confidence which characterizes the especially autonomous person. Nor is my concern with the psychological antecedents and effects of self-respect. Nevertheless, my conclusions, if correct, should be of interest; for they imply that, given a common view of morality, there are nonutilitarian moral reasons for each person, regardless of his merits, to respect himself. To avoid servility to the extent that one can is not simply a right but a duty, not simply a duty to others but a duty to oneself.

I

Three examples may give a preliminary idea of what I mean by *servility*. Consider, first, an extremely deferential black, whom I shall call the *Uncle Tom*. He always steps aside for white men; he does not complain when less qualified whites take over his job; he gratefully accepts whatever benefits his all-white government and employers allot him, and he would not think of protesting its insufficiency. He displays the symbols of deference to whites, and of contempt towards blacks: he faces the former with bowed stance and a ready 'sir' and 'Ma'am'; he reserves his strongest obscenities for the latter. Imagine, too, that he is not playing a game. He is not the shrewdly prudent calculator, who knows how to make the best of a bad lot and mocks his masters behind their backs. He accepts without question the idea that, as a black, he is owed less than whites. He may believe that blacks are mentally inferior and of less social utility, but that is not the crucial point. The attitude which he displays is that what he values, aspires for, and can demand is of less importance than what whites value, aspire for, and can demand. He is far from the picture book's carefree, happy servant, but he does not feel that he has a right to expect anything better.

Another pattern of servility is illustrated by a person I shall call the *Self-Deprecator*. Like the Uncle Tom, he is reluctant to make demands. He says nothing when others take unfair advantage of him. When asked for his preferences or opinions, he tends to shrink away as if what he said should make no difference. His problem, however, is not a sense of racial inferiority but rather an acute awareness of his own inadequacies and failures as an individual. These defects are not imaginary: he has in fact done poorly by his own standards and others'. But, unlike many of us in the same situation, he acts as if his failings warrant quite unrelated maltreatment even by strangers. His sense of shame and self-contempt make him content to be the instrument of others. He feels that nothing is owed him until he has earned it and that he has earned very little. He is not simply playing a masochist's game of winning sympathy by disparaging himself. On the contrary, he assesses his individual merits with painful accuracy.

A rather different case is that of the *Deferential Wife*. This is a woman who is utterly devoted to serving her husband. She buys the clothes *he* prefers, invites the guests *he* wants to entertain, and makes love whenever *he* is in the mood. She willingly moves to a new city in order for him to have a more attractive job, counting her own friendships and geographical preferences insignificant by comparison. She loves her husband, but her conduct is not simply an expression of love. She is happy, but she does not subordinate herself as a means to happiness. She does not simply defer to her husband in certain spheres as a trade-off for his deference in other spheres. On the contrary, she tends not to form her own interests, values, and ideals; and, when she does, she counts them as less important than her husband's. When confronted by appeals from Women's Liberation she grants that women are mentally and physically equal, if not superior, to men. She just believes that the proper role for a woman is to serve her family. As a matter of fact, much of her happiness derives from her belief that she fulfills this role very well. No one is trampling on her rights, she says; for she is quite glad, and proud, to serve her husband as she does.

Each one of these cases reflects the attitude which I call servility.[2] It betrays the absence of a certain kind of self-respect. What I take this attitude to be, more specifically, will become clearer later on. It is important at the outset, however, not to confuse the three cases sketched above with other, superficially similar cases. In particular, the cases I have sketched are not simply cases in which someone refuses to press his rights, speaks disparagingly of himself, or devotes himself to another. A black, for example, is not necessarily servile because he does not demand a just wage; for, seeing that such a demand would result in his being fired, he might forbear for the sake of his children. A self-critical person is not necessarily servile by virtue of bemoaning his faults in public; for his behavior may be merely a complex way of satisfying his own inner needs quite independent of a willingness to accept abuse from others. A woman need not be servile whenever she works to make her husband happy and prosperous; for she might freely and knowingly choose to do so from love or from a desire to share the rewards of his success. If the effort did not require her to submit to humiliation or maltreatment, her choice would not mark her as servile. There may, of course, be grounds for objecting to the attitudes in these cases; but the defect is not servility of the sort I want to consider. It should also be noted that my cases of servility are not simply instances of deference to superior knowledge or judgment. To defer to an expert's judgment on matters of fact is not to be servile; to defer to his every wish and whim is. Similarly, the belief that one's talents and achievements are comparatively low does not, by itself, make one servile. It is no vice to acknowledge the truth, and one

---

[2]Each of the cases is intended to represent only one possible pattern of servility. I make no claims about how often these patterns are exemplified, nor do I mean to imply that only these patterns could warrant the labels "Deferential Wife", "Uncle Tom", etc. All the more, I do not mean to imply any comparative judgments about the causes or relative magnitude of the problems of racial and sexual discrimination. One person, e.g. a self-contemptuous woman with a sense of racial inferiority, might exemplify features of several patterns at once; and, of course, a person might view her being a woman the way an Uncle Tom views his being black, etc.

may in fact have achieved less, and have less ability, than others. To be servile is not simply to hold certain empirical beliefs but to have a certain attitude concerning one's rightful place in a moral community.

II

Are there grounds for regarding the attitudes of the Uncle Tom, the Self-Deprecator, and the Deferential Wife as morally objectionable? Are there moral arguments we could give them to show that they ought to have more self-respect? None of the more obvious replies is entirely satisfactory.

One might, in the first place, adduce utilitarian considerations. Typically the servile person will be less happy than he might be. Moreover, he may be less prone to make the best of his own socially useful abilities. He may become a nuisance to others by being overly dependent. He will, in any case, lose the special contentment that comes from standing up for one's rights. A submissive attitude encourages exploitation, and exploitation spreads misery in a variety of ways. These considerations provide a prima facie case against the attitudes of the Uncle Tom, the Deferential Wife, and the Self-Deprecator, but they are hardly conclusive. Other utilities tend to counterbalance the ones just mentioned. When people refuse to press their rights, there are usually others who profit. There are undeniable pleasures in associating with those who are devoted, understanding, and grateful for whatever we see fit to give them—as our fondness for dogs attests. Even the servile person may find his attitude a source of happiness, as the case of the Deferential Wife illustrates. There may be comfort and security in thinking that the hard choices must be made by others, that what I would say has little to do with what ought to be done. Self-condemnation may bring relief from the pangs of guilt even if it is not deliberately used for that purpose. On balance, then, utilitarian considerations may turn out to favor servility as much as they oppose it.

For those who share my moral intuitions, there is another sort of reason for not trying to rest a case against servility on utilitarian considerations. Certain utilities seem irrelevant to the issue. The utilitarian must weigh them along with others, but to do so seems morally inappropriate. Suppose, for example, that the submissive attitudes of the Uncle Tom and the Deferential Wife result in positive utilities for those who dominate and exploit them. Do we need to tabulate *these* utilities before conceding that servility is objectionable? The Uncle Tom, it seems, is making an error, a moral error, quite apart from consideration of how much others in fact profit from his attitude. The Deferential Wife may be quite happy; but if her happiness turns out to be contingent on her distorted view of her own rights and worth as a person, then it carries little moral weight against the contention that she ought to change that view. Suppose I could cause a woman to find her happiness in denying all her rights and serving my every wish. No doubt I could do so only by nonrational manipulative techniques, which I ought not to use. But is this the only objection? My efforts would be wrong, it seems, not only because of the techniques they require but also because the resultant attitude is itself objectionable. When a person's happiness stems from a morally objectionable attitude, it ought to be discounted. That a sadist gets pleasure from seeing others suffer should not count even as a partial justification for his attitude. That a servile person derives pleasure from denying her moral status, for similar reasons, cannot make her attitude acceptable. These brief intuitive remarks are not intended as a refutation of utilitarianism, with all its many varieties; but they do suggest that it is well to look elsewhere for adequate grounds for rejecting the attitudes of the Uncle Tom, the Self-Deprecator, and the Deferential Wife.

One might try to appeal to meritarian considerations. That is, one might argue that the servile person *deserves* more than he allows himself. This line of argument, however, is no more adequate than the utilitarian one. It may be wrong to deny others what they deserve, but it is not so obviously wrong to demand less for oneself than one deserves. In any case, the Self-Deprecator's problem is not that he underestimates his merits. By hypothesis, he assesses his merits quite accurately. We cannot reasonably tell him to have more respect for himself because he *deserves* more respect; he knows that he has not *earned* better treatment. His problem, in fact, is that he thinks of his moral status with regard to others as entirely dependent upon his merits. His interests and choices are important, he feels, only if he has earned the right to make demands; or if he had rights by birth, they were forfeited by his subsequent failures and misdeeds. My Self-Deprecator is no doubt an atypical person, but nevertheless he illustrates an important point. Normally when we find a self-contemptuous person, we can plausibly argue that he is not so bad as he thinks, that his self-contempt is an overreaction prompted more by inner needs than by objective assessment of his merits. Because this argument cannot work with the Self-Deprecator, his case draws attention to a distinction, applicable in other cases as well, between saying that someone deserves respect for his merits and saying that he is owed respect as a person. On meritarian grounds we can only say 'You deserve better than this,' but the defect of the servile person is not merely failure to recognize his merits.

Other common arguments against the Uncle Tom, et al., may have some force but seem not to strike to the heart of the problem. For example, philosophers sometimes appeal to the value of human potentialities. As a human being, it is said, one at least has a capacity for rationality, morality, excellence, or autonomy, and this capacity is worthy of respect. Although such arguments have the merit of making respect independent of a person's actual deserts, they seem quite misplaced in some cases. There comes a time when we have sufficient evidence that a person is not ever going to *be* rational, moral, excellent, or autonomous even if he still has a capacity, in some sense, for being so. As a person approaches death with an atrocious record so far, the chances of his realizing his diminishing capacities become increasingly slim. To make these capacities the basis of his self-respect is to rest it on a shifting and unstable ground. We do, of course, respect persons for capacities which they are not exercising at the moment; for example, I might respect a person as a good philosopher even though he is just now blundering into gross confusion. In these cases, however, we respect the person for an active capacity, a ready disposition, which he has displayed on many occasions.

On this analogy, a person should have respect for himself only when his capacities are developed and ready, needing only to be triggered by an appropriate occasion or the removal of some temporary obstacle. The Uncle Tom and the Deferential Wife, however, may in fact have quite limited capacities of this sort, and, since the Self-Deprecator is already overly concerned with his own inadequacies, drawing attention to his capacities seems a poor way to increase his self-respect. In any case, setting aside the Kantian nonempirical capacity for autonomy, the capacities of different persons vary widely; but what the servile person seems to overlook is something by virtue of which he is equal with every other person.

III

Why, then, is servility a moral defect? There is, I think, another sort of answer which is worth exploring. The first part of this answer must be an attempt to isolate the objectionable features of the servile person; later we can ask why these features are objectionable. As a step in this direction, let us examine again our three paradigm cases. The moral defect in each case, I suggest, is a failure to understand and acknowledge one's own moral rights. I assume, without argument here, that each person has moral rights.[3] Some of these rights may be basic human rights; that it, rights for which a person needs only to be human to qualify. Other rights will be derivative and contingent upon his special commitments, institutional affiliations, etc. Most rights will be prima facie ones; some may be absolute. Most can be waived under appropriate conditions; perhaps some cannot. Many rights can be forfeited; but some, presumably, cannot. The servile person does not, strictly speaking, violate his own rights. At least in our paradigm cases he fails to acknowledge fully his own moral status because he does not fully understand what his rights are, how they can be waived, and when they can be forfeited.

The defect of the Uncle Tom, for example, is that he displays an attitude that denies his moral equality with whites. He does not realize, or apprehend in an effective way, that he has as much right to a decent wage and a share of political power as any comparable white. His gratitude is misplaced; he accepts benefits which are his by right as if they were gifts. The Self-Deprecator is servile in a more complex way. He acts as if he has forfeited many important rights which in fact he has not. He does not understand, or fully realize in his own case, that certain rights to fair and decent treatment do not have to be earned. He sees his merits clearly enough, but he fails to see that what he can expect from others is not merely a function of his merits. The Deferential Wife *says* that she understands her rights vis-à-vis her husband, but what she fails to appreciate is that her consent to serve him is a valid waiver of her rights only under certain conditions. If her consent is

[3]As will become evident, I am also presupposing some form of cognitive or "naturalistic" interpretation of rights. If, to accommodate an emotivist or prescriptivist, we set aside talk of moral knowledge and ignorance, we might construct a somewhat analogous case against servility from the point of view of those who adopt principles ascribing rights to all; but the argument, I suspect, would be more complex and less persuasive.

coerced, say, by the lack of viable options for women in her society, then her consent is worth little. If socially fostered ignorance of her own talents and alternatives is responsible for her consent, then her consent should not count as a fully legitimate waiver of her right to equal consideration within the marriage. All the more, her consent to defer constantly to her husband is not a legitimate setting aside of her rights if it results from her mistaken belief that she has a moral duty to do so. (Recall: "The *proper* role for a woman is to serve her family.") If she believes that she has a *duty* to defer to her husband, then, whatever she may say, she cannot fully understand that she has a *right* not to defer to him. When she says that she freely gives up such a right, she is confused. Her confusion is rather like that of a person who has been persuaded by an unscrupulous lawyer that it is legally incumbent on him to refuse a jury trial but who nevertheless tells the judge that he understands that he has a right to a jury trial and freely waives it. He does not really understand what it is to have and freely give up the right if he thinks that it would be an offense for him to exercise it.

Insofar as servility results from moral ignorance or confusion, it need not be something for which a person is to blame. Even self-reproach may be inappropriate; for at the time a person is in ignorance he cannot feel guilty about his servility, and later he may conclude that his ignorance was unavoidable. In some cases, however, a person might reasonably believe that he should have known better. If, for example, the Deferential Wife's confusion about her rights resulted from a motivated resistance to drawing the implications of her own basic moral principles, then later she might find some ground for self-reproach. Whether blameworthy or not, servility could still be morally objectionable at least in the sense that it ought to be discouraged, that social conditions which nourish it should be reformed, and the like. Not all morally undesirable features of a person are ones for which he is responsible, but that does not mean that they are defects merely from an esthetic or prudential point of view.

In our paradigm cases, I have suggested, servility is a kind of deferential attitude towards others resulting from ignorance or misunderstanding of one's moral rights. A sufficient remedy, one might think, would be moral enlightenment. Suppose, however, that our servile persons come to know their rights but do not substantially alter their behavior. Are they not still servile in an objectionable way? One might even think that reproach is more appropriate now because they know what they are doing.

The problem, unfortunately, is not as simple as it may appear. Much depends on what they tolerate and why. Let us set aside cases in which a person merely refuses to *fight* for his rights, chooses not to exercise certain rights, or freely waives many rights which he might have insisted upon. Our problem concerns the previously servile person who continues to display the same marks of deference even after he fully knows his rights. Imagine, for example, that even after enlightenment our Uncle Tom persists in his old pattern of behavior, giving all the typical signs of believing that the injustices done to him are not really wrong. Suppose, too, that the newly enlightened Deferential Wife continues to defer to her husband, refusing to disturb the old way of life by introducing her new ideas. She acts as if she accepts the idea that she is merely doing her duty though actually she no longer believes it. Let us suppose, further, that the Uncle Tom and the Deferential Wife are not merely generous with their time and property; they also accept without protest, and even appear to sanction, treatment which is humiliating and degrading. That is, they do not simply consent to waive mutually acknowledged rights; they tolerate violations of their rights with apparent approval. They pretend to give their permission for subtle humiliations which they really believe no permission can make legitimate. Are such persons still servile despite their moral knowledge?

The answer, I think, should depend upon why the deferential role is played. If the motive is a morally commendable one, or a desire to avert dire consequences to oneself, or even an ambition to set an oppressor up for a later fall, then I would not count the role player as servile. The Uncle Tom, for instance, is not servile in my sense if he shuffles and bows to keep the Klan from killing his children, to save his own skin, or even to buy time while he plans the revolution. Similarly, the Deferential Wife is not servile if she tolerates an abusive husband because he is so ill that further strain would kill him, because protesting would deprive her of her only means of survival, or because she is collecting atrocity stories for her book against marriage. If there is fault in these situations, it seems inappropriate to call it *servility*. The story is quite different, however, if a person continues in his deferential role just from laziness, timidity, or a desire for some minor advantage. He shows too little concern for his moral status as a person, one is tempted to say, if he is willing to deny it for a small profit or simply because it requires some effort and courage to affirm it openly. A black who plays the Uncle Tom merely to gain an advantage over other blacks is harming them, of course; but he is also displaying disregard for his own moral position as an equal among human beings. Similarly, a woman throws away her rights too lightly if she continues to play the subservient role because she is used to it or is too timid to risk a change. A Self-Deprecator who readily accepts what he knows are violations of his rights may be indulging his peculiar need for punishment at the expense of denying something more valuable. In these cases, I suggest, we have a kind of servility independent of any ignorance or confusion about one's rights. The person who has it may or may not be blameworthy, depending on many factors; and the line between servile and nonservile role playing will often be hard to draw. Nevertheless, the objectionable feature is perhaps clear enough for present purposes: it is a willingness to disavow one's moral status, publicly and systematically, in the absence of any strong reason to do so.

My proposal, then, is that there are at least two types of servility: one resulting from misunderstanding of one's rights and the other from placing a comparatively low value on them. In either case, servility manifests the absence of a certain kind of self-respect. The respect which is missing is not respect for one's merits but respect for one's rights. The servile person displays this absence of respect not directly by acting contrary to his own rights but indirectly by acting as if his rights were nonexistent or insignificant. An arrogant person ignores the rights of others, thereby arrogating for himself a higher status than he is entitled to; a servile person denies his own rights, thereby assuming a lower position than he is entitled to. Whether rooted in ignorance or simply lack of concern for moral rights, the attitudes in both cases may be incompatible with a proper regard for morality. That this is so is obvious in the case of arrogance; but to see it in the case of servility requires some further argument.

IV

The objectionable feature of the servile person, as I have described him, is his tendency to disavow his own moral rights either because he misunderstands them or because he cares little for them. The question remains: why should anyone regard this as a moral defect? After all, the rights which he denies are his own. He may be unfortunate, foolish, or even distasteful; but why *morally* deficient? One sort of answer, quite different from those reviewed earlier, is suggested by some of Kant's remarks. Kant held that servility is contrary to a perfect nonjuridical duty to oneself.[4] To say that the duty is perfect is roughly to say that it is stringent, never overridden by other considerations (e.g., beneficence). To say that the duty is nonjuridical is to say that a person cannot legitimately be coerced to comply. Although Kant did not develop an explicit argument for this view, an argument can easily be constructed from materials which reflect the spirit, if not the letter, of his moral theory. The argument which I have in mind is prompted by Kant's contention that respect for persons, strictly speaking, is respect for moral law.[5] If taken as a claim about all sorts of respect, this seems quite implausible. If it means that we respect persons only for their moral character, their capacity for moral conduct, or their status as "authors" of the moral law, then it seems unduly moralistic. My strategy is to construe the remark as saying that at least one sort of respect for persons is respect for the rights which the moral law accords them. If one respects the moral law, then one must respect one's own moral rights; and this amounts to having a kind of self-respect incompatible with servility.

The premises for the Kantian argument, which are all admittedly vague, can be sketched as follows:

First, let us assume, as Kant did, that all human beings have equal basic human rights. Specific rights vary with different conditions, but all must be justified from a point of view under which all are equal. Not all rights need to be earned, and some cannot be forfeited. Many rights can be waived but only under certain conditions of knowledge and freedom. These conditions are complex and

---

[4]See Immanuel Kant, *The Doctrine of Virtue,* Part II of *The Metaphysics of Morals,* ed. by M. J. Gregor (New York: Harper & Row, 1964), pp. 99–103; Prussian Academy edition, Vol. VI, pp. 434–37.

[5]Immanuel Kant, *Groundwork of the Metaphysics of Morals,* ed. by H. J. Paton (New York: Harper & Row, 1964), p. 69; Prussian Academy edition, Vol. IV, p. 401; *The Critique of Practical Reason,* ed. by Lewis W. Beck (New York: Bobbs-Merrill, 1956), pp. 81, 84; Prussian Academy edition, Vol. V, pp. 78, 81. My purpose here is not to interpret what Kant meant but to give a sense to his remark.

difficult to state; but they include something like the condition that a person's consent releases others from obligation only if it is autonomously given, and consent resulting from underestimation of one's moral status is not autonomously given. Rights can be objects of knowledge, but also of ignorance, misunderstanding, deception, and the like.

Second, let us assume that my account of servility is correct; or, if one prefers, we can take it as a definition. That is, in brief, a servile person is one who tends to deny or disavow his own moral rights because he does not understand them or has little concern for the status they give him.

Third, we need one formal premise concerning moral duty, namely, that each person ought, as far as possible, to respect the moral law. In less Kantian language, the point is that everyone should approximate, to the extent that he can, the ideal of a person who fully adopts the moral point of view. Roughly, this means not only that each person ought to do what is morally required and refrain from what is morally wrong but also that each person should treat all the provisions of morality as valuable—worth preserving and prizing as well as obeying. One must, so to speak, take up the spirit of morality as well as meet the letter of its requirements. To keep one's promises, avoid hurting others, and the like, is not sufficient; one should also take an attitude of respect towards the principles, ideals, and goals of morality. A respectful attitude towards a system of rights and duties consists of more than a disposition to conform to its definite rules of behavior; it also involves holding the system in esteem, being unwilling to ridicule it, and being reluctant to give up one's place in it. The essentially Kantian idea here is that morality, as a system of equal fundamental rights and duties, is worthy of respect, and hence a completely moral person would respect it in word and manner as well as in deed. And what a completely moral person would do, in Kant's view, is our duty to do so far as we can.

The assumptions here are, of course, strong ones, and I make no attempt to justify them. They are, I suspect, widely held though rarely articulated. In any case, my present purpose is not to evaluate them but to see how, if granted, they constitute a case against servility. The objection to the servile person, given our premises, is that he does not satisfy the basic requirement to respect morality. A person who fully respected a system of moral rights would be disposed to learn his proper place in it, to affirm it proudly, and not to tolerate abuses of it lightly. This is just the sort of disposition that the servile person lacks. If he does not understand the system, he is in no position to respect it adequately. This lack of respect may be no fault of his own, but it is still a way in which he falls short of a moral ideal. If, on the other hand, the servile person knowingly disavows his moral rights by pretending to approve of violations of them, then, barring special explanations, he shows an indifference to whether the provisions of morality are honored and publicly acknowledged. This avoidable display of indifference, by our Kantian premises, is contrary to the duty to respect morality. The disrespect in this second case is somewhat like the disrespect a religious believer might show towards his religion if, to avoid embarrassment, he laughed congenially while nonbelievers were mocking the beliefs which he secretly held. In any case, the servile person, as such, does not express disrespect for the system of moral rights in the obvious way by violating the rights of others. His lack of respect is more subtly manifested by his acting before others as if he did not know or care about his position of equality under that system.

The central idea here may be illustrated by an analogy. Imagine a club, say, an old German dueling fraternity. By the rules of the club, each member has certain rights and responsibilities. These are the same for each member regardless of what titles he may hold outside the club. Each has, for example, a right to be heard at meetings, a right not to be shouted down by the others. Some rights cannot be forfeited: for example, each may vote regardless of whether he has paid his dues and satisfied other rules. Some rights cannot be waived: for example, the right to be defended when attacked by several members of the rival fraternity. The members show respect for each other by respecting the status which the rules confer on each member. Now one new member is careful always to allow the others to speak at meetings; but when they shout him down, he does nothing. He just shrugs as if to say, 'Who am I to complain?' When he fails to stand up in defense of a fellow member, he feels ashamed and refuses to vote. He does not deserve to vote, he says. As the only commoner among illustrious barons, he feels that it is his place to serve them and defer to their decisions. When attackers from the rival fraternity come at him with swords drawn, he tells his companions to run and save themselves. When they defend him, he expresses immense gratitude— as if they had done him a gratuitous favor. Now one might argue that our new member fails to show respect for the fraternity and its rules. He does not actually violate any of the rules by refusing to vote, asking others not to defend him, and deferring to the barons, but he symbolically disavows the equal status which the rules confer on him. If he ought to have respect for the fraternity, he ought to change his attitude. Our servile person, then, is like the new member of the dueling fraternity in having insufficient respect for a system of rules and ideals. The difference is that everyone ought to respect morality whereas there is no comparable moral requirement to respect the fraternity.

The conclusion here is, of course, a limited one. Self-sacrifice is not always a sign of servility. It is not a duty always to press one's rights. Whether a given act is evidence of servility will depend not only on the attitude of the agent but also on the specific nature of his moral rights, a matter not considered here. Moreover, the extent to which a person is responsible, or blameworthy, for his defect remains an open question. Nevertheless, the conclusion should not be minimized. In order to avoid servility, a person who gives up his rights must do so with a full appreciation for what they are. A woman, for example, may devote herself to her husband if she is uncoerced, knows what she is doing, and does not pretend that she has no decent alternative. A self-contemptuous person may decide not to press various unforfeited rights but only if he does not take the attitude that he is too rotten to deserve them. A black may demand less than is due to him provided he is prepared to acknowledge that no one has a right to expect this of him. Sacrifices of this sort, I suspect, are extremely rare. Most people, if they fully acknowledged their rights, would not autonomously refuse to press them.

An even stronger conclusion would emerge if we could assume that some basic rights cannot be waived. That is, if there are some rights that others are bound to respect regardless of what we say, then, barring special explanation, we would be obliged not only to acknowledge these rights but also to avoid any appearance of consenting to give them up. To act as if we could release others from their obligation to grant these rights, apart from special circumstances, would be to fail to respect morality. Rousseau held, for example, that at least a minimal right to liberty cannot be waived. A man who consents to be enslaved, giving up liberty without *quid pro quo,* thereby displays a conditioned slavish mentality that renders his consent worthless. Similarly, a Kantian might argue that a person cannot release others from the obligation to refrain from killing him: consent is no defense against the charge of murder. To accept principles of this sort is to hold that rights to life and liberty are, as Kant believed, rather like a trustee's rights to preserve something valuable entrusted to him: he has not only a right but a duty to preserve it.

Even if there are no specific rights which cannot be waived, there might be at least one formal right of this sort. This is the right to some minimum degree of respect from others. No matter how willing a person is to submit to humiliation by others, they ought to show him some respect as a person. By analogy with self-respect, as presented here, this respect owed by others would consist of a willingness to acknowledge fully, in word as well as action, the person's basically equal moral status as defined by his other rights. To the extent that a person gives even tacit consent to humiliations incompatible with this respect, he will be acting as if he waives a right which he cannot in fact give up. To do this, barring special explanations, would mark one as servile.

V

Kant held that the avoidance of servility is a duty to oneself rather than a duty to others. Recent philosophers, however, tend to discard the idea of a duty to oneself as a conceptual confusion. Although admittedly the analogy between a duty to oneself and a duty to others is not perfect, I suggest that something important is reflected in Kant's contention.

Let us consider briefly the function of saying that a duty is *to* someone. *First,* to say that a duty is *to* a given person sometimes merely indicates who is the object of that duty. That is, it tells us that the duty is concerned with how that person is to be treated, how his interests and wishes are to be taken into account, and the like. Here we might as well say that we have a duty *towards,* or *regarding* that person. Typically the person in question is the beneficiary of the fulfillment of the duty. For example, in this sense I have a duty to my children and even a duty to a distant stranger if I promised a third party that I would help that stranger. Clearly a duty to avoid servility would be a duty to oneself at least in this minimal sense, for it is a duty to avoid, so far as possible, the denial of one's own moral status. The duty is concerned with understanding and affirming one's rights, which are, at least as a rule, for one's own benefit.

Second, when we say that a duty is *to* a certain person, we often indicate thereby the person especially entitled to complain in case the duty is not fulfilled. For example, if I fail in my duty to my colleagues, then it is they who can most appropriately reproach me. Others may sometimes speak up on their behalf, but, for the most part, it is not the business of strangers to set me straight. Analogously, to say that the duty to avoid servility is a duty to oneself would indicate that, though sometimes a person may justifiably reproach himself for being servile, others are not generally in the appropriate position to complain. Outside encouragement is sometimes necessary, but, if any blame is called for, it is primarily self-recrimination and not the censure of others.

Third, mention of the person to whom a duty is owed often tells us something about the source of that duty. For example, to say that I have a duty to another person may indicate that the argument to show that I have such a duty turns upon a promise to that person, his authority over me, my having accepted special benefits from him, or, more generally, his rights. Accordingly, to say that the duty to avoid servility is a duty to oneself would at least imply that it is not entirely based upon promises to others, their authority, their beneficence, or an obligation to respect their rights. More positively, the assertion might serve to indicate that the source of the duty is one's own rights rather than the rights of others, etc. That is, one ought not to be servile because, in some broad sense, one ought to respect one's own rights as a person. There is, to be sure, an asymmetry: one has certain duties to others because one ought not to violate their rights, and one has a duty to oneself because one ought to affirm one's own rights. Nevertheless, to dismiss duties to oneself out of hand is to overlook significant similarities.

Some familiar objections to duties to oneself, moreover, seem irrelevant in the case of servility. For example, some place much stock in the idea that a person would have no duties if alone on a desert island. This can be doubted, but in any case is irrelevant here. The duty to avoid servility is a duty to take a certain stance towards others and hence would be inapplicable if one were isolated on a desert island. Again, some suggest that if there were duties to oneself then one could make promises to oneself or owe oneself a debt of gratitude. Their paradigms are familiar ones. Someone remarks, 'I promised myself a vacation this year' or 'I have been such a good boy I owe myself a treat.' Concentration on these facetious cases tends to confuse the issue. In any case the duty to avoid servility, as presented here, does not presuppose promises to oneself or debts of gratitude to oneself. Other objections stem from the intuition that a person has no duty to promote his own happiness. A duty to oneself, it is sometimes assumed, must be a duty to promote one's own happiness. From a utilitarian point of view, in fact, this is what a duty to oneself would most likely be. The problems with such alleged duties, however, are irrelevant to the duty to avoid servility. This is a duty to understand and affirm one's rights, not to promote one's own welfare. While it is usually in the interest of a person to affirm his rights, our Kantian argument against servility was not based upon this premise. Finally, a more subtle line of objection turns on the idea that, given that rights and duties are correlative, a person who acted contrary to a duty to oneself would have to be violating his own rights, which seems absurd.[6] This objection raises issues too complex to examine here. One should note, however, that I have tried to give a sense to saying that servility is contrary to a duty to oneself without presupposing that the servile person violates his own rights. If acts contrary to duties to others are always violations of their rights, then duties to oneself are not parallel with duties to others to that extent. But this does not mean that it is empty or pointless to say that a duty is to oneself.

My argument against servility may prompt some to say that the duty is "to morality" rather than "to oneself." All this means, however, is that the duty is derived from a basic requirement to respect the provisions of morality; and in this sense every duty is a duty "to morality." My duties to my children are also derivative from a general requirement to respect moral principles, but they are still duties *to* them.

Kant suggests that duties to oneself are a precondition of duties to others. On our account of servility, there is at least one sense in which this is so. Insofar as the servile person is ignorant of his own rights, he is not in an adequate position to appreciate the rights of others. Misunderstanding the moral basis for his equal status with others, he is necessarily liable to underestimate the rights of those with whom he classifies himself. On the other hand, if he plays the servile role knowingly, then, barring special explanation, he displays a lack of concern to see the principles of morality acknowledged and respected and thus the absence of one motive which can move a moral person to respect the rights of others. In either case, the servile person's lack of self-respect necessarily puts him in a less than ideal position to respect others. Failure to fulfill one's duty to oneself, then, renders a person liable to violate duties to others. This, however, is a consequence of our argument against servility, not a presupposition of it.

[6]This, I take it, is part of M. G. Singer's objection to duties to oneself in *Generalization in Ethics* (New York: Alfred A. Knopf, 1961), pp. 311–318. I have attempted to examine Singer's arguments in detail elsewhere.

Bentham on Legal Rights[1]
•
H. L. A. Hart

I. Introductory

Most English students of jurisprudence learn to take the first steps towards the analysis of the notion of a legal right from Hohfeld's *Fundamental Legal
Conceptions*. [2] In my view Bentham is a more thought-provoking guide than Hohfeld,
and indeed than any other writer on the subject, though unfortunately his doctrine
has to be collected from observations scattered through his voluminous and not
always very readable works. Bentham certainly anticipated much of Hohfeld's work
and he has moreover much to say about important aspects of the subject on which

From *Oxford Essays in Jurisprudence (second series)*, ed. A. W. B. Simpson (Oxford: The Clarendon Press, 1973), pp. 171–201. © Oxford University Press 1973. Reprinted by permission
of the author and Oxford University Press.

[1]The present account of Bentham's doctrine of rights is collected from his *An Introduction to
the Principles of Morals and Legislation* (referred to here as *P.M.L.*), *Of Laws in General* (referred
to here as *O.L.G.*) and passages in *Bentham's Works* (Bowring ed. 1843), vol. III (referred to
here as Bowring, vol. III). All references here to *P.M.L.* and *O.L.G.* are to the 1970 edition
of these works in the *Collected Works of Jeremy Bentham* (University of London: Athlone Press).
A brief exposition and criticism of part of Bentham's doctrine, based mainly on Bowring, vol.
III, was given in my lecture on 'Bentham': *British Academy Proceedings*, 48 (1962), 313–17. This
was criticized by David Lyons in 'Rights, Claimants, and Beneficiaries', (1969) 6 *American
Philosophical Quarterly*, 173 [this volume, pp. 58–77—*Ed.*], and the present fuller and, I hope,
more precise account and criticism of Bentham owes much to the stimulus of his article.

[2]1919 (3rd reprint 1964).

Hohfeld did not touch. But his account of legal rights is by no means free from objections; for at some important points his utilitarianism gets in the way of his analytical vision. Bentham's doctrine has however the supreme merit of confronting problems ignored by other theories, even where as in the case of 'interest-theories' of rights, they are similar to or even derived from his own.

The notion of a legal right has proved in the history of jurisprudence to be very elusive: how elusive may be judged not only from the well-known division of theories into 'Will theories' and 'Interest theories' but also from some of the interesting though also strange things that jurists and others have said about rights. They have on the whole hammered rights with sceptical doubts much harder than obligations or duties. Duguit, for example, held that there were legal duties but no legal rights;[3] Austin,[4] Bentham,[5] and in our own day, Ross,[6] while apparently admitting that there may be nonlegal obligations or duties insist that 'strictly' the only rights are legal rights. It has moreover often been observed that the concept of a right, legal or moral, is not to be found in the work of the Greek philosophers, and certainly there is no noun or noun phrase in Plato or Aristotle which is the equivalent of our expression 'a right', as distinct from the 'right action' or 'the right thing to do'. Jurists of stature[7] have even held that lawyers of some sophisticated systems of law, including Roman Law, never achieved a clear concept of a legal right. Thus Maine wrote: 'singular as the fact may appear to those unacquainted with it, the Romans had not attained, or had not fully attained, to the conception of a legal Right, which seems to us elementary'[8] and 'The clear conception of a legal right . . . belongs distinctively to the modern world.'[9] He added that 'unquestionably a clear and consistent meaning was for the first time given to the expression "a right" by the searching analysis of Bentham and Austin.'[10]

Maine's reference to Bentham not as discovering or revealing the meaning of the expression 'a right', but as *giving* a clear meaning to it is accurate; and raises a methodological issue of some importance. When we ask for the analysis of such notions as that of a legal right, what precisely is it that we are seeking and by what criteria should success or failure be judged? Bentham's views on these matters are astonishingly modern and are still worth attention. He thought that the expression 'a right' was one of a fairly short list of terms including the term 'law' which were the subject matter of 'universal expository jurisprudence',[11] and its task was to expound the ideas annexed to these terms. But he did not think that in discharging

---

[3]*Traité de droit constitutionel* (1911), 1: 64, 130–45, discussed by Allen, *Legal Duties* (1931), p. 158, and Ross, *On Law and Justice* (1958), p. 186.

[4]*Lectures on Jurisprudence* (5th ed.), ch. XII, p. 344.

[5]Bowring II. 501; III. 221.

[6]Ross, op. cit., pp. 248, 365.

[7]Besides Maine (see n. 8) Buckland, *Text Book of Roman Law,* 2nd ed. (1950), 58 and Villey, *Leçons d'histoire de la philosophie de droit* (1957), chs. XI and XIV.

[8]*Early Law and Custom* (1891), p. 365; cf. p. 366.

[9]Op. cit., p. 390.

[10]Op. cit., p. 366.

[11]*P.M.L.,* pp. 6, 295.

this task he was strictly bound by common usage, or that definitions, if they were to be useful in jurisprudence, should merely follow or reflect that usage, which at points he found to be confused, arbitrary, and vague and in various other ways unsatisfactory. Quite frequently and explicitly, he departed from usage in order to construct a meaning for a term which, while generally coinciding with usage and furnishing an explanation of its main trends, would not only be clear, but would pick out and collect clusters of features frequently recurrent in the life of a legal system, to which it was important to attend for some statable theoretical or practical purpose. Hence Bentham spoke of himself as expounding the meaning of terms by 'fixing' rather than 'teaching' their import;[12] and when he came in *Of Laws in General* to elaborate his definition of a law he spoke of 'rather a meaning which I wish to see annexed to the term law than one which it has any settled and exclusive possession of already'.[13] In modern terminology, Bentham's conception of analysis is that of 'rational reconstruction' or refinement of concepts in use: his general standpoint is critical and corrective, and in the sequel I shall appeal to it in criticism of part of Bentham's own doctrine concerning legal rights.

II. Survey of Bentham's Doctrine

Bentham distinguishes three principal kinds of right which correspond roughly to Hohfeld's 'claim-right', 'liberty' or 'privilege', and 'power', though he does not include an element corresponding to Hohfeld's 'immunity'. In spite of this rough correspondence there are many differences of which perhaps the most important is that unlike Bentham, Hohfeld considers that the very common use of the expression of a right to cover all the four cases which he distinguishes to be a 'loose'[14] and even 'nebulous'[15] usage: the 'proper meaning'[16] of the term according to Hohfeld is to designate the element which he terms a claim-right, and the broad or loose use is described as 'unfortunate'[17] because it leads to confusion of thought. Notwithstanding these strictures Hohfeld recognizes that the use of the term to cover claim-right, liberty, power, and immunity is a use of the term in a 'generic'[18] sense and hints that the characteristic common to the genus is 'any sort of legal advantage'[19] though he does not explain this idea further. Bentham does not express any similar misgivings concerning the wide extension of the term in ordinary usage, and though in the cases of other terms he is prepared to distinguish what is 'strictly and properly so called' from what is not, he does not do so in the case of rights.

[12]Bowring III. 217.

[13]*O.L.G.*, p. 11.

[14]Hohfeld, op. cit., pp. 42, 51.

[15]Op. cit., p. 54.

[16]Op. cit., pp. 38, 39.

[17]Op. cit., p. 51.

[18]Op. cit., p. 42.

[19]Op. cit., p. 71.

Bentham starts by making what he says is a fundamental distinction between two sorts of rights distinguished by different relationships to the idea of obligation or duty.[20] The first sort of rights owe their existence to (or as he says 'result from') the absence of legal obligation:[21] the second sort result from obligations imposed by law.[22] Rights of the first sort are rights to do or abstain from some action, and rights of the second sort are rights to what Bentham calls the 'services',[23] i.e. the actions or forbearance, of others. Corresponding to these two different sorts of rights are two different sorts of law or states of the law. Rights resulting from obligation are conferred by (or as Bentham puts it, 'have as their base') coercive laws; rights resulting from the absence of obligation have as their base discoercive or permissive laws.[24] In this last phrase Bentham includes three different cases. These are (i) *active* permission[25] or countermand: where the law permits some action, previously legally prohibited or obligatory, to be done or not done; (ii) *inactive* or original permission:[26] where the law simply declares that some action not previously prohibited or obligatory may be done or not done; (iii) the case where the law is silent.[27] Such permissive laws or legal silence leave the individual who is the right-holder free or at liberty to do or not to do some action; I shall use the expression 'liberty-right' instead of Bentham's more explicit though clumsy circumlocution for this sort of right, and I shall use instead of Bentham's expression 'right resulting from obligation' the more familiar 'right correlative to obligation' for his second sort of right, which arises when the law imposes a duty not on the right-holder, but on another and thus restricts the other's freedom to act as he chooses.

A. Liberty-Rights

Bentham in my view was certainly justified in regarding liberty-rights as of very great importance. Some later theorists have thought that so negative an idea could be of little significance for jurisprudence and could not represent 'a legal relation'.[28] This I am sure is a great mistake. Without attention to this negative and apparently insignificant element there cannot be any clear understanding of such important ideas as that of ownership, or of the legal character of the sphere left open by the law to economic competition, or any clear formulation of many legal

---

[20]Obligation and duty are treated as synonymous terms by Bentham: see *O.L.G.*, p. 294.
[21]Bowring III. 181, 217–18; *P.M.L.*, p. 212.
[22]Bowring III, loc. cit., *O.L.G.*, pp. 57–8, 294.
[23]Bowring III. 159, *O.L.G.*, pp. 57–8.
[24]Bowring III. 181, *P.M.L.*, p. 302.
[25]*O.L.G.*, pp. 57–8.
[26]Ibid.
[27]*O.L.G.*, pp. 98–9, Bowring III. 159.
[28]e.g. Pollock, *Jurisprudence* (2nd ed., 1902), p. 62, but see Hohfeld, op. cit., p. 48 n.

problems to which that has given rise.[29] Indeed in the sequel I shall claim that this element of a liberty-right is involved in all the most important kinds of legal right at least in the civil law. But the notion of a liberty-right needs some further characterization beyond that given to it by Bentham's phrase, 'right resulting from the absence of obligation'. The following points in particular deserve attention.

The Bilateral Character of Liberty-Rights. In England and in most other countries a man has a right to look over his garden fence at his neighbour; he is under no obligation not to look at him and under no obligation to look at him. In this example the liberty is therefore bilateral; both the obligation not to look and the obligation to look are in Bentham's phrase 'absent'. Most of Bentham's examples of a liberty-right and his general account of them represent them as bilateral; they are, he says, such rights as men have in the state of nature where there are no obligations. But he occasionally speaks as if a unilateral liberty, that is the absence of *either* an obligation not to do something *or* an obligation to do it were enough to constitute a right of this kind.[30] On that footing a right to do an action would merely exclude an obligation not to do it, and men always have a right to do what they have an obligation to do. Hohfeld's 'liberty' or 'privilege' is by his definition a unilateral liberty,[31] and, in some special contexts, to treat unilateral liberties as rights accords with a common and intelligible usage for which I offer an explanation below.[32] But I shall treat Bentham as committed to regarding bilateral liberties as the standard type of liberty-right.

Liberty-Rights and Correlative Obligations Not to Interfere. The fact that a man has a right to look at his neighbour over the garden fence does not entail that the neighbour has a correlative obligation to let himself be looked at or not to interfere with the exercise of this specific liberty-right. So he could, for example, erect a screen on his side of the fence to block the view. But though a neighbour may do this if he wishes, and so has himself a liberty-right or bilateral liberty to erect or not to erect such a fence, there are other things that, in most countries, he cannot legally do to prevent his tormentor looking at him. For he has certain legal obligations or duties, civil or criminal, or both, which preclude some, though not all forms of interference, and these in practice more or less adequately protect the exercise of the liberty-right. Thus he cannot enter the next-door garden and beat up his tormentor, for this would be a breach of certain duties not indeed correlative to his tormentor's liberty-right to look at him, but correlative at least in the case of civil duties to certain other rights, which his tormentor has and which are not mere liberties. These are the tormentor's rights not to be assaulted and his right that others should not enter on his land without his consent. These are rights correlative to obligations and to Bentham's account of these I now turn.

[29]See below p. 133 n. 53.
[30]e.g. Bowring III. 218 but cf. III. 159.
[31]Hohfeld, op. cit., p. 39.
[32]Below, pp. 134, 145 n. 93.

B. Rights Correlative to Obligations

The right not to be assaulted and the right of an owner or occupier of land that others should not enter on it without his consent are rights to what Bentham terms a negative service,[33] that is to the abstention from 'hurtful action';[34] in other cases of rights correlative to obligations, where the obligation is to *do* something rather than abstain from action the right is to an 'affirmative' or 'positive' service,[35] or, as Bentham paraphrases it, to 'a useful action'.[36] All rights correlative to obligations are rights to services which consist in the performance of their correlative obligation and with two exceptions all legal obligations or duties have correlative rights. One exception is the case of 'self-regarding duties'[37] where the duty is imposed by law solely for the benefit of the agent on whom it is imposed. Bentham's examples of self-regarding duties include duties to abstain from suicide, from 'indecency not in public', incest, idleness, gaming, and 'other species of prodigality'.[38] The other more important exception to the principle that all legal obligations have correlative rights is where the legislator has disregarded entirely the dictates of utility and created obligations by which no one at all benefits. Such obligations Bentham terms 'ascetic', 'pure', or 'barren', or 'useful to no one'[39] and he thought they had been all too numerous in the history of human law. But apart from these two cases, whenever the law creates civil or criminal obligations, it always thereby creates what Bentham terms 'an enforced service' negative or positive, for the benefit of others; and to have a right correlative to an obligation is to be the person or persons intended to benefit from the performance of the obligation.[40] But not only individuals have rights; the public and also distinct classes included in it have, according to Bentham, rights in those cases where the persons intended to benefit are what he terms 'unassignable individuals'.[41]

Accordingly, with the two exceptions mentioned, every offence, crime or civil wrong, is a violation of some right and a case of 'wrongful withholding of services'[42] so that 'there is no law whatsoever that does not confer on some person or other a right'.[43] I shall call this identification of a right-holder by reference to the person or persons intended to benefit by the performance of an obligation 'the benefit theory' of rights; and when I come to criticize it I shall try to make precise the sense not only of benefit but of a person intended to benefit and to clarify the distinction which Bentham makes between assignable and unassignable individuals.

[33]Bowring III. 159; *O.L.G.*, pp. 58–9.
[34]Bowring III. 159.
[35]*O.L.G.*, pp. 58–9; Bowring III. 159.
[36]Bowring III. 159.
[37]*O.L.G.*, pp. 58, 294; *P.M.L.*, p. 206.
[38]*P.M.L.*, pp. 225 n., 296 n., 232 n.
[39]Bowring III. 181, 221.
[40]*P.M.L.*, p. 206; *O.L.G.*, p. 58.
[41]See below, pp. 137–8.
[42]*P.M.L.*, p. 228 n.
[43]*O.L.G.*, p. 220.

C. Powers

Legal powers are for Bentham a species of right[44] and his works contain a most elaborate taxonomy of the different kinds of legal powers together with a sophisticated analysis of the idea of a legal power and of the legal provisions by which powers are conferred on individuals.[45] The simplest kind of power is that which a man has when he is allowed by law to interfere with or physically control things or the bodies of persons or animals. Bentham subsumes such interference (which of course may take a great variety of forms such as touching, holding, moving, confining) under the general notion of handling and he calls such powers 'powers of contrectation': examples are an owner's power to make physical use of his property or a policeman's power of arrest. Such powers are in fact liberty-rights differing from other liberty-rights in two respects: first the action which, in such cases, there is liberty to do is restricted to actions physically affecting things or bodies; secondly in such cases the liberty is exclusive or exceptional[46] in the sense that it is a liberty to do something that others are generally under an obligation not to do. Such powers are conferred by permissive laws,[47] but like other liberty-rights they may be protected or 'corroborated'[48] by duties imposed on others not to obstruct, or even requiring them to assist, their exercise. If they are not so corroborated, they exist as 'bare' liberties: and then like other liberty-rights their existence does not entail the existence of any correlative obligations.

More important for our present purpose is the kind of power which Bentham calls 'investitive' and 'divestitive'.[49] These are the powers which a man has when he is enabled by law to change the legal position of others, or of himself and others as he does for example when he alienates property or makes a will or contract. In entering into such legal transactions he does an act (usually the writing or saying of certain words according to more or less strictly prescribed forms) which manifest certain intentions as to future rights and duties of himself and others. Such acts, or acts in the law, are not only *permitted* by the law but are *recognized* by the law as having certain legal consequences: given certain circumstances, a duly executed conveyance of land is 'valid', i.e. legally effective in divesting the transferor of certain rights and duties and in investing the transferee with similar ones. Bentham's elaborate account of the legal provisions by which such investitive and divestitive powers are conferred is designed to reconcile their existence with his general 'imperative' theory of law according to which all laws either impose duties or grant permissions.[50] There is not according to Bentham a further special

---

[44]*O.L.G.*, pp. 84, 220.

[45]See *O.L.G.*, *passim*, and esp. ch. IX and my 'Bentham on Legal Powers', (1972) 81 *Yale Law Journal* 799.

[46]For an examination of Bentham's notion of powers of contrectation as exclusive or exceptional liberties see my 'Bentham on Legal Powers', loc. cit.

[47]*O.L.G.*, pp. 81, 86–7, 137 n.

[48]*P.M.L.*, p. 302; *O.L.G.*, p. 260 (48); *O.L.G.*, p. 261.

[49]*O.L.G.*, pp. 82–4; cf. *P.M.L.*, p. 217 n., Bowring III. 186–90 on 'collative and ablative events'.

[50]*O.L.G.*, pp. 95–9 and *passim*. *P.M.L.*, p. 302.

kind of laws which confer powers; but powers are conferred when laws imposing duties or granting permissions are 'imperfect mandates',[51] i.e. incomplete in some respects and so contain 'blanks'[52] left to 'power-holders' to 'fill up', and when they do this they thereby determine or vary the incidence of existing 'imperfect' laws.

III. Criticism of Bentham's Doctrine

A. Liberty-Rights

Liberty-Rights and Their Protective Perimeter. Those who have doubted the importance of liberties or mere absence of obligation for the analysis of legal rights have felt that so negative a notion without some positive correlate is not worth a lawyer's attention. This is a mistaken way of presenting the important fact that where a man is left free by the law to do or not to do some particular action, the exercise of this liberty will always be protected by the law to some extent, even if there is no strictly correlative obligation upon others not to interfere with it. This is so because at least the cruder forms of interference, such as those involving physical assault or trespass, will be criminal or civil offences or both, and the duties or obligations not to engage in such modes of interference constitute a protective perimeter behind which liberties exist and may be exercised. Thus, to take a trivial example, my right to scratch my head is protected, not by a correlative obligation upon others not to interfere with my doing that specific kind of act, but by the fact that obligations to refrain from assault or trespass to my person will generally preclude effective interference to it. In most cases the protection of my liberty afforded by this perimeter of obligations will be adequate but it may not be complete: if others could stop me scratching my head without any breach of these obligations e.g. by hypnotizing me, they may do so. This makes clear the difference between a liberty-right to do some kind of act protected by a strictly correlative obligation upon others not to interfere with it, and a liberty-right protected only by a normally adequate perimeter of general obligations.

It may be that jurists who have doubted the importance of the negative notion of absence of obligation or liberty have done so because the protective perimeter has obscured their view of it; but it is in fact important not to lose sight of either the liberty or the perimeter. Both are required in the analysis of many legal phenomena including that of economic competition. Two people walking in an empty street see a purse lying on the pavement: each has a liberty so far as the law is concerned to pick it up and each may prevent the other doing so if he can race him to the spot. But though each has this liberty there are also several specific things which each has a right that the other should not do: these are rights with correlative obligations and these correlative obligations together with the duties of the criminal law protect (and also restrict) each party's liberty. Thus neither of the

[51]O.L.G., pp. 26, 80–91.
[52]Bowring III. 222; cf. III. 197

competitors may hit or trip up the other, or threaten him with violence in order to get the prize. The perimeter of obligations to abstain from such actions constitutes the ring within which the competitors compete in the exercise of their liberties. Of course where competition is not in question, as in the case of 'fundamental' human rights or liberties, great importance may be attached to their unimpeded exercise and in such cases the law may protect the liberty by a strictly correlative obligation not to interfere by any means with a specific form of activity. But most liberties are not so protected.[53]

Bentham appreciated the importance of this combination of a liberty with a protective perimeter of obligations, but his formulations on the point are casual and somewhat ambiguous. He distinguishes between a 'naked' right and a 'vested' or 'established' one.[54] A naked right is a liberty unprotected by any obligation and are the rights which men have in the state of nature; a man has a vested or established right when he has a right that others should abstain from interfering with a liberty which he has. This language suggests that Bentham thought of rights as vested only where there was a strictly correlative obligation not to interfere, but in other passages in discussing liberty-rights he envisages their protection by a perimeter of general obligations not strictly correlative to the liberty.

> I may stand or sit down—I may go in or out—I may eat or not eat etc.: the law says nothing upon the matter. Still, the right which I exercise I derive from the law because it is the law which erects into an offence every species of violence by which one may seek to prevent me from doing what I like.[55]

Notwithstanding his appreciation of the importance of the combination of liberties with a perimeter of protective though not correlative obligation, Bentham, like Hobbes in describing the state of nature, treats liberties even when 'naked' as rights. But it is not at all clear that lawyers or anyone else would speak of a completely naked or unprotected liberty as a right, or that any useful purpose would be served if they did. The state of nature, if worth describing at all, can be described adequately in other terms. So far as organized society is concerned there would be something not only strange but misleading in describing naked liberties as rights: if we said, for example, that a class of helots whom free citizens were allowed to treat as they wished or interfere with at will, yet had rights to do those acts which they were not forbidden by the law to do. All the very important points

---

[53]Thus the famous cases *Allen* v. *Flood* (1898) A.C. 1, *Mogul Steamship* v. *Macgregor & Others* (1892) A.C. 25, *Quinn* v. *Leathern* (1901) A.C. 495 and (in part) *Rookes* v. *Barnard* (1964) A.C. 1129, are best understood as raising the question whether an individual's liberty-rights to trade or employ labour or sell his labour are protected by a perimeter consisting only of duties corresponding to the specific torts of conspiracy, intimidation, and inducement of breach of contract, or by a perimeter consisting also of a duty corresponding to a more general tort of interfering with the trade, business, or employment of a person without lawful justification or excuse.

[54]Bowring III. 218.

[55]Bowring III. 159–60.

in Bentham's doctrine distinguishing between liberty-rights and rights correlative to obligations can be preserved by treating bilateral liberty as an essential *element* in the analysis of liberty-rights but only constituting a liberty-right in conjunction with a perimeter of some protecting obligations or duties. It is not necessary, nor I think useful for any purpose, to treat liberties without any such protection as a distinct kind of legal right.

Unilateral Liberty-Rights. Bentham, as I have said, occasionally speaks as if a unilateral liberty were sufficient to constitute a liberty-right. On this footing a liberty-right to do an act would be compatible with, and indeed entailed by, an obligation to do it. The right-holder would not, as in the case of bilateral liberty, be free to choose whether to do an act or not; he would be at liberty to do an act only in the sense that he was not under an obligation not to do it. Bentham does not discuss the appropriateness or otherwise of extending the notion of rights to include unilateral liberty; but it seems clear that a general extension to include all unilateral liberties would neither accord with usage nor be useful. In the ordinary case, where the law imposes general obligations, e.g. to pay taxes, or to abstain from assault or trespass, it would be pointless or even confusing to describe those who had these obligations as having rights to pay taxes or to abstain from assault. Yet there undoubtedly are certain specific contexts where unilateral liberties are intelligibly spoken of as rights to do actions even where there is also an obligation to do the same action. Among these are cases where individuals by way of exception to a general rule are not merely permitted but also legally required to do some act generally prohibited.

Thus a policeman ordered to arrest a man might be asked 'What right have you to arrest him?' and might well produce his orders as showing that he had a right to arrest. In general the query 'What right have you to do that?' invites the person addressed to show that some act of his which is prima facie wrongful because generally prohibited is one which in the particular case he is at liberty to do. The questioner is not concerned to know whether the liberty is unilateral, i.e. accompanied by an obligation, or bilateral; so the form of his question covers both.[56]

B. The Benefit Theory of Rights
Correlative to Obligation

The most striking feature of Bentham's analysis of legal rights is his benefit theory of rights correlative to obligation: the view that with the exception of 'barren'

[56]Further examples of unilateral liberties spoken of as rights are afforded by cases where duties in Bentham's phrase, are 'superadded' to liberty-rights (*O.L.G.*, pp. 270–1, 296). Thus a trustee who has equitable duties to put the trust property to a certain use may be said to have a right to do this since the equitable duty is for historical reasons conceived as something distinct grafted on to his still persistent legal bilateral liberty-rights, though its actual effect is to render the liberty-right unilateral.

and 'self regarding' obligation *all* obligations, civil or criminal, have correlative rights held by those intended to benefit by their performance. In considering this doctrine certain features of Bentham's elaborate classification of offences[57] must be kept in mind, since, according to him, every offence, i.e. every breach of obligation with the two exceptions mentioned, violates a right. Bentham distinguishes between offences which are primarily or in the first instance detrimental to 'assignable persons' (which he terms 'offences against individuals' or 'private offences')[58] and offences detrimental only to unassignable individuals.[59] Of the latter there are two kinds, viz. public offences against a whole community or state, or semi-public offences against classes of persons within the community distinguished either by some class characteristic or by residence in a particular area. Offences of the first kind violate individual rights: examples of them are murder, assault, theft, and breach of contract:[60] offences of the second kind violate the rights of the public or a class, and examples of them are failure to pay taxes or desertion from the army (public offences)[61] and violation of health regulations imposed for the protection of a particular neighbourhood (semi-public offences).[62]

Intended Benefits to Assignable versus Unassignable Individuals. Before attempting any general criticism of Bentham's benefit theory, it is necessary to explore the ambiguities of the central ideas involved in it. These ambiguities are, I think, involved in all theories which attempt to define the notion of an individual's right in terms of benefits or interests, and they concern (a) the ideas of benefit and detriment, (b) the distinction between assignable and unassignable persons, and (c) the idea of a person intended by the law to benefit. These are difficult notions requiring fuller investigation than is attempted here, but the following may suffice for the present purposes.

(a) *Benefit and Detriment.* Bentham, though committed to the doctrine that pleasure and pain are the only things good and bad in themselves,[63] does not in his account of rights and offences simply identify benefit with pleasure or avoidance of pain or detriment with pain or loss of pleasure. Hence, for him, as for others, theft of £1 from a millionaire indifferent to the loss constitutes a detriment to him and an offence against him; while forbearance from such theft constitutes a negative service and a benefit to which he has a legal right. So, too, security of the person or of reputation are benefits, even if in some cases the particular individual concerned would have welcomed an attack or found it pleasurable or otherwise desirable. So in general the idea of benefit or services, positive or neg-

[57]*P.M.L.*, ch. XVI, pp. 187 ff.
[58]*P.M.L.*, p. 188.
[59]Op. cit., p. 189.
[60]Op. cit., pp. 223–4, 228 n.
[61]Op. cit., p. 262.
[62]Op. cit., pp. 194 n., 225 n.
[63]*P.M.L.*, pp. 88–9, 100.

ative, includes the provision or maintenance of conditions or treatment which are regarded by human beings generally, or in a particular society, as desirable or 'in their interest' and so to be sought from others. Correspondingly the idea of a detriment or harm includes the loss of such benefits and conditions and treatment generally regarded as undesirable and to be avoided. No doubt Bentham thought also that what makes anything a benefit or desirable is its general tendency to produce pleasure or to avoid pain,[64] and if, in a particular society, the notion of benefits or detriments had no such connection with pleasure and pain, this was an aberration to be deplored.

Given this conception of benefits and detriments, it follows that in the case of those offences which Bentham calls offences against individuals and regards as violating the rights of assignable individuals, the breach of the law necessarily, and not merely contingently, constitutes a detriment to individuals, and compliance with the law in such cases necessarily, and not merely contingently, constitutes a benefit to individuals. This feature is secured simply by the definition of the offence in terms of actions which constitute in themselves detriments to individuals even if they do not always cause pain. For killing or wounding or slandering an individual or thieving from him or false imprisonment or 'wife-stealing' (abduction), given the above account of detriments, necessarily constitute detriments and do not merely contingently cause them or make them more likely. Since it is perfectly reasonable, without further investigation of 'legislative intent', to ascribe to laws prohibiting offences which thus necessarily constitute a detriment to individuals, an intention to benefit them, it is by reference to this feature that Bentham's central conception of assignable individuals intended to benefit from the law is mainly to be explained.

In such cases we may call the benefit or detriment 'direct' and it is to be observed that in the case of Bentham's public and semi-public offences benefits and detriments are not involved in the same direct way. As Bentham points out[65] compliance with laws requiring payment of taxes will make funds available to a government, but whether or not benefits as above defined will result for any individuals is a contingent matter, depending on what Bentham terms 'a various and remote concatenation of causes and effects',[66] including the nature of the government's policies for use of the funds and their skill or even luck in implementing them. The same is true of laws requiring military service or prohibiting treason. General compliance with such laws will constitute certain conditions without which it would be impossible or less likely that various benefits will be ultimately received by individuals, and in that sense these conditions may be said to make their receipt more likely than would otherwise be the case. Such contingently beneficial laws may be said to provide indirect benefits.[67]

---

[64]*P.M.L.*, pp. 191–3. Bowring III. 214.

[65]*O.L.G.*, pp. 62–3; *P.M.L.*, pp. 149–51.

[66]*O.L.G.*, p. 62.

[67]Of course the distinction between direct and indirect benefits will present disputable borderline cases, since whether anything is to be counted as in itself a benefit or only making

(b) *Assignable and Unassignable Individuals.* This distinction appears in many places in Bentham's works[68] and he uses it to explain what is meant by saying that certain offences are against the public or against a class, and that the public or a class are intended to benefit by a law and so have rights resulting from the obligations which it imposes. Bentham does not conceive of the public or of a class as an entity distinct from its members, and for him to speak of the public or class of persons as having rights is still to speak only of individuals, but of individuals who cannot be 'individually assigned' included in the community or class.[69] What then is it for an individual to be 'assignable'? Bentham's most explicit statement on this subject is in a footnote which merely tells us that an individual may be assignable 'by name or at least by description in such manner as to be sufficiently distinguished from all others'.[70] This leaves the notion of a law intended to benefit assignable individuals still obscure; because the various laws, such as the laws forbidding murder or assault which he does in fact regard as intended to benefit assignable individuals (and so as conferring rights upon them), do not refer to individuals either by name or by some uniquely applicable description, nor on any account of legislative intent does it seem that they are intended only to benefit individuals so identified,[71] if that means identified at the time when the law comes into existence.

None the less Bentham's brief explanation of his distinction can be used indirectly to determine whether or not the individuals intended to be benefited by a law are assignable, since the corresponding question whether or not an *offence*[72] is against assignable individuals can be answered by direct reference to it. Thus the laws which Bentham regards as creating offences against assignable individuals and so as conferring rights upon them are such that to establish that the offence

the receipt of benefits more likely will often depend on degrees of likelihood, numbers of contingencies and and also on analogies with standard direct individual benefits. Thus compliance by an employer with a duty to provide each of his workmen working in dangerous conditions with protective clothing might, like a law requiring him to pay each of them a sum of money, be considered as constituting a direct benefit, and its breach as constituting a direct detriment; whereas a law requiring him to fit a fence or guard on dangerous machinery while men are at work, might be considered not as constituting a direct benefit for them but only as making the avoidance of harm more likely, and so constituting an indirect benefit. It is also to be noted that if provision of such a fence or guard is treated as constituting a direct benefit it would be a *common* benefit, in contrast with the *separate* or *individual* benefits constituted by the provision of each workman with protective clothing. It seems likely that Bentham would regard all laws providing such common benefits as intended to benefit classes not 'assignable individuals'. (See below, p. 138, with regard to statutory duties.)

[68]e.g. *P.M.L.*, pp. 143, 188–9; *O.L.G.*, p. 37. It also appears in John Stuart Mill's account of rights in *Utilitarianism*, ch. V.

[69]*P.M.L.*, p. 189.

[70]*P.M.L.*, p. 188 n.

[71]Of course they may be said to be intended to benefit 'each individual' in the community but this does not make the individuals 'assignable' in Bentham's sense.

[72]Bentham observes that rights may best be 'expounded' by considering the corresponding offences: *P.M.L.*, p. 206 and see *O.L.G.*, p. 58.

has been committed it must be shown that an individual who *is* 'assignable' in Bentham's sense, i.e. distinguished from others in some way and so uniquely identified, has suffered some individual detriment from the commission of the offence. It seems therefore that we may interpret the statement that a law is intended to benefit assignable individuals (and so confers rights upon them) as meaning no more than that to establish its breach an assignable individual must be shown to have suffered an individual detriment.[73] This seems to give the required contrast with those laws creating offences which Bentham classes as against unassignable individuals, such as failure to pay taxes or military desertion; for in such cases it is not necessary to show that any individual has suffered any detriment and it may often be the case that no individual has suffered or will suffer thereby. On this footing, an offence may be said to be against unassignable individuals, and so one which violates the rights not of individuals but of the public or a class, if (a) it is not an offence against assignable individuals, and (b) general compliance with the law creating an offence is intended to constitute an indirect benefit for any one or more individuals who are or may be included in the community or in a class within it but who are not otherwise identified.[74]

---

[73]This interpretation is not I think inconsistent with Bentham's remark *(P.M.L.,* p. 189 n.) that the divisions between private, semi-public, and public offences are liable to be 'confounded'. He points out that 'the fewer the individuals of which a class is composed . . . the more likely are the persons to whom an offence is detrimental to *become* assignable.' This seems merely to point out that though an offence (e.g. breach of health regulations imposed for the benefit of a particular area) is correctly regarded as one against a class in accordance with the interpretation offered above, it will in the case of small *closed* classes be possible to determine which individuals ultimately suffer from a given offence even though proof of their suffering is not, as in the case of offences against individuals, necessary to establish that the offence has been committed. But Bentham's point here is certainly not clear.

[74]It should be observed that Bentham's distinction between laws which confer rights on individuals and those which confer them on the public or classes, based as it is on assignability as interpreted above, is *not* the same as the apparently similar distinction which has sometimes been invoked by English courts in their attempts to formulate tests for determining whether breach of a statutory duty, such as the duty to fence dangerous machinery or provide specified forms of fire-escape, gives rise to an action for damages on the part of individuals for injuries caused by the breach. Breach of most such statutory duties would, according to Bentham's assignability test, not be offences against individuals and so would not confer a right upon them to performance of the statutory duty; since to establish their breach it would not be necessary to show that any individual had suffered any individual detriment, but only that e.g. the machinery had not been fenced as required: such an offence, for Bentham, would either be against a class (e.g. of workmen) or against the public. It is on the other hand true that in determining whether the legislature in creating such statutory duties also by implication created a statutory tort, courts have flirted with the idea that this depended on whether the statutory duty was 'owed to' individuals or imposed in their interests and not merely imposed for the general welfare of the public (see *Solomons* v. *R. Gertzenstein* [1954] 2 Q.B. 243). This test has been rejected by some judges (see per Atkin L.J. in *Phillips* v. *Britannia Hygienic Laundry* [1923] 2 K.B. 832) and indeed the finding that a statutory duty was owed to or for the benefit of individuals seems rather to be a conclusion from a finding, made on other grounds, that the statute conferred a right of action upon individuals, than a reason for such a finding. But whatever this distinction is it does not, for the reasons stated above,

(c) Intended by the Law to Benefit. If the statement that a law intends to benefit an individual and so confers a right upon him is interpreted as meaning no more than that its breach constitutes a direct individual detriment, then we have a criterion for determining when laws confer individual rights which avoids difficult inquiries into 'actual' legislative intent. Moreover this criterion will give a decisive and at least an intelligible answer to some questions which have confronted theorists who, within the general framework of an interest- or benefit-theory of rights, have wished to limit, in some reasonable way, the class of intended beneficiaries who should count as having rights. Thus, to take an example, famous from Ihering's[75] discussion of it, in a similar context, should a law, forbidding in general terms the importation of manufactured goods, which was in fact enacted solely in order to benefit a particular domestic manufacturer be taken to confer a right upon him? Ihering was anxious to distinguish such a case as a mere *'Reflexwirkung,* (reflex operation) of a duty and not as a right, and he sought for, but never clearly formulated, some criterion which would distinguish a right violated by a demonstrable 'individual breach of the law' (*Individuelle Rechtsverletzung*) from a mere reflex operation of duty.[76] Kelsen believed that no such distinction could be drawn; but Bentham's conception of a direct detriment to an assignable individual, interpreted as above, might well have served this purpose and the test later suggested by Ross[77] in discussing Ihering's case is in substance identical with it.

For the purpose of criticism of the benefit theory I shall assume that the above interpretation of Bentham is correct.[78] I do so because this is the strongest form of the benefit theory and if it is vulnerable to criticism it is not likely that a theory depending on a more extended sense of 'intended by the law to benefit' is

turn, as Bentham's does, upon assignability. It appears rather to be a distinction (which the Courts have found very difficult to apply in practice) between the cases where, on the construction of the statute, it can be said that its main purpose was to secure to each individual of a specific class some specific benefit or protection from some specific harm and those cases where either there was no such discernible purpose, or, if there was, this was merely ancillary to a dominant purpose to create or maintain conditions (e.g. the conservation of manpower or resources) whereby all or any unspecified members of the public might benefit in various unspecified ways.

[75]*Geist des römischen Rechts* (1924 ed.), III. 351–3, discussed by Kelsen in *Haupt probleme des Staatrechts* (1960 ed.), pp. 578–81, and Ross in *Towards a Realistic Jurisprudence* (1946), pp. 167–8, 179 ff.

[76]Ihering's earlier account of rights (op. cit., 2nd ed., III. 339) had avoided this problem since it restricted rights to cases where the enforcement by legal proceedings of duties protecting interests was left to the individual concerned. (Selbstschutz des Interesses.')

[77]Op. cit., pp. 179 ff. Lyons's account of the 'qualified beneficiary theory' which he favours and considers may be attributable to Bentham (op. cit., pp. 173–4, 176–80 [this volume, pp. 58–60, 63–69—*Ed.*] is very close to the above interpretation of Bentham.

[78]There are certainly passages in Bentham (e.g. *O.L.G.*, pp. 55–6) where he seems to contemplate that if the legislator intended an 'assignable' individual to benefit even very indirectly from the performance of an obligation this would confer a right to its performance on him. On this view the favoured manufacturer in Ihering's case would have a right that the goods should not be imported.

likely to be successful. For the same reason I shall not consider further Bentham's account of rights of the public or a class.[79]

Absolute and Relative Duties. The principal advocates of benefit or 'interest' theories of rights correlative to obligations have shown themselves sensitive to the criticism that, if to say that an individual has such a right means no more than that he is the intended beneficiary of a duty, then 'a right' in this sense may be an unnecessary, and perhaps confusing, term in the description of the law; since all that can be said in a terminology of such rights can be and indeed is best said in the indispensable terminology of duty. So the benefit theory appears to make nothing more of rights than an alternative formulation of duties: yet nothing seems to be gained in significance or clarity by translating, e.g. the statement that men are under a legal duty not to murder, assault, or steal from others into the statement that individuals have a right not to be murdered, assaulted, or stolen from, or by saying, when a man has been murdered, that his right not to be killed has been violated.[80]

Ihering as I have said was visited by just such doubts. Bentham confronted them in his codification proposals in the form of an inquiry whether the law should be expounded at length in a list of rights or a list of obligations. The test which he proposed was 'Present the entire law to that one of the parties that has most need to be instructed'[81] and he thought that the law should generally be expounded at length in terms of obligations but need 'only be mentioned' in a list of rights; his principal reason for this was that because of the penalties imposed the party on whom the law imposed the obligation had most need for instruction.[82]

(a) Criminal versus *Civil Law.* The most cogent criticisms of the benefit theory are those that on the one hand press home the charge of redundancy or uselessness to a lawyer of the concept of right correlative to obligation defined simply in terms of the intended beneficiary of the obligation, and on the other hand constructively present an alternative selective account of those obligations which are for legal purposes illuminatingly regarded as having correlative rights. This latter task amounts to a redrawing of the lines between 'absolute'[83] and relative duties which for Bentham merely separated 'barren' and self-regarding duties from duties

---

[79]In fact Bentham seems to have made very little use of his idea that in the sense explained the public or a class within it have legal rights. Nearly all of his examples of rights are rights of individuals. Austin expressly confines legal rights to the rights of 'determinate persons' (op. cit., Lecture XVII, p. 401).

[80]Under the American Civil Rights Act 1964 suits were brought against white men who had murdered Negroes alleging 'that they had deprived their victims of their civil rights'. This desperate expedient was necessary because murder is a state crime and prosecutions in such cases were not likely to succeed in Southern state courts. I owe this point to Mrs. Carolyn Irish.

[81]Bowring III. 195.

[82]Ibid.

[83]So Austin (op. cit., Lecture XVII, 401–2).

'useful to others'. This has been done sometimes in too sweeping a fashion as a distinction precisely coinciding with that between the criminal and civil law, and on the assumption, which seems dogmatic, if not plainly mistaken, that the purpose of the criminal law is not to secure the separate interests of individuals but 'security and order', and that all its duties are really duties not to behave in certain ways which are prejudicial to the 'general interests of society'.[84]

None the less a line may be drawn between most duties of the criminal law and those of the civil law which does not depend on this assumption, but would, on principles quite distinct from those of the benefit theory, reserve the notion of relative duties and correlative rights mainly for the obligations of the civil law, such as those which arise under contracts or under the law of tort, and other civil wrongs. For what is distinctive about these obligations is not their content which sometimes overlaps with the criminal law, since there are some actions, e.g. assault, which are both a crime and a civil wrong; nor is the only distinction of importance the familiar one that crime has as its characteristic consequence liability to punishment, and civil wrong liability to pay compensation for harm done. The crucial distinction, according to this view of relative duties, is the special manner in which the civil law as distinct from the criminal law provides for individuals: it recognizes or gives them a place or *locus standi* in relation to the law quite different from that given by the criminal law. Instead of utilitarian notions of benefit or intended benefit we need, if we are to reproduce this distinctive concern for the individual, a different idea. The idea is that of one individual being given by the law exclusive control, more or less extensive, over another person's duty so that in the area of conduct covered by that duty the individual who has the right is a small-scale sovereign to whom the duty is owed. The fullest measure[85] of control comprises three distinguishable elements: (i) the right holder may waive or extinguish the duty or leave it in existence; (ii) after breach or threatened breach of a duty he may leave it 'unenforced' or may 'enforce' it by suing for compensation or, in certain cases, for an injunction or mandatory order to restrain the continued or further breach of duty; and (iii) he may waive or extinguish the obligation to pay compensation to which the breach gives rise. It is obvious that not all who benefit or are intended to benefit by another's legal obligation are in this unique sovereign position in relation to the duty. A person protected only by the criminal law has no power to release anyone from its duties, and though, as in England, he may in theory be entitled to prosecute along with any other member of the public he has no unique power to determine whether the duties of the criminal law should be enforced or not.

[84] Allen, *Legal Duties,* pp. 184–6.

[85] The right holder will have less than the full measure of control if, as in the case of statutory duties, he is unable to release or extinguish the duty or if principles of public policy prevent him, even after breach of the duty, making a binding agreement not to sue for injury caused by its breach (see e.g. *Bowmaker Ltd.* v. *Tabor* (1942) 2 K.B. 1). In such cases the choice left to him is only to sue or not to sue. There are suggestions, never fully developed, that such a choice is a necessary element in a legal system in Bentham's *A Fragment on Government,* Ch. V para. 6 n. 1 s. 2.

These legal powers (for such they are) over a correlative obligation are of great importance to lawyers: both laymen and lawyers will need, in Bentham's phrase, 'to be instructed' about them; and their exercise calls for the specific skills of the lawyer. They are therefore a natural focus of legal attention, and there are I think many signs of the centrality of those powers to the conception of a legal right. Thus it is hard to think of rights except as capable of *exercise* and this conception of rights correlative to obligations as containing legal powers accommodates this feature.[86] Moreover, we speak of a breach of duty in the civil law, whether arising in contract or in tort, not only as wrong, or detrimental to the person who has the correlative right, but as *a wrong to* him and a breach of an obligation *owed to* him;[87] we also speak of the person who has the correlative right as *possessing* it or even *owning* it. The conception suggested by these phrases is that duties with correlative rights are a species of normative property belonging to the right holder, and this figure becomes intelligible by reference to the special form of control over a correlative duty which a person with such a right is given by the law. Whenever an individual has this special control, as he has in most cases in the civil law but not over the duties of the criminal law, there is a contrast of importance to be marked and many jurists have done so by distinguishing the duties of the criminal law as 'absolute duties' from the 'relative' duties of the civil law.[88]

It is an incidental, though substantial merit of this approach that it provides an intelligible explanation of the fact that animals, even though directly protected by the duties of the criminal law prohibiting cruelty to them, are not spoken or thought of as having rights. However it is to be observed that if the distinction between absolute and relative duties is drawn as above suggested, this does not entail that only duties of the civil law have correlative rights. For there are cases

[86]Where infants or other persons not *sui juris* have rights, such powers and the correlative obligations are exercised on their behalf by appointed representatives and their exercise may be subject to approval by a court. But since (a) what such representatives can and cannot do by way of exercise of such power is determined by what those whom they represent could have done if *sui juris* and (b) when the latter become *sui juris* they can exercise these powers without any transfer or fresh assignment; the powers are regarded as belonging throughout to them and not to their representatives, though they are only exercisable by the latter during the period of disability.

[87]Lyons (loc. cit., p. 178 [this volume, p. 66—*Ed.*]) assumes that 'rights under the civil law' arise only from 'special relations or transactions between the parties' (e.g. contracts) and that only in such cases are the right holders 'claimants' to whom duties are 'owed'. But individuals have rights corresponding to the primary duties in tort which do not arise from such special relations or transactions and such duties are 'owed' to them.

[88]It is sometimes argued that in the case of persons not *sui juris* e.g. infants, it is only the fact that they are direct beneficiaries of the correlative duties which explains the ascription of rights to them, rather than to their representatives who alone can exercise the powers over the correlative duties. But the explanation offered above (p. 142, n. 86) seems adequate; even if it is not, this would only show that being the direct beneficiary of a duty was a *necessary* condition of a person not *sui juris* having a right. Hence it would still be possible so far as this argument goes, to distinguish the duties of the criminal law (over which there are no such powers of control exercisable by the beneficiaries' representatives) as not having correlative rights.

made prominent by the extension of the welfare functions of the state where officials of public bodies are under a legal duty to provide individuals if they satisfy certain conditions, with benefits which may take the form of money payments (e.g. public assistance, unemployment relief, farming subsidies) or supply of goods or services, e.g. medical care. In such cases it is perfectly common and natural to speak of individuals who have satisfied the prescribed conditions as being legally entitled to and having a right to such benefits. Yet it is commonly not the case that they have the kind of control over the official's duties which, according to the view suggested above, is a defining feature of legal rights correlative to obligations. For though such obligations are not always supported by criminal sanctions they cannot be extinguished or waived by beneficiaries, nor does their breach necessarily give rise to any secondary obligation to make compensation which the beneficiaries can enforce, leave unenforced or extinguish. None the less there are in most of such cases two features which link them to the paradigm cases of rights correlative to obligations as these appear in the civil law. In most cases where such public duties are thought of as having correlative rights, the duty to supply the benefits are conditional upon their being demanded and the beneficiary of the duty is free to demand it or not. Hence, though he has no power to waive or extinguish the duty he has a power by presenting a demand to substitute for a conditional duty not requiring present performance an unconditional duty which does, and so has a choice. Secondly, though breach of such duties may not give rise to any secondary duties of compensation, there are in many such cases steps which the beneficiary if he has suffered some peculiar damage may take to secure its performance, and in regard to which he has a special *locus standi* so that on his application a court may make a peremptory or mandatory order or injunction directing the official body to carry out the duty or restraining its breach.[89] These two features of the case differentiate the beneficiary of such public duties from that of the ordinary duties of the criminal law. This explains why, though it is generally enough to describe the criminal law only in terms of duties, so to describe the law creating these public welfare duties would obscure important features. For the necessity that such beneficiaries if they wish the duty to be performed must present demands, and the availability to them of means of enforcement, make their position under the law a focus for legal attention needing separate description from that of the duties beneficial to them.[90]

(b) *Contracts and Third Parties*. The identification of a rightholder with the person who is merely benefited by the performance of a duty not only obscures a very important general dividing line between criminal and civil law, but is ill adapted to the law relating to contract. Whereas in the last paragraph it was urged that to be an intended beneficiary of an obligation is not a satisfactory *sufficient*

[89]Difficult questions may arise concerning the nature of the interest which a successful applicant for such relief must possess. See *R.* v. *Manchester Corp.* [1911] 1 K.B. 560.

[90]But so far as such public welfare duties are thought of as providing for essential human needs they may on that ground alone be regarded as constituting legal rights. See below, pp. 147–8.

condition of having a right, the present criticism is that it is not satisfactory as a *necessary* condition. For where there is a contract between two people, not all those who benefit and are intended to benefit by the performance of its obligations have a legal right correlative to them. In many jurisdictions contracts expressly made for the benefit of third parties, e.g. a contract between two people to pay a third party a sum of money, is not enforceable by the third party and he cannot waive or release the obligation. In such a case although the third party is a direct beneficiary since breach of the contract constitutes a direct detriment to him, he has no legal control over the duty and so no legal right. On the other hand the contracting party having the appropriate control has the legal right, though he is not the person intended to benefit by the performance of the contract.[91] Where, however, the law is modified as it is in some jurisdictions so as to give the third party power to enforce the contract then he is consistently with the view presented here spoken of as having legal right.[92]

The analysis of a right correlative to obligation which is suggested by the foregoing criticisms of the benefit theory is that for such a right to exist it is neither sufficient nor necessary for the person who has the right to be the beneficiary of the obligation; what is sufficient and necessary is that he should have at least some measure of the control, described above, over the correlative obligation.

IV. The Limits of a General Theory

If the arguments of the last section are accepted and if we substitute for the utilitarian idea of benefit, as a defining feature of a right correlative to obligation, the individual's legal powers of control, full or partial, over that obligation, a generalization may be made concerning all three kinds of right distinguished by Bentham. This is attractive because it imposes a pattern of order on a wide range of apparently disparate legal phenomena. Thus in all three kinds of right the idea of a bilateral liberty is present and the difference between the kinds of right lies only in the kind of act which there is liberty to do. In the case of liberty-rights such as a man's right to look at his neighbour, his act may be called a natural act in the

---

[91]It is sometimes argued that the fact that in some jurisdictions a third-party beneficiary may sue shows this point against the beneficiary theory of rights to be mistaken. But of course a third party entitled to sue or not to sue would on *that* account be recognized as having a legal right and this does nothing to confirm the beneficiary theory.

[92]Lyons, loc. cit., pp. 183–4 [this volume, pp. 74–5—*Ed.*], argues that 'one of the conditions of a valid and binding promise and thus a condition of a right accruing to a promisee is that he really wants what is promised' (even if this is true of 'promises' it scarcely seems applicable to legal contracts). He then suggests that performance of a contract for the benefit of a third party must 'assure a good' to the promisee, since this satisfies his want to have what is promised done, and that it is this, not his control over the promisor's obligation, which accounts for the ascription of a right to him. But if the performance of the obligation beneficial to the third party is not sufficient to lead lawyers to recognize the third party as having a legal right, surely the secondary benefit to the promisee consisting in gratification of his wish to benefit the third party is not sufficient to account for his right.

sense that it is not endowed by the law with a special legal significance or legal effect. On the other hand in the case of rights which are powers, such as the right to alienate property, the act which there is a bilateral liberty[93] to do is an act-in-the-law, just in the sense that it is specifically recognized by the law as having legal effects in varying the legal position of various parties. The case of a right correlative to obligation then emerges as only a special case of legal power in which the right-holder is at liberty to waive or extinguish or to enforce or leave unenforced another's obligation. It would follow from these considerations that in each of these three types of case one who has a right has a choice respected by the law. On this view there would be only one sense of legal right—a legally respected choice—though it would be one with different exemplifications, depending on the kind of act or act-in-the-law which there is liberty to do.

The merits of this analysis are therefore threefold. First, it coincides with a very wide area of common and legal usage. Secondly it explains why liberty-rights, powers, and rights correlative to obligations are all described as rights and does so by identifying as common to three superficially diverse types of case, an element which, on any theory of law or morals, is of great importance; namely an individual choice respected by the law. Thirdly, the concept which it defines is well adapted to a lawyer's purpose; for it will lead him to talk in terms of rights only where there is something of importance to the lawyer to talk about which cannot be equally well said in terms of obligation or duty, and this is pre-eminently so in the case of the civil law.[94]

However, in spite of its attractions, this theory, centred on the notion of a legally respected individual choice, cannot be taken as exhausting the notion of a legal right: the notion of individual benefit must be brought in, though *not* as the benefit theory brings it in, to supplement the notion of individual choice. Unless this is done no adequate account can be given of the deployment of the language of rights, in two main contexts, when certain freedoms and benefits are regarded as essential for the maintenance of the life, the security, the development, and the dignity of the individual. Such freedoms and benefits are recognized as rights in the constitutional law of many countries by Bills of Rights, which afford to the individual protection even against the processes of legislation. In countries such as our own, where the doctrine of legislative sovereignty is held to preclude limiting the powers of the legislature by Bills of Rights, they are, though given only the lesser measure of legal protection in the form of duties of the criminal law, thought and spoken of as legal rights by social theorists or critics of the law who

---

[93]As in the case of liberty-rights, duties may be superimposed on rights which are powers and such duties will render the liberty to exercise the power unilateral (a simple example from property law is where an owner of property binds himself by contract either to sell it or not to sell it). In general where there is a duty to exercise a power the resultant unilateral liberty is not described as a right nor is there usually any point in so describing it. Exceptions to this are again cases such as that of a trustee whose legal rights are theoretically distinguishable from his equitable duties (see above, p. 134, n. 56) and are thought of as coexisting even where they in fact conflict.

[94]But not exclusively, see pp. 142–3 above.

are accustomed to view the law in a wider perspective than the lawyer concerned only with its day-to-day working.

Immunity Rights

Both the benefit theory of rights and the alternative theory of a right as a legally respected choice are designed primarily as accounts of the rights of citizen against citizen; that is of rights under the 'ordinary' law. From that point of view the benefit theory was criticized above (*inter alia*) for offering no more than a redundant translation of duties of the criminal law into a terminology of rights, e.g. not be murdered or assaulted. But this accusation of redundancy is no longer pertinent when what is to be considered are not rights under the ordinary law, but fundamental rights which may be said to be against the legislature, limiting its powers to make (or unmake) the ordinary law, where so to do would deny to individuals certain freedoms and benefits now regarded as essentials of human well-being, such as freedom of speech and of association, freedom from arbitrary arrest, security of life and person, education, and equality of treatment in certain respects.

The various elements which the benefit theory uses to analyse rights correlative to obligations and those which the rival 'choice' theory uses to analyse these and other kinds of right (that is: duty, absence of duty, benefit, act, and act-in-the-law) are not sufficient to provide an analysis of such constitutionally guaranteed individual rights. These require for their analysis the notion of an immunity. Bentham, unlike Hohfeld, did not isolate this notion in distinguishing different kinds or meanings of legal right, and indeed his attention was never seriously given to the analysis of fundamental legal rights. This was, no doubt, because, although, unlike Austin, he did not think that there were logical or conceptual objections to the notion of legal limitations of a sovereign legislature[95] he viewed with extreme suspicion any legal arrangements which would prevent the legislature enacting whatever measures appeared from time to time to be required by the dictates of general utility; and suspicion became contempt at the suggestion that such arrangements should be used to give legal form to doctrines of natural or fundamental individual rights. Hohfeld, who identified among the various 'loose' uses of the expression 'a right' its use to refer to an immunity, defined an immunity as the correlative of 'disability' or 'no power';[96] so that to say that a man, X, had a certain immunity meant that someone else lacked legal power to alter X's legal position in some respect. But, plainly, even in the loosest usage, the expression 'a right' is not used to refer to the fact that a man is thus immune from an *advantageous* change; the facts that the City Council cannot legally, i.e. has 'no power', to award me a pension, and my neighbour has no power to exempt me from my

---

[95]See for his discussion of such limitations, O.L.G., pp. 18, 64–71, 306, and *A Fragment of Government*, ch. IV, paras. 23–36, and my 'Bentham on Sovereignty' (1967) *Irish Jurist* 327.
[96]Hohfeld, op. cit., p. 60.

duty to pay my income-tax, do not constitute any legal rights for me. An individual's immunity from legal change at the hands of others is spoken and thought of as a right only when the change in question is *adverse,* that is, would deprive him of legal rights of other kinds (liberty-rights, powers, rights correlative to obligations) or benefits secured to him by law.

The chief, though not the only employment[97] of this notion of an immunity from adverse legal change which we may call an 'immunity right' is to characterize distinctively the position of individuals protected from such adverse change by constitutional limitations or, as Hohfeld would say, by disabilities of the legislature. Such immunity rights are obviously of extreme importance to individuals and may usually be asserted in the form of justiciable claims that some purported enactment is invalid because it infringes them. There is here an illuminating contrast with the redundancy of rights as defined by the beneficiary theory; for whereas, as I have urged above, nothing is to be gained for the lawyer, either in clarity or the focusing of legal attention, by expounding, say, the law of murder or assault in terms of rights, the case is altered if a constitutional Bill of Rights precludes the legislature from depriving individuals of the protections of the criminal law. For then there is every reason why lawyers and others should have picked out for them, as rights to life or security of the person, legal immunities the assertion of which on behalf of the individual calls for their advice and skill. That is why I said above that though certain legally secured individual benefits would have to be brought in to any adequate account of legal rights, they would not be brought in as the benefit theory brings them in.

Wider Perspectives

Law is however too important a thing to leave to lawyers—even to constitutional lawyers; and the ways of thinking about rights common among serious critics of the law and social theorists must be accommodated even though they are different from and may not serve any of the specific purposes of the lawyer. Here also a concept of legal rights limited to those cases where the law, in the ways described above, respects the choice of individuals would be too narrow. For there is a distinct form of the moral criticism of law which, like the constitutional immunity rights already described, is inspired by regard for the needs of the individual for certain fundamental freedoms and protections or benefits. Criticism of the law for its failure to provide for such individual needs is distinct from, and sometimes at war with, the criticism with which Bentham was perhaps too exclusively concerned, that the law often fails to maximize aggregate utility. A critic of the former, individualistic kind will of course not address himself only to those legal systems in which there are immunity rights guaranteed by Bills of Rights; but in scrutinizing systems like our own, where the maximum form of provision for

[97]Immunities against divestment of various kinds of rights are involved in the notion of ownership. See A. M. Honoré, 'Ownership' in *Oxford Essays on Jurisprudence,* First Series (1961), p. 119.

such individual needs must fall short of constitutional immunity rights, he will count the measure of protection afforded by the ordinary criminal law as a provision for those needs, together with the duties to provide for them which fall on public bodies or officials. Viewed in this light the law against murder and assault will be considered and described quite properly as securing rights to life and security of the person; though if it were a question simply of expounding the criminal law this would be redundant and even confusing.

Hence in cases where the criminal law provides for such essential human needs the individualistic critic of the law would agree with the benefit-theorist in speaking of rights corresponding to certain duties of the criminal law. They would however differ in two ways: first the critic need entertain no *general* theory that every direct beneficiary of a legal obligation had a corresponding legal right and he could therefore consistently subscribe to all the criticisms of the beneficiary theory made above; secondly the individualistic critic implicitly draws a distinction quite foreign to the letter and the spirit of the beneficiary theory between the legal provision of benefits simply as a contribution to general utility and as a contribution to the satisfaction of individual needs. It is the latter which leads him to talk of rights secured by the duties of the criminal law.

The upshot of these considerations is that instead of a general analytical and explanatory theory covering the whole field of legal rights I have provided a general theory in terms of the notion of a legally respected individual choice which is satisfactory only at one level—the level of the lawyer concerned with the working of the 'ordinary' law. This requires supplementation in order to accommodate the important deployment of the language of rights by the constitutional lawyer and the individualistic critic of the law, for whom the core of the notion of rights is neither individual choice nor individual benefit but basic or fundamental individual needs. This result may be felt as distressingly untidy by some, and they may be tempted to combine the perspectives which I have distinguished of the ordinary lawyer, the constitutional lawyer, and the individualistic critic of the law in some general formula embracing all three. Such a general formula is suggested by Hohfeld's statement that the generic sense of a right means 'any legal advantage'.[98] But I fear that, behind the comfortable appearance of generality, we would have only an unilluminating combination or mere juxtaposition of the choice theory together with the benefit theory; and this would fail to be sensitive to the important reasons for describing only some legally secured benefits, only in some contexts, as legal rights.

[98]Op. cit., pp. 42, 71. Cf. also Bentham's discussion in *O.L.G.*, pp. 55–9 of the inclusion in the idea of a 'party favoured by the law' of two kinds of favour: favour in 'point of interest' and 'in point of agency'. A party is 'favoured in point of agency' when he has an *exceptional* liberty, i.e. a liberty to do some act generally prohibited.

The Entitlement Theory
•
Robert Nozick

The subject of justice in holdings consists of three major topics. The first is the *original acquisition of holdings,* the appropriation of unheld things. This includes the issues of how unheld things may come to be held, the process, or processes, by which unheld things may come to be held, the things that may come to be held by these processes, the extent of what comes to be held by a particular process, and so on. We shall refer to the complicated truth about this topic, which we shall not formulate here, as the principle of justice in acquisition. The second topic concerns the *transfer of holdings* from one person to another. By what processes may a person transfer holdings to another? How may a person acquire a holding from another who holds it? Under this topic come general descriptions of voluntary exchange, and gift and (on the other hand) fraud, as well as reference to particular conventional details fixed upon in a given society. The complicated truth about this subject (with placeholders for conventional details) we shall call the principle of justice in transfer. (And we shall suppose it also includes principles governing how a person may divest himself of a holding, passing it into an unheld state.)

If the world were wholly just, the following inductive definition would exhaustively cover the subject of justice in holdings.

From chapter 7, section I of *Anarchy, State, and Utopia* by Robert Nozick (New York: Basic Books, 1974), pp. 150–182. © 1974 by Basic Books, Inc., Publishers, New York. First published in *Philosophy & Public Affairs,* Vol. 3 (Fall 1973), 46–78. Reprinted by permission of the author and Basic Books.

1. A person who acquires a holding in accordance with the principle of justice in acquisition is entitled to that holding.

2. A person who acquires a holding in accordance with the principle of justice in transfer, from someone else entitled to the holding, is entitled to the holding.

3. No one is entitled to a holding except by (repeated) applications of 1 and 2.

The complete principle of distributive justice would say simply that a distribution is just if everyone is entitled to the holdings they possess under the distribution.

A distribution is just if it arises from another just distribution by legitimate means. The legitimate means of moving from one distribution to another are specified by the principle of justice in transfer. The legitimate first "moves" are specified by the principle of justice in acquisition.[1] Whatever arises from a just situation by just steps is itself just. The means of change specified by the principle of justice in transfer preserve justice. As correct rules of inference are truth-preserving, and any conclusion deduced via repeated application of such rules from only true premises is itself true, so the means of transition from one situation to another specified by the principle of justice in transfer are justice-preserving, and any situation actually arising from repeated transitions in accordance with the principle from a just situation is itself just. The parallel between justice-preserving transformations and truth-preserving transformations illuminates where it fails as well as where it holds. That a conclusion could have been deduced by truth-preserving means from premises that are true suffices to show its truth. That from a just situation a situation *could* have arisen via justice-preserving means does *not* suffice to show its justice. The fact that a thief's victims voluntarily *could* have presented him with gifts does not entitle the thief to his ill-gotten gains. Justice in holdings is historical; it depends upon what actually has happened. We shall return to this point later.

Not all actual situations are generated in accordance with the two principles of justice in holdings: the principle of justice in acquisition and the principle of justice in transfer. Some people steal from others, or defraud them, or enslave them, seizing their product and preventing them from living as they choose, or forcibly exclude others from competing in exchanges. None of these are permissible modes of transition from one situation to another. And some persons acquire holdings by means not sanctioned by the principle of justice in acquisition. The existence of past injustice (previous violations of the first two principles of justice in holdings) raises the third major topic under justice in holdings: the rectification of injustice in holdings. If past injustice has shaped present holdings in various ways, some identifiable and some not, what now, if anything, ought to be done to rectify these injustices? What obligations do the performers of injustice have toward those

---

[1]Applications of the principle of justice in acquisition may also occur as part of the move from one distribution to another. You may find an unheld thing now and appropriate it. Acquisitions also are to be understood as included when, to simplify, I speak only of transitions by transfers.

whose position is worse than it would have been had the injustice not been done? Or, than it would have been had compensation been paid promptly? How, if at all, do things change if the beneficiaries and those made worse off are not the direct parties in the act of injustice, but, for example, their descendants? Is an injustice done to someone whose holding was itself based upon an unrectified injustice? How far back must one go in wiping clean the historical slate of injustices? What may victims of injustice permissibly do in order to rectify the injustices being done to them, including the many injustices done by persons acting through their government? I do not know of a thorough or theoretically sophisticated treatment of such issues.[2] Idealizing greatly, let us suppose theoretical investigation will produce a principle of rectification. This principle uses historical information about previous situations and injustices done in them (as defined by the first two principles of justice and rights against interference), and information about the actual course of events that flowed from these injustices, until the present, and it yields a description (or descriptions) of holdings in the society. The principle of rectification presumably will make use of its best estimate of subjunctive information about what would have occurred (or a probability distribution over what might have occurred, using the expected value) if the injustice had not taken place. If the actual description of holdings turns out not to be one of the descriptions yielded by the principle, then one of the descriptions yielded must be realized.[3]

The general outlines of the theory of justice in holdings are that the holdings of a person are just if he is entitled to them by the principles of justice in acquisition and transfer, or by the principle of rectification of injustice (as specified by the first two principles). If each person's holdings are just, then the total set (distribution) of holdings is just. To turn these general outlines into a specific theory we would have to specify the details of each of the three principles of justice in holdings: the principle of acquisition of holdings, the principle of transfer of holdings, and the principle of rectification of violations of the first two principles. I shall not attempt that task here. (Locke's principle of justice in acquisition is discussed below.)

Historical Principles
and End-Result Principles

The general outlines of the entitlement theory illuminate the nature and defects of other conceptions of distributive justice. The entitlement theory of justice

---

[2]See, however, the useful book by Boris Bittker, *The Case for Black Reparations* (New York: Random House, 1973).

[3]If the principle of rectification of violations of the first two principles yields more than one description of holdings, then some choice must be made as to which of these is to be realized. Perhaps the sort of considerations about distributive justice and equality that I argue against play a legitimate role in *this* subsidiary choice. Similarly, there may be room for such considerations in deciding which otherwise arbitrary features a statute will embody, when such features are unavoidable because other considerations do not specify a precise line; yet a line must be drawn.

in distribution is *historical;* whether a distribution is just depends upon how it came about. In contrast, *current time-slice principles* of justice hold that the justice of a distribution is determined by how things are distributed (who has what) as judged by some *structural* principle(s) of just distribution. A utilitarian who judges between any two distributions by seeing which has the greater sum of utility and, if the sums tie, applies some fixed equality criterion to choose the more equal distribution, would hold a current time-slice principle of justice. As would someone who had a fixed schedule of trade-offs between the sum of happiness and equality. According to a current time-slice principle, all that needs to be looked at, in judging the justice of a distribution, is who ends up with what; in comparing any two distributions one need look only at the matrix presenting the distributions. No further information need be fed into a principle of justice. It is a consequence of such principles of justice that any two structurally identical distributions are equally just. (Two distributions are structurally identical if they present the same profile, but perhaps have different persons occupying the particular slots. My having ten and your having five, and my having five and your having ten are structurally identical distributions.) Welfare economics is the theory of current time-slice principles of justice. The subject is conceived as operating on matrices representing only current information about distribution. This, as well as some of the usual conditions (for example, the choice of distribution is invariant under relabeling of columns), guarantees that welfare economics will be a current time-slice theory, with all of its inadequacies.

Most persons do not accept current time-slice principles as constituting the whole story about distributive shares. They think it relevant in assessing the justice of a situation to consider not only the distribution it embodies, but also how that distribution came about. If some persons are in prison for murder or war crimes, we do not say that to assess the justice of the distribution in the society we must look only at what this person has, and that person has, and that person has, . . . at the current time. We think it relevant to ask whether someone did something so that he *deserved* to be punished, deserved to have a lower share. Most will agree to the relevance of further information with regard to punishments and penalties. Consider also desired things. One traditional socialist view is that workers are entitled to the product and full fruits of their labor; they have earned it; a distribution is unjust if it does not give the workers what they are entitled to. Such entitlements are based upon some past history. No socialist holding this view would find it comforting to be told that because the actual distribution *A* happens to coincide structurally with the one he desires *D*, *A* therefore is no less just than *D;* it differs only in that the "parasitic" owners of capital receive under *A* what the workers are entitled to under *D*, and the workers receive under *A* what the owners are entitled to under *D*, namely very little. This socialist rightly, in my view, holds onto the notions of earning, producing, entitlement, desert, and so forth, and he rejects current time-slice principles that look only to the structure of the resulting set of holdings. (The set of holdings resulting from what? Isn't it implausible that how holdings are produced and come to exist has no effect at all on who should hold what?) His mistake lies in his view of what entitlements arise out of what sorts of productive processes.

We construe the position we discuss too narrowly by speaking of *current* time-slice principles. Nothing is changed if structural principles operate upon a time sequence of current time-slice profiles and, for example, give someone more now to counterbalance the less he has had earlier. A utilitarian or an egalitarian or any mixture of the two over time will inherit the difficulties of his more myopic comrades. He is not helped by the fact that *some* of the information others consider relevant in assessing a distribution is reflected, unrecoverably, in past matrices. Henceforth, we shall refer to such unhistorical principles of distributive justice, including the current time-slice principles, as *end-result principles* or *end-state principles*.

In contrast to end-result principles of justice, *historical principles* of justice hold that past circumstances or actions of people can create differential entitlements or differential deserts to things. An injustice can be worked by moving from one distribution to another structurally identical one, for the second, in profile the same, may violate people's entitlements or deserts; it may not fit the actual history.

Patterning

The entitlement principles of justice in holdings that we have sketched are historical principles of justice. To better understand their precise character, we shall distinguish them from another subclass of the historical principles. Consider, as an example, the principle of distribution according to moral merit. This principle requires that total distributive shares vary directly with moral merit; no person should have a greater share than anyone whose moral merit is greater. (If moral merit could be not merely ordered but measured on an interval or ratio scale, stronger principles could be formulated.) Or consider the principle that results by substituting "usefulness to society" for "moral merit" in the previous principle. Or instead of "distribute according to moral merit," or "distribute according to usefulness to society," we might consider "distribute according to the weighted sum of moral merit, usefulness to society, and need," with the weights of the different dimensions equal. Let us call a principle of distribution *patterned* if it specifies that a distribution is to vary along with some natural dimension, weighted sum of natural dimensions, or lexicographic ordering of natural dimensions. And let us say a distribution is patterned if it accords with some patterned principle. (I speak of natural dimensions, admittedly without a general criterion for them, because for any set of holdings some artificial dimensions can be gimmicked up to vary along with the distribution of the set.) The principle of distribution in accordance with moral merit is a patterned historical principle, which specifies a patterned distribution. "Distribute according to I.Q." is a patterned principle that looks to information not contained in distributional matrices. It is not historical, however, in that it does not look to any past actions creating differential entitlements to evaluate a distribution; it requires only distributional matrices whose columns are labeled by I.Q. scores. The distribution in a society, however, may be composed of such simple patterned distributions, without itself being simply patterned. Different sectors may operate different patterns, or some combination of patterns may operate in different proportions across a society. A distribution composed in this manner, from a small number of patterned distributions, we also shall term "patterned." And we extend the use of "pattern" to include the overall designs put forth by combinations of end-state principles.

Almost every suggested principle of distributive justice is patterned: to each according to his moral merit, or needs, or marginal product, or how hard he tries, or the weighted sum of the foregoing, and so on. The principle of entitlement we have sketched is *not* patterned.[4] There is no one natural dimension or weighted sum or combination of a small number of natural dimensions that yields the distributions generated in accordance with the principle of entitlement. The set of holdings that results when some persons receive their marginal products, others win at gambling, others receive a share of their mate's income, others receive gifts from foundations, others receive interest on loans, others receive gifts from admirers, others receive returns on investment, others make for themselves much of what they have, others find things, and so on, will not be patterned. Heavy strands of patterns will run through it; significant portions of the variance in holdings will be accounted for by pattern-variables. If most people most of the time choose to transfer some of their entitlements to others only in exchange for something from them, then a large part of what many people hold will vary with what they held that others wanted. More details are provided by the theory of marginal productivity. But gifts to relatives, charitable donations, bequests to children, and the like, are not best conceived, in the first instance, in this manner. Ignoring the strands of pattern, let us suppose for the moment that a distribution actually arrived at by the operation of the principle of entitlement is random with respect to any pattern. Though the resulting set of holdings will be unpatterned, it will not be incomprehensible, for it can be seen as arising from the operation of a small number of principles. These principles specify how an initial distribution may arise (the principle of acquisition of holdings) and how distributions may be transformed into others (the principle of transfer of holdings). The process whereby the set of hold-

---

[4]One might try to squeeze a patterned conception of distributive justice into the framework of the entitlement conception, by formulating a gimmicky obligatory "principle of transfer" that would lead to the pattern. For example, the principle that if one has more than the mean income one must transfer everything one holds above the mean to persons below the mean so as to bring them up to (but not over) the mean. We can formulate a criterion for a "principle of transfer" to rule out such obligatory transfers, or we can say that no correct principle of transfer, no principle of transfer in a free society will be like this. The former is probably the better course, though the latter also is true.

Alternatively, one might think to make the entitlement conception instantiate a pattern, by using matrix entries that express the relative strength of a person's entitlements as measured by some real-valued function. But even if the limitation to natural dimensions failed to exclude this function, the resulting edifice would *not* capture our system of entitlements to *particular* things.

ings is generated will be intelligible, though the set of holdings itself that results from this process will be unpatterned.

The writings of F. A. Hayek focus less than is usually done upon what patterning distributive justice requires. Hayek argues that we cannot know enough about each person's situation to distribute to each according to his moral merit (but would justice demand we do so if we did have this knowledge?); and he goes on to say, "our objection is against all attempts to impress upon society a deliberately chosen pattern of distribution, whether it be an order of equality or of inequality."[5] However, Hayek concludes that in a free society there will be distribution in accordance with value rather than moral merit; that is, in accordance with the perceived value of a person's actions and services to others. Despite his rejection of a patterned conception of distributive justice, Hayek himself suggests a pattern he thinks justifiable: distribution in accordance with the perceived benefits given to others, leaving room for the complaint that a free society does not realize exactly this pattern. Stating this patterned strand of a free capitalist society more precisely, we get "To each according to how much he benefits others who have the resources for benefiting those who benefit them." This will seem arbitrary unless some acceptable initial set of holdings is specified, or unless it is held that the operation of the system over time washes out any significant effects from the initial set of holdings. As an example of the latter, if almost anyone would have bought a car from Henry Ford, the supposition that it was an arbitrary matter who held the money then (and so bought) would not place Henry Ford's earnings under a cloud. In any event, *his* coming to hold it is not arbitrary. Distribution according to benefits to others *is* a major patterned strand in a free capitalist society, as Hayek correctly points out, but it is only a strand and does not constitute the whole pattern of a system of entitlements (namely, inheritance, gifts for arbitrary reasons, charity, and so on) or a standard that one should insist a society fit. Will people tolerate for long a system yielding distributions that they believe are unpatterned?[6] No doubt people will not long accept a distribution they believe is *unjust*. People want their society to be and to look just. But must the look of justice reside in a resulting pattern rather than in the underlying generating principles? We are in no position to conclude that the inhabitants of a society embodying an entitlement conception of justice in holdings will find it unacceptable. Still, it must be granted that were people's reasons for transferring some of their holdings to others always irrational or arbitrary, we would find this disturbing. (Suppose people always determined what holdings they would transfer, and to whom, by using a random

[5] F. A. Hayek, *The Constitution of Liberty* (Chicago: University of Chicago Press, 1960), p. 87.
[6] This question does not imply that they will tolerate any and every patterned distribution. In discussing Hayek's views, Irving Kristol has recently speculated that people will not long tolerate a system that yields distributions patterned in accordance with value rather than merit. (" 'When Virtue Loses All Her Loveliness'—Some Reflections on Capitalism and 'The Free Society,'" *The Public Interest*, Fall 1970, pp. 3–15.) Kristol, following some remarks of Hayek's, equates the merit system with justice. Since some case can be made for the external standard of distribution in accordance with benefit to others, we ask about a weaker (and therefore more plausible) hypothesis.

device.) We feel more comfortable upholding the justice of an entitlement system if most of the transfers under it are done for reasons. This does not mean necessarily that all deserve what holdings they receive. It means only that there is a purpose or point to someone's transferring a holding to one person rather than to another; that usually we can see what the transferrer thinks he's gaining, what cause he thinks he's serving, what goals he thinks he's helping to achieve, and so forth. Since in a capitalist society people often transfer holdings to others in accordance with how much they perceive these others benefiting them, the fabric constituted by the individual transactions and transfers is largely reasonable and intelligible.[7] (Gifts to loved ones, bequests to children, charity to the needy also are nonarbitrary components of the fabric.) In stressing the large strand of distribution in accordance with benefit to others, Hayek shows the point of many transfers, and so shows that the system of transfer of entitlements is not just spinning its gears aimlessly. The system of entitlements is defensible when constituted by the individual aims of individual transactions. No overarching aim is needed, no distributional pattern is required.

To think that the task of a theory of distributive justice is to fill in the blank in "to each according to his _____" is to be predisposed to search for a pattern; and the separate treatment of "from each according to his _____" treats production and distribution as two separate and independent issues. On an entitlement view these are *not* two separate questions. Whoever makes something, having bought or contracted for all other held resources used in the process (transferring some of his holdings for these cooperating factors), is entitled to it. The situation is *not* one of something's getting made, and there being an open question of who is to get it. Things come into the world already attached to people having entitlements over them. From the point of view of the historical entitlement conception of justice in holdings, those who start afresh to complete "to each according to his _____" treat objects as if they appeared from nowhere, out of nothing. A complete theory of justice might cover this limit case as well; perhaps here is a use for the usual conceptions of distributive justice.[8]

---

[7]We certainly benefit because great economic incentives operate to get others to spend much time and energy to figure out how to serve us by providing things we will want to pay for. It is not mere paradox mongering to wonder whether capitalism should be criticized for most rewarding and hence encouraging, not individualists like Thoreau who go about their own lives, but people who are occupied with serving others and winning them as customers. But to defend capitalism one need not think businessmen are the finest human types. (I do not mean to join here the general maligning of businessmen, either.) Those who think the finest should acquire the most can try to convince their fellows to transfer resources in accordance with *that* principle.

[8]Varying situations continuously from that limit situation to our own would force us to make explicit the underlying rationale of entitlements and to consider whether entitlement considerations lexicographically precede the considerations of the usual theories of distributive justice, so that the *slightest* strand of entitlement outweighs the considerations of the usual theories of distributive justice.

So entrenched are maxims of the usual form that perhaps we should present the entitlement conception as a competitor. Ignoring acquisition and rectification, we might say:

> *From each according to what he chooses to do, to each according to what he makes for himself (perhaps with the contracted aid of others) and what others choose to do for him and choose to give him of what they've been given previously (under this maxim) and haven't yet expended or transferred.*

This, the discerning reader will have noticed, has its defects as a slogan. So as a summary and great simplification (and not as a maxim with any independent meaning) we have:

> *From each as they choose, to each as they are chosen.*

How Liberty Upsets Patterns

It is not clear how those holding alternative conceptions of distributive justice can reject the entitlement conception of justice in holdings. For suppose a distribution favored by one of these nonentitlement conceptions is realized. Let us suppose it is your favorite one and let us call this distribution D_1; perhaps everyone has an equal share, perhaps shares vary in accordance with some dimension you treasure. Now suppose that Wilt Chamberlain is greatly in demand by basketball teams, being a great gate attraction. (Also suppose contracts run only for a year, with players being free agents.) He signs the following sort of contract with a team: In each home game, twenty-five cents from the price of each ticket of admission goes to him. (We ignore the question of whether he is "gouging" the owners, letting them look out for themselves.) The season starts, and people cheerfully attend his team's games; they buy their tickets, each time dropping a separate twenty-five cents of their admission price into a special box with Chamberlain's name on it. They are excited about seeing him play; it is worth the total admission price to them. Let us suppose that in one season one million persons attend his home games, and Wilt Chamberlain winds up with $250,000, a much larger sum than the average income and larger even than anyone else has. Is he entitled to this income? Is this new distribution D_2, unjust? If so, why? There is *no* question about whether each of the people was entitled to the control over the resources they held in D_1; because that was the distribution (your favorite) that (for the purposes of argument) we assumed was acceptable. Each of these persons *chose* to give twenty-five cents of their money to Chamberlain. They could have spent it on going to the movies, or on candy bars, or on copies of *Dissent* magazine, or of *Monthly Review*. But they all, at least one million of them, converged on giving it to Wilt Chamberlain in exchange for watching him play basketball. If D_1 was a just distribution, and people voluntarily moved from it to D_2, transferring parts of their shares they were given under D_1 (what was it for if not to do something with?), isn't D_2 also just? If the people were entitled to dispose of the resources to which they were entitled (under D_1), didn't this include their being entitled to give it to, or exchange it with, Wilt Chamberlain? Can anyone else complain on grounds of justice? Each other person already has his legitimate share under D_1. Under D_1, there is nothing that anyone has that anyone else has a claim of justice against. After someone transfers something to Wilt Chamberlain, third parties *still* have their legitimate shares; *their* shares are not changed. By what process could such a transfer among two persons give rise to a legitimate claim of distributive justice on a portion of what was transferred, by a third party who had no claim of justice on any holding of the others *before* the transfer?[9] To cut off objections irrelevant here, we might imagine the exchanges occurring in a socialist society, after hours. After playing whatever basketball he does in his daily work, or doing whatever other daily work he does, Wilt Chamberlain decides to put in *overtime* to earn additional money. (First his work quota is set; he works time over that.) Or imagine it is a skilled juggler people like to see, who puts on shows after hours.

Why might someone work overtime in a society in which it is assumed their needs are satisfied? Perhaps because they care about things other than needs. I like to write in books that I read, and to have easy access to books for browsing at odd hours. It would be very pleasant and convenient to have the resources of Widener Library in my back yard. No society, I assume, will provide such resources close to each person who would like them as part of his regular allotment (under D_1). Thus, persons either must do without some extra things that they want, or be allowed to do something extra to get some of these things. On what basis could the inequalities that would eventuate be forbidden? Notice also that small factories would spring up in a socialist society, unless forbidden. I melt down some of my personal possessions (under D_1) and build a machine out of the material. I offer you, and others, a philosophy lecture once a week in exchange for your cranking the handle on my machine, whose products I exchange for yet other things, and

[9]Might not a transfer have instrumental effects on a third party, changing his feasible options? (But what if the two parties to the transfer independently had used their holdings in this fashion?) I discuss this question below, but note here that this question concedes the point for distributions of ultimate intrinsic noninstrumental goods (pure utility experiences, so to speak) that are transferrable. It also might be objected that the transfer might make a third party more envious because it worsens his position relative to someone else. I find it incomprehensible how this can be thought to involve a claim of justice. On envy, see [*Anarchy, State, and Utopia,*] Chapter 8.

Here and elsewhere in this chapter, a theory which incorporates elements of pure procedural justice might find what I say acceptable, *if* kept in its proper place; that is, if background institutions exist to ensure the satisfaction of certain conditions on distributive shares. But if these institutions are not themselves the sum or invisible-hand result of people's voluntary (nonaggressive) actions, the constraints they impose require justification. At no point does *our* argument assume any background institutions more extensive than those of the minimal night-watchman state, a state limited to protecting persons against murder, assault, theft, fraud, and so forth.

so on. (The raw materials used by the machine are given to me by others who possess them under D_1, in exchange for hearing lectures.) Each person might participate to gain things over and above their allotment under D_1. Some persons even might want to leave their job in socialist industry and work full time in this private sector. I shall say something more about these issues in the next chapter, [*Anarchy, State, and Utopia,* Chapter 8—*Ed.*]. Here I wish merely to note how private property even in means of production would occur in a socialist society that did not forbid people to use as they wished some of the resources they are given under the socialist distribution D_1.[10] The socialist society would have to forbid capitalist acts between consenting adults.

The general point illustrated by the Wilt Chamberlain example and the example of the entrepreneur in a socialist society is that no end-state principle or distributional patterned principle of justice can be continuously realized without continuous interference with people's lives. Any favored pattern would be transformed into one unfavored by the principle, by people choosing to act in various ways; for example, by people exchanging goods and services with other people, or giving things to other people, things the transferrers are entitled to under the favored distributional pattern. To maintain a pattern one must either continually interfere to stop people from transferring resources as they wish to, or continually (or periodically) interfere to take from some persons resources that others for some reason chose to transfer to them. (But if some time limit is to be set on how long people may keep resources others voluntarily transfer to them, why let them keep these resources for *any* period of time? Why not have immediate confiscation?) It might be objected that all persons voluntarily will choose to refrain from actions which would upset the pattern. This presupposes unrealistically (1) that all will most want to maintain the pattern (are those who don't, to be "reeducated" or forced to undergo "self-criticism"?), (2) that each can gather enough information

---

[10]See the selection from John Henry MacKay's novel, *The Anarchists,* reprinted in Leonard Krimmerman and Lewis Perry, eds., *Patterns of Anarchy* (New York: Doubleday Anchor Books, 1966), in which an individualist anarchist presses upon a communist anarchist the following question: "Would you, in the system of society which you call 'free Communism' prevent individuals from exchanging their labor among themselves by means of their own medium of exchange? And further: Would you prevent them from occupying land for the purpose of personal use?" The novel continues: "[the] question was not to be escaped. If he answered 'Yes!' he admitted that society had the right of control over the individual and threw overboard the autonomy of the individual which he had always zealously defended; if on the other hand, he answered 'No!' he admitted the right of private property which he had just denied so emphatically. . . . Then he answered 'In Anarchy any number of men must have the right of forming a voluntary association, and so realizing their ideas in practice. Nor can I understand how any one could justly be driven from the land and house which he uses and occupies . . . every serious man must declare himself: for Socialism, and thereby for force and against liberty, or for Anarchism, and thereby for liberty and against force.'" In contrast, we find Noam Chomsky writing, "Any consistent anarchist must oppose private ownership of the means of production," "the consistent anarchist then . . . will be a socialist . . . of a particular sort." Introduction to Daniel Guerin, *Anarchism: From Theory to Practice* (New York: Monthly Review Press, 1970), pages xiii, xv.

about his own actions and the ongoing activities of others to discover which of his actions will upset the pattern, and (3) that diverse and far-flung persons can co-ordinate their actions to dovetail into the pattern. Compare the manner in which the market is neutral among persons' desires, as it reflects and transmits widely scattered information via prices, and coordinates persons' activities.

It puts things perhaps a bit too strongly to say that every patterned (or end-state) principle is liable to be thwarted by the voluntary actions of the indi-vidual parties transferring some of their shares they receive under the principle. For perhaps some *very* weak patterns are not so thwarted.[11] Any distributional pattern with any egalitarian component is overturnable by the voluntary actions of individual persons over time; as is every patterned condition with sufficient con-tent so as actually to have been proposed as presenting the central core of distrib-utive justice. Still, given the possibility that some weak conditions or patterns may not be unstable in this way, it would be better to formulate an explicit description of the kind of interesting and contentful patterns under discussion, and to prove a theorem about their instability. Since the weaker the patterning, the more likely it is that the entitlement system itself satisfies it, a plausible conjecture is that any patterning either is unstable or is satisfied by the entitlement system.

Sen's Argument

Our conclusions are reinforced by considering a recent general argument of Amartya K. Sen.[12] Suppose individual rights are interpreted as the right to choose which of two alternatives is to be more highly ranked in a social ordering of the alternatives. Add the weak condition that if one alternative unanimously is preferred to another then it is ranked higher by the social ordering. If there are two different individuals each with individual rights, interpreted as above, over different pairs of alternatives (having no members in common), then for some pos-sible preference rankings of the alternatives by the individuals, there is no linear

[11]Is the patterned principle stable that requires merely that a distribution be Pareto-optimal? One person might give another a gift or bequest that the second could exchange with a third to their mutual benefit. Before the second makes this exchange, there is not Pareto-optimality. Is a stable pattern presented by a principle choosing that among the Pareto-optimal positions that satisfies some further condition C? It may seem that there cannot be a counterexample, for won't any voluntary exchange made away from a situation show that the first situation wasn't Pareto-optimal? (Ignore the implausibility of this last claim for the case of bequests.) But principles are to be satisfied over time, during which new possibilities arise. A distri-bution that at one time satisfies the criterion of Pareto-optimality might not do so when some new possibilities arise (Wilt Chamberlain grows up and starts playing basketball); and though people's activities will tend to move then to a new Pareto-optimal position, *this* new one need not satisfy the contentful condition C. Continual interference will be needed to insure the continual satisfaction of C. (The theoretical possibility of a pattern's being maintained by some invisible-hand process that brings it back to an equilibrium that fits the pattern when deviations occur should be investigated.)

[12]*Collective Choice and Social Welfare,* Holden-Day, Inc., 1970, chaps. 6 and 6*.

social ordering. For suppose that person A has the right to decide among (X, Y) and person B has the right to decide among (Z, W); and suppose their individual preferences are as follows (and that there are no other individuals). Person A prefers W to X to Y to Z, and person B prefers Y to Z to W to X. By the unanimity condition, in the social ordering W is preferred to X (since each individual prefers it to X), and Y is preferred to Z (since each individual prefers it to Z). Also in the social ordering, X is preferred to Y, by person A's right of choice among these two alternatives. Combining these three binary rankings, we get W preferred to X preferred to Y preferred to Z, in the social ordering. However, by person B's right of choice, Z must be preferred to W in the social ordering. There is no transitive social ordering satisfying all these conditions, and the social ordering, therefore, is nonlinear. Thus far, Sen.

The trouble stems from treating an individual's right to choose among alternatives as the right to determine the relative ordering of these alternatives within a social ordering. The alternative which has individuals rank *pairs* of alternatives, and separately rank the individual alternatives is no better; their ranking of pairs feeds into some method of amalgamating preferences to yield a social ordering of pairs; and the choice among the alternatives in the highest ranked pair in the social ordering is made by the individual with the right to decide between this pair. This system also has the result that an alternative may be selected although *everyone* prefers some other alternative; for example, A selects X over Y, where (X, Y) somehow is the highest ranked *pair* in the social ordering of pairs, although everyone, including A, prefers W to X. (But the choice person A was given, however, was only between X and Y.)

A more appropriate view of individual rights is as follows. Individual rights are co-possible; each person may exercise his rights as he chooses. The exercise of these rights fixes some features of the world. Within the constraints of these fixed features, a choice may be made by a social choice mechanism based upon a social ordering; if there are any choices left to make! Rights do not determine a social ordering but instead set the constraints within which a social choice is to be made, by excluding certain alternatives, fixing others, and so on. (If I have a right to choose to live in New York or in Massachusetts, and I choose Massachusetts, then alternatives involving my living in New York are not appropriate objects to be entered in a social ordering.) Even if all possible alternatives are ordered first, apart from anyone's rights, the situation is not changed: for then the highest ranked alternative *that is not excluded by anyone's exercise of his rights* is instituted. Rights do not determine the position of an alternative or the relative position of two alternatives in a social ordering; they *operate upon* a social ordering to constrain the choice it can yield.

If entitlements to holdings are rights to dispose of them, then social choice must take place *within* the constraints of how people choose to exercise these rights. If any patterning is legitimate, it falls within the domain of social choice, and hence is constrained by people's rights. *How else can one cope with Sen's result?* The alternative of first having a social ranking with rights exercised within *its* constraints is no alternative at all. Why not just select the top-ranked alternative and forget about rights? If that top-ranked alternative itself leaves some room for individual choice (and here is where "rights" of choice is supposed to enter in) there must be something to stop these choices from transforming it into another alternative. Thus Sen's argument leads us again to the result that patterning requires continuous interference with individuals' actions and choices.[13]

Redistribution and Property Rights

Apparently, patterned principles allow people to choose to expend upon themselves, but not upon others, those resources they are entitled to (or rather, receive) under some favored distributional pattern D_1. For if each of several persons chooses to expend some of his D_1 resources upon one other person, then that other person will receive more than his D_1 share, disturbing the favored distributional pattern. Maintaining a distributional pattern is individualism with a vengeance! Patterned distributional principles do not give people what entitlement principles do, only better distributed. For they do not give the right to choose what to do with what one has; they do not give the right to choose to pursue an end involving (instrinsically, or as a means) the enhancement of another's position. To such views, families are disturbing; for within a family occur transfers that upset the favored distributional pattern. Either families themselves become units to which distribution takes place, the column occupiers (on what rationale?), or loving behavior is forbidden. We should note in passing the ambivalent position of radicals toward the family. Its loving relationships are seen as a model to be emulated and extended across the whole society, at the same time that it is denounced as a suffocating institution to be broken and condemned as a focus of parochial concerns that interfere with achieving radical goals. Need we say that it is not appropriate to enforce across the wider society the relationships of love and care appropriate within a family, relationships which are voluntarily undertaken?[14] Incidentally, love is an interesting instance of another relationship that is historical, in that (like justice) it depends upon what actually occurred. An adult may come to love another because of the other's characteristics; but it is the other person, and not the

---

[13]Oppression will be less noticeable if the background institutions do not prohibit certain actions that upset the patterning (various exchanges or transfers of entitlement), but rather prevent them from being done, by nullifying them.

[14]One indication of the stringency of Rawls' difference principle, which we attend to in the second part of this chapter [in Chap. 7, Sec. II, of *Anarchy, State, and Utopia*—Ed.] is its inappropriateness as a governing principle even within a family of individuals who love one another. Should a family devote its resources to maximizing the position of its least well off and least talented child, holding back the other children or using resources for their education and development only if they will follow a policy through their lifetimes of maximizing the position of their least fortunate sibling? Surely not. How then can this even be considered as the appropriate policy for enforcement in the wider society? (I discuss below [in Chap. 7, Sec. II, of *Anarchy, State, and Utopia*—Ed.] what I think would be Rawls' reply: that some principles apply at the macro level which do not apply to micro-situations.)

characteristics, that is loved.[15] The love is not transferrable to someone else with the same characteristics, even to one who "scores" higher for these characteristics. And the love endures through changes of the characteristics that gave rise to it. One loves the particular person one actually encountered. Why love is historical, attaching to persons in this way and not to characteristics, is an interesting and puzzling question.

Proponents of patterned principles of distributive justice focus upon criteria for determining who is to receive holdings; they consider the reasons for which someone should have something, and also the total picture of holdings. Whether or not it is better to give than to receive, proponents of patterned principles ignore giving altogether. In considering the distribution of goods, income, and so forth, their theories are theories of recipient justice; they completely ignore any right a person might have to give something to someone. Even in exchanges where each party is simultaneously giver and recipient, patterned principles of justice focus only upon the recipient role and its supposed rights. Thus discussions tend to focus on whether people (should) have a right to inherit, rather than on whether people (should) have a right to bequeath or on whether persons who have a right to hold also have a right to choose that others hold in their place. I lack a good explanation of why the usual theories of distributive justice are so recipient oriented; ignoring givers and transferrers and their rights is of a piece with ignoring producers and their entitlements. But why is it *all* ignored?

Patterned principles of distributive justice necessitate *re*distributive activities. The likelihood is small that any actual freely-arrived-at set of holdings fits a given pattern; and the likelihood is nil that it will continue to fit the pattern as people exchange and give. From the point of view of an entitlement theory, redistribution is a serious matter indeed, involving, as it does, the violation of people's rights. (An exception is those takings that fall under the principle of the rectification of injustices.) From other points of view, also, it is serious.

Taxation of earnings from labor is on a par with forced labor.[16] Some persons find this claim obviously true: taking the earnings of n hours labor is like taking n hours from the person; it is like forcing the person to work n hours for another's purpose. Others find the claim absurd. But even these, *if* they object to forced labor, would oppose forcing unemployed hippies to work for the benefit of the needy.[17] And they would also object to forcing each person to work five extra hours each week for the benefit of the needy. But a system that takes five hours'

---

[15]See Gregory Vlastos, "The Individual as an Object of Love in Plato" in his *Platonic Studies* (Princeton: Princeton University Press, 1973), pp. 3–34.

[16]I am unsure as to whether the arguments I present below show that such taxation merely *is* forced labor; so that "is on a par with" means "is one kind of." Or alternatively, whether the arguments emphasize the great similarities between such taxation and forced labor, to show it is plausible and illuminating to view such taxation in the light of forced labor. This latter approach would remind one of how John Wisdom conceives of the claims of metaphysicians.

[17]Nothing hangs on the fact that here and elsewhere I speak loosely of *needs*, since I go on, each time, to reject the criterion of justice which includes it. If, however, something did

wages in taxes does not seem to them like one that forces someone to work five hours, since it offers the person forced a wider range of choice in activities than does taxation in kind with the particular labor specified. (But we can imagine a gradation of systems of forced labor, from one that specifies a particular activity, to one that gives a choice among two activities, to . . . ; and so on up.) Furthermore, people envisage a system with something like a proportional tax on everything above the amount necessary for basic needs. Some think this does not force someone to work extra hours, since there is no fixed number of extra hours he is forced to work, and since he can avoid the tax entirely by earning only enough to cover his basic needs. This is a very uncharacteristic view of forcing for those who *also* think people are forced to do something *whenever* the alternatives they face are considerably worse. However, *neither* view is correct. The fact that others intentionally intervene, in violation of a side constraint against aggression, to threaten force to limit the alternatives, in this case to paying taxes or (presumably the worse alternative) bare subsistence, makes the taxation system one of forced labor and distinguishes it from other cases of limited choices which are not forcings.[18]

The man who chooses to work longer to gain an income more than sufficient for his basic needs prefers some extra goods or services to the leisure and activities he could perform during the possible nonworking hours; whereas the man who chooses not to work the extra time prefers the leisure activities to the extra goods or services he could acquire by working more. Given this, if it would be illegitimate for a tax system to seize some of a man's leisure (forced labor) for the purpose of serving the needy, how can it be legitimate for a tax system to seize some of a man's goods for that purpose? Why should we treat the man whose happiness requires certain material goods or services differently from the man whose preferences and desires make such goods unnecessary for his happiness? Why should the man who prefers seeing a movie (and who has to earn money for a ticket) be open to the required call to aid the needy, while the person who prefers looking at a sunset (and hence need earn no extra money) is not? Indeed, isn't it surprising that redistributionists choose to ignore the man whose pleasures are so easily attainable without extra labor, while adding yet another burden to the poor unfortunate who must work for his pleasures? If anything, one would have expected the reverse. Why is the person with the nonmaterial or nonconsumption desire allowed to proceed unimpeded to his most favored feasible alternative, whereas the man whose pleasures or desires involve material things and who must work for extra money (thereby serving whomever considers his activities valuable enough to pay him) is constrained in what he can realize? Perhaps there is no difference in principle. And perhaps some think the answer concerns merely administrative convenience. (These questions and issues will not disturb those who think that forced labor to serve the needy or to realize some favored-end-state

depend upon the notion, one would want to examine it more carefully. For a skeptical view, see Kenneth Minogue, *The Liberal Mind*, (New York: Random House, 1963), pp. 103–112.

[18]Further details which this statement should include are contained in my essay "Coercion," in *Philosophy, Science, and Method*, ed. S. Morgenbesser, P. Suppes, and M. White (New York: St. Martin, 1969).

pattern is acceptable.) In a fuller discussion we would have (and want) to extend our argument to include interest, entrepreneurial profits, and so on. Those who doubt that this extension can be carried through, and who draw the line here at taxation of income from labor, will have to state rather complicated patterned *historical* principles of distributive justice, since end-state principles would not distinguish *sources* of income in any way. It is enough for now to get away from end-state principles and to make clear how various patterned principles are dependent upon particular views about the sources or the illegitimacy or the lesser legitimacy of profits, interest, and so on; which particular views may well be mistaken.

What sort of right over others does a legally institutionalized end-state pattern give one? The central core of the notion of a property right in *X*, relative to which other parts of the notion are to be explained, is the right to determine what shall be done with *X*; the right to choose which of the constrained set of options concerning *X* shall be realized or attempted.[19] The constraints are set by other principles or laws operating in the society; in our theory, by the Lockean rights people possess (under the minimal state). My property rights in my knife allow me to leave it where I will, but not in your chest. I may choose which of the acceptable options involving the knife is to be realized. This notion of property helps us to understand why earlier theorists spoke of people as having property in themselves and their labor. They viewed each person as having a right to decide what would become of himself and what he would do, and as having a right to reap the benefits of what he did.

This right of selecting the alternative to be realized from the constrained set of alternatives may be held by an *individual* or by a *group* with some procedure for reaching a joint decision; or the right may be passed back and forth, so that one year I decide what's to become of *X*, and the next year you do (with the alternative of destruction, perhaps, being excluded). Or, during the same time period, some types of decisions about *X* may be made by me, and others by you. And so on. We lack an adequate, fruitful, analytical apparatus for classifying the *types* of constraints on the set of options among which choices are to be made, and the *types* of ways decision powers can be held, divided, and amalgamated. A *theory* of property would, among other things, contain such a classification of constraints and decision modes, and from a small number of principles would follow a host of interesting statements about the *consequences* and effects of certain combinations of constraints and modes of decision.

When end-result principles of distributive justice are built into the legal structure of a society, they (as do most patterned principles) give each citizen an enforceable claim to some portion of the total social product; that is, to some portion of the sum total of the individually and jointly made products. This total product is produced by individuals laboring, using means of production others have saved to bring into existence, by people organizing production or creating means to produce new things or things in a new way. It is on this batch of individual activities that patterned distributional principles give each individual an enforce-

---

[19]On the themes in this and the next paragraph, see the writings of Armen Alchian.

able claim. Each person has a claim to the activities and the products of other persons, independently of whether the other persons enter into particular relationships that give rise to these claims, and independently of whether they voluntarily take these claims upon themselves, in charity or in exchange for something.

Whether it is done through taxation on wages or on wages over a certain amount, or through seizure of profits, or through there being a big *social pot* so that it's not clear what's coming from where and what's going where, patterned principles of distributive justice involve appropriating the actions of other persons. Seizing the results of someone's labor is equivalent to seizing hours from him and directing him to carry on various activities. If people force you to do certain work, or unrewarded work, for a certain period of time, they decide what you are to do and what purposes your work is to serve apart from your decisions. This process whereby they take this decision from you makes them a *part-owner* of you; it gives them a property right in you. Just as having such partial control and power of decision, by right, over an animal or inanimate object would be to have a property right in it.

End-state and most patterned principles of distributive justice institute (partial) ownership by others of people and their actions and labor. These principles involve a shift from the classical liberals' notion of self-ownership to a notion of (partial) property rights in *other* people.

Considerations such as these confront end-state and other patterned conceptions of justice with the question of whether the actions necessary to achieve the selected pattern don't themselves violate moral side constraints. Any view holding that there are moral side constraints on actions, that not all moral considerations can be built into end states that are to be achieved (see [*Anarchy, State, and Utopia,*] Chapter 3, pp. 28–30), must face the possibility that some of its goals are not achievable by any morally permissible available means. An entitlement theorist will face such conflicts in a society that deviates from the principles of justice for the generation of holdings, if and only if the only actions available to realize the principles themselves violate some moral constraints. Since deviation from the first two principles of justice (in acquisition and transfer) will involve other persons' direct and aggressive intervention to violate rights, and since moral constraints will not exclude defensive or retributive action in such cases, the entitlement theorist's problem rarely will be pressing. And whatever difficulties he has in applying the principle of rectification to persons who did not themselves violate the first two principles are difficulties in balancing the conflicting considerations so as correctly to formulate the complex principle of rectification itself; he will not violate moral side constraints by applying the principle. Proponents of patterned conceptions of justice, however, often will face head-on clashes (and poignant ones if they cherish each party to the clash) between moral side constraints on how individuals may be treated and their patterned conception of justice that presents an end-state or other pattern that *must* be realized.

May a person emigrate from a nation that has institutionalized some end-state or patterned distributional principle? For some principles (for example, Hayek's) emigration presents no theoretical problem. But for others it is a tricky matter.

Consider a nation having a compulsory scheme of minimal social provision to aid the neediest (or one organized so as to maximize the position of the worst-off group); no one may opt out of participating in it. (None may say, "Don't compel me to contribute to others and don't provide for me via this compulsory mechanism if I am in need.") Everyone above a certain level is forced to contribute to aid the needy. But if emigration from the country were allowed, anyone could choose to move to another country that did not have compulsory social provision but otherwise was (as much as possible) identical. In such a case, the person's *only* motive for leaving would be to avoid participating in the compulsory scheme of social provision. And if he does leave, the needy in his initial country will receive no (compelled) help from him. What rationale yields the result that the person be permitted to emigrate, yet forbidden to stay and opt out of the compulsory scheme of social provision? If providing for the needy is of overriding importance, this does militate against allowing internal opting out; but it also speaks against allowing external emigration. (Would it also support, to some extent, the kidnapping of persons living in a place without compulsory social provision, who could be forced to make a contribution to the needy in your community?) Perhaps the crucial component of the position that allows emigration solely to avoid certain arrangements, while not allowing anyone internally to opt out of them, is a concern for fraternal feelings within the country. "We don't want anyone here who doesn't contribute, who doesn't care enough about the others to contribute." That concern, in this case, would have to be tied to the view that forced aiding tends to produce fraternal feelings between the aided and the aider (or perhaps merely to the view that the knowledge that someone or other voluntarily is not aiding produces unfraternal feelings).

Locke's Theory of Acquisition

Before we turn to consider other theories of justice in detail, we must introduce an additional bit of complexity into the structure of the entitlement theory. This is best approached by considering Locke's attempt to specify a principle of justice in acquisition. Locke views property rights in an unowned object as originating through someone's mixing his labor with it. This gives rise to many questions. What are the boundaries of what labor is mixed with? If a private astronaut clears a place on Mars, has he mixed his labor with (so that he comes to own) the whole planet, the whole uninhabited universe, or just a particular plot? Which plot does an act bring under ownership? The minimal (possibly disconnected) area such that an act decreases entropy in that area, and not elsewhere? Can virgin land (for the purposes of ecological investigation by high-flying airplane) come under ownership by a Lockean process? Building a fence around a territory presumably would make one the owner of only the fence (and the land immediately underneath it).

Why does mixing one's labor with something make one the owner of it? Perhaps because one owns one's labor, and so one comes to own a previously unowned thing that becomes permeated with what one owns. Ownership seeps over into the rest. But why isn't mixing what I own with what I don't own a way of losing what I own rather than a way of gaining what I don't? If I own a can of tomato juice and spill it in the sea so that its molecules (made radioactive, so I can check this) mingle evenly throughout the sea, do I thereby come to own the sea, or have I foolishly dissipated my tomato juice? Perhaps the idea, instead, is that laboring on something improves it and makes it more valuable; and anyone is entitled to own a thing whose value he has created. (Reinforcing this, perhaps, is the view that laboring is unpleasant. If some people made things effortlessly, as the cartoon characters in *The Yellow Submarine* trail flowers in their wake, would they have lesser claim to their own products whose making didn't *cost* them anything?) Ignore the fact that laboring on something may make it less valuable (spraying pink enamel paint on a piece of driftwood that you have found). Why should one's entitlement extend to the whole object rather than just to the *added value* one's labor has produced? (Such reference to value might also serve to delimit the extent of ownership; for example, substitute "increases the value of" for "decreases entropy in" in the above entropy criterion.) No workable or coherent value-added property scheme has yet been devised, and any such scheme presumably would fall to objections (similar to those) that fell the theory of Henry George.

It will be implausible to view improving an object as giving full ownership to it, if the stock of unowned objects that might be improved is limited. For an object's coming under one person's ownership changes the situation of all others. Whereas previously they were at liberty (in Hohfeld's sense) to use the object, they now no longer are. This change in the situation of others (by removing their liberty to act on a previously unowned object) need not worsen their situation. If I appropriate a grain of sand from Coney Island, no one else may now do as they will with *that* grain of sand. But there are plenty of other grains of sand left for them to do the same with. Or if not grains of sand, then other things. Alternatively, the things I do with the grain of sand I appropriate might improve the position of others, counterbalancing their loss of the liberty to use that grain. The crucial point is whether appropriation of an unowned object worsens the situation of others.

Locke's proviso that there be "enough and as good left in common for others" (sect. 27) is meant to ensure that the situation of others is not worsened. (If this proviso is met is there any motivation for his further condition of nonwaste?) It is often said that this proviso once held but now no longer does. But there appears to be an argument for the conclusion that if the proviso no longer holds, then it cannot even have held so as to yield permanent and inheritable property rights. Consider the first person Z for whom there is not enough and as good left to appropriate. The last person Y to appropriate left Z without his previous liberty to act on an object, and so worsened Z's situation. So Y's appropriation is not allowed under Locke's proviso. Therefore the next to last person X to appropriate left Y in a worse position, for X's act ended permissible appropriation. Therefore X's appropriation wasn't permissible. But then the appropriator two from last, W, ended permissible appropriation and so, since it worsened X's position, W's appropriation wasn't permissible. And so on back to the first person A to appropriate a permanent property right.

This argument, however, proceeds too quickly. Someone may be made worse off by another's appropriation in two ways: first, by losing the opportunity to improve his situation by a particular appropriation or any one; and second, by no longer being able to use freely (without appropriation) what he previously could. A *stringent* requirement that another not be made worse off by an appropriation would exclude the first way if nothing else counterbalances the diminution in opportunity, as well as the second. A *weaker* requirement would exclude the second way, though not the first. With the weaker requirement, we cannot zip back so quickly from Z to A, as in the above argument; for though person Z can no longer *appropriate,* there may remain some for him to *use* as before. In this case Y's appropriation would not violate the weaker Lockean condition. (With less remaining that people are at liberty to use, users might face more inconvenience, crowding, and so on; in that way the situation of others might be worsened, unless appropriation stopped far short of such a point.) It is arguable that no one legitimately can complain if the weaker provision is satisfied. However, since this is less clear than in the case of the more stringent proviso, Locke may have intended this stringent proviso by "enough and as good" remaining, and perhaps he meant the nonwaste condition to delay the end point from which the argument zips back.

Is the situation of persons who are unable to appropriate (there being no more accessible and useful unowned objects) worsened by a system allowing appropriation and permanent property? Here enter the various familiar social considerations favoring private property: it increases the social product by putting means of production in the hands of those who can use them most efficiently (profitably); experimentation is encouraged, because with separate persons controlling resources, there is no one person or small group whom someone with a new idea must convince to try it out; private property enables people to decide on the pattern and types of risks they wish to bear, leading to specialized types of risk bearing; private property protects future persons by leading some to hold back resources from current consumption for future markets; it provides alternate sources of employment for unpopular persons who don't have to convince any one person or small group to hire them, and so on. These considerations enter a Lockean theory to support the claim that appropriation of private property satisfies the intent behind the "enough and as good left over" proviso, *not* as a utilitarian justification of property. They enter to rebut the claim that because the proviso is violated no natural right to private property can arise by a Lockean process. The difficulty in working such an argument to show that the proviso is satisfied is in fixing the appropriate baseline for comparison. Lockean appropriation makes people no worse off than they would be *how?*[20] This question of fixing the baseline needs

---

[20]Compare this with Robert Paul Wolff's "A Refutation of Rawls' Theorem on Justice," *Journal of Philosophy,* March 31, 1966, sect. 2. Wolff's criticism does not apply to Rawls' conception under which the baseline is fixed by the difference principle.

more detailed investigation than we are able to give it here. It would be desirable to have an estimate of the general economic importance of original appropriation in order to see how much leeway there is for differing theories of appropriation and of the location of the baseline. Perhaps this importance can be measured by the percentage of all income that is based upon untransformed raw materials and given resources (rather than upon human actions), mainly rental income representing the unimproved value of land, and the price of raw material *in situ,* and by the percentage of current wealth which represents such income in the past.[21]

We should note that it is not only persons favoring *private* property who need a theory of how property rights legitimately originate. Those believing in collective property, for example those believing that a group of persons living in an area jointly own the territory, or its mineral resources, also must provide a theory of how such property rights arise; they must show why the persons living there have rights to determine what is done with the land and resources there that persons living elsewhere don't have (with regard to the same land and resources).

The Proviso

Whether or not Locke's particular theory of appropriation can be spelled out so as to handle various difficulties, I assume that any adequate theory of justice in acquisition will contain a proviso similar to the weaker of the ones we have attributed to Locke. A process normally giving rise to a permanent bequeathable property right in a previously unowned thing will not do so if the position of others no longer at liberty to use the thing is thereby worsened. It is important to specify *this* particular mode of worsening the situation of others, for the proviso does not encompass other modes. It does not include the worsening due to more limited opportunities to appropriate (the first way above, corresponding to the more stringent condition), and it does not include how I "worsen" a seller's position if I appropriate materials to make some of what he is selling, and then enter into competition with him. Someone whose appropriation otherwise would violate the proviso still may appropriate provided he compensates the others so that their situation is not thereby worsened; unless he does compensate these others, his appropriation will violate the proviso of the principle of justice in acquisition and will be an illegitimate one.[22] A theory of appropriation incorporating this Lockean

[21]I have not seen a precise estimate. David Friedman, *The Machinery of Freedom* (N.Y.: Harper & Row, 1973), pp. xiv, xv, discusses this issue and suggests 5 percent of U.S. national income as an upper limit for the first two factors mentioned. However he does not attempt to estimate the percentage of current wealth which is based upon such income in the past. (The vague notion of "based upon" merely indicates a topic needing investigation.)

[22]Fourier held that since the process of civilization had deprived the members of society of certain liberties (to gather, pasture, engage in the chase), a socially guaranteed minimum provision for persons was justified as compensation for the loss (Alexander Gray, *The Socialist Tradition* [New York: Harper & Row, 1968], p. 188). But this puts the point too strongly. This compensation would be due those persons, if any, for whom the process of civilization was

proviso will handle correctly the cases (objections to the theory lacking the proviso) where someone appropriates the total supply of something necessary for life.[23]

A theory which includes this proviso in its principle of justice in acquisition must also contain a more complex principle of justice in transfer. Some reflection of the proviso about appropriation constrains later actions. If my appropriating all of a certain substance violates the Lockean proviso, then so does my appropriating some and purchasing all the rest from others who obtained it without otherwise violating the Lockean proviso. If the proviso excludes someone's appropriating all the drinkable water in the world, it also excludes his purchasing it all. (More weakly, and messily, it may exclude his charging certain prices for some of his supply.) This proviso (almost?) never will come into effect; the more someone acquires of a scarce substance which others want, the higher the price of the rest will go, and the more difficult it will become for him to acquire it all. But still, we can imagine, at least, that something like this occurs: someone makes simultaneous secret bids to the separate owners of a substance, each of whom sells assuming he can easily purchase more from the other owners; or some natural catastrophe destroys all of the supply of something except that in one person's possession. The total supply could not be permissibly appropriated by one person at the beginning. His later acquisition of it all does not show that the original appropriation violated the proviso (even by a reverse argument similar to the one above that tried to zip back from Z to A). Rather, it is the combination of the original appropriation *plus* all the later transfers and actions that violates the Lockean proviso.

Each owner's title to his holding includes the historical shadow of the Lockean proviso on appropriation. This excludes his transferring it into an agglomeration that does violate the Lockean proviso and excludes his using it in a way, in coordination with others or independently of them, so as to violate the proviso by making the situation of others worse than their baseline situation. Once it is known that someone's ownership runs afoul of the Lockean proviso, there are stringent limits on what he may do with (what it is difficult any longer unreservedly

a *net loss,* for whom the benefits of civilization did not counterbalance being deprived of these particular liberties.

[23]For example, Rashdall's case of someone who comes upon the only water in the desert several miles ahead of others who also will come to it and appropriates it all. Hastings Rashdall, "The Philosophical Theory of Property," in *Property, its Duties and Rights* (London: MacMillan, 1915).

We should note Ayn Rand's theory of property rights ("Man's Rights" in *The Virtue of Self-ishness* [New York: New American Library, 1964], p. 94), wherein these follow from the right to life, since people need physical things to live. But a right to life is not a right to whatever one needs to live; other people may have rights over these other things (see [*Anarchy, State, and Utopia,*] Chapter 3). At most, a right to life would be a right to have or strive for whatever one needs to live, provided that having it does not violate anyone else's rights. With regard to material things, the question is whether having it does violate any right of others. (Would appropriation of all unowned things do so? Would appropriating the water hole in Rashdall's example?) Since special considerations (such as the Lockean proviso) may enter with regard to material property, one *first* needs a theory of property rights before one can apply any supposed right to life (as amended above). Therefore the right to life cannot provide the foundation for a theory of property rights.

to call) "his property." Thus a person may not appropriate the only water hole in a desert and charge what he will. Nor may he charge what he will if he possesses one, and unfortunately it happens that all the water holes in the desert dry up, except for his. This unfortunate circumstance, admittedly no fault of his, brings into operation the Lockean proviso and limits his property rights.[24] Similarly, an owner's property right in the only island in an area does not allow him to order a castaway from a shipwreck off his island as a trespasser, for this would violate the Lockean proviso.

Notice that the theory does not say that owners do have these rights, but that the rights are overridden to avoid some catastrophe. (Overridden rights do not disappear; they leave a trace of a sort absent in the cases under discussion.)[25] There is no such external (and *ad hoc?*) overriding. Considerations internal to the theory of property itself, to its theory of acquisition and appropriation, provide the means for handling such cases. The results, however, may be coextensive with some condition about catastrophe, since the baseline for comparison is so low as compared to the productiveness of a society with private appropriation that the question of the Lockean proviso being violated arises only in the case of catastrophe (or a desert-island situation).

The fact that someone owns the total supply of something necessary for others to stay alive does *not* entail that his (or anyone's) appropriation of anything left some people (immediately or later) in a situation worse than the baseline one. A medical researcher who synthesizes a new substance that effectively treats a certain disease and who refuses to sell except on his terms does not worsen the situation of others by depriving them of whatever he has appropriated. The others easily can possess the same materials he appropriated; the researcher's appropriation or purchase of chemicals didn't make those chemicals scarce in a way so as to violate the Lockean proviso. Nor would someone else's purchasing the total supply of the synthesized substance from the medical researcher. The fact that the medical researcher uses easily available chemicals to synthesize the drug no more violates the Lockean proviso than does the fact that the only surgeon able to perform a particular operation eats easily obtainable food in order to stay alive and to have the energy to work. This shows that the Lockean proviso is not an "end-state principle"; it focuses on a particular way that appropriative actions affect others, and not on the structure of the situation that results.[26]

---

[24]The situation would be different if his water hole didn't dry up, due to special precautions he took to prevent this. Compare our discussion of the case in the text with Hayek, *The Constitution of Liberty*, p. 136; and also with Ronald Hamowy, "Hayek's Concept of Freedom; A Critique," *New Individualist Review*, April 1961, pp. 28–31.

[25]I discuss overriding and its moral traces in "Moral Complications and Moral Structures," *Natural Law Forum*, 1968, pp. 1–50.

[26]Does the principle of compensation ([*Anarchy, State, and Utopia,*] Chapter 4) introduce patterning considerations? Though it requires compensation for the disadvantages imposed by those seeking security from risks, it is not a patterned principle. For it seeks to remove only those disadvantages which prohibitions inflict on those who might present risks to others,

Intermediate between someone who takes all of the public supply and someone who makes the total supply out of easily obtainable substances is someone who appropriates the total supply of something in a way that does not deprive the others of it. For example, someone finds a new substance in an out-of-the-way place. He discovers that it effectively treats a certain disease and appropriates the total supply. He does not worsen the situation of others; if he did not stumble upon the substance no one else would have, and the others would remain without it. However, as time passes, the likelihood increases that others would have come across the substance; upon this fact might be based a limit to his property right in the substance so that others are not below their baseline position; for example, its bequest might be limited. The theme of someone worsening another's situation by depriving him of something he otherwise would possess may also illuminate the example of patents. An inventor's patent does not deprive others of an object which would not exist if not for the inventor. Yet patents would have this effect on others who independently invent the object. Therefore, these independent inventors, upon whom the burden of proving independent discovery may rest, should not be excluded from utilizing their own invention as they wish (including selling it to others). Furthermore, a known inventor drastically lessens the chances of actual independent invention. For persons who know of an invention usually will not try to reinvent it, and the notion of independent discovery here would be murky at best. Yet we may assume that in the absence of the original invention, sometime later someone else would have come up with it. This suggests placing a time limit on patents, as a rough rule of thumb to approximate how long it would have taken, in the absence of knowledge of the invention, for independent discovery.

I believe that the free operation of a market system will not actually run afoul of the Lockean proviso. (Recall that crucial to our story in Part I of how a protective agency becomes dominant and a *de facto* monopoly is the fact that it wields force in situations of conflict, and is not merely in competition, with other agencies. A similar tale cannot be told about other businesses.) [See *Anarchy, State, and Utopia*, Part I—*Ed.*] If this is correct, the proviso will not play a very important role in the activities of protective agencies and will not provide a significant opportunity for future state action. Indeed, were it not for the effects of previous *illegitimate* state action, people would not think the possibility of the proviso's being violated as of more interest than any other logical possibility. (Here I make an empirical historical claim; as does someone who disagrees with this.) This completes our indication of the complication in the entitlement theory introduced by the Lockean proviso.

not all disadvantages. It specifies an obligation on those who impose the prohibition, which stems from their own particular acts, to remove a particular complaint those prohibited may make against them.

Human Rights and the General Welfare

•

David Lyons

Our Constitution tells us that it aims "to form a more perfect union, establish justice, insure domestic tranquility, provide for the common defense, promote the general welfare, and secure the blessings of liberty to ourselves and our posterity." But these grand words must to some extent be discounted. Because of the "three-fifths rule,"[1] which tacitly condoned human slavery, for example, the original Constitution fell short of promising liberty and justice for *all*. At best, the document seems to represent a compromise. But with what? Consider the other aims mentioned: a more perfect union, domestic tranquility, the common defense—these might easily be viewed as either means to, or else included under an enlarged conception of, the general welfare, and it might be thought that this last-mentioned standard is what the Constitution was truly designed to serve—the general welfare, at the expense, if necessary, of those "inalienable rights" and that universal equality which the Declaration of Independence had earlier maintained governments are supposed to serve. At least in that early, critical period of the republic, it might have been argued that the interests of the nation as a whole could be served only through sacrificing the interests of some, even if those interests—in life, liberty, and the pursuit of happiness—amount to basic rights. The Bill of Rights, after all, had to be added to the original document to secure some of the rights of concern to the drafters of the Declaration of Independence. The general

From *Philosophy & Public Affairs* 6, no. 2 (Winter 1977), 113–129. Copyright © 1977 by Princeton University Press. Reprinted by permission of *Philosophy & Public Affairs*.

This essay was originally presented as the Special Bicentennial Invited Address to the Pacific Division A.P.A. Meetings in Berkeley, 25 March 1976. I am grateful to Sharon Hill for her comments on that occasion.

[1]In Article 1, section 2—just after the Preamble.

idea behind this interpretation cannot lightly be dismissed; at any rate, critics of utilitarianism have often objected that the general welfare standard condones immoral inequalities, injustice, and exploitation, because the interests of a community as a whole might sometimes most efficiently be served by benefiting some individuals at the expense of others. One might be tempted, therefore, to identify the Declaration of Independence with the doctrine of human rights and the Constitution with a commitment to the general welfare, and then conceive of the differences between these documents as transcending their distinct functions and representing a fundamental conflict between commitment to the general welfare and the principles of rights and justice.

These issues need examination now, not just because this nation's Bicentennial obliges us to acknowledge its original ideologies. Thanks to a convergence of political and philosophical developments—including movements to secure equal rights at home and a less barbaric policy abroad, and the somewhat connected resuscitation of political and legal theory—substantive questions of public policy are being discussed more fully today than they have been for many years. Nevertheless, the philosophical attitudes expressed sometimes threaten to become, in their way, just as trite and unreflective as the average politician's Bicentennial claptrap. It is very widely assumed that the general welfare standard, or more specifically utilitarianism, is essentially defective; but the grounds on which this conclusion is reached are often so slender as to make it seem like dogma, not a proper philosophic judgment. Our professional obligations make it incumbent on us, I believe, to challenge such dogmas.

I wish to explore the connections between human rights and the general welfare (where I assume that commitment to the general welfare standard does not entail commitment to full-blown utilitarianism, which regards all other standards as either derivative or else invalid). These matters were not pursued very deeply in the eighteenth century, so my historical references, indeed the basis for my suggestions on behalf of the general welfare, go back only half way, to John Stuart Mill (who was, fittingly, a champion of rights and liberty as well as of the general welfare). Mill's contributions to this area have been neglected and so, I believe, somewhat misunderstood. I hope to throw some light on Mill while seeking a better grasp upon the principles that our republic in its infancy endorsed.

Rights as well as justice have been problems for utilitarians. Aside from Mill, only Bentham gave much thought to rights, and Bentham thought enforcement was essential. He could conceive of rights within an institution but not of rights one might invoke when designing or criticizing institutions. He thus rejected what we call "moral" rights. Recent views of utilitarianism seem to imply that this neglect of rights is theoretically unavoidable. Critics and partisans alike generally suppose that a commitment to the general welfare means that rights are not to count in our deliberations except as conduct affecting them also affects the general welfare, and critics contend that this fails to take rights seriously.[2] Rights are sup-

[2]See, for example, Ronald Dworkin, "Taking Rights Seriously," *New York Review of Books,* 18 December 1970; reprinted in A.W.B. Simpson, ed., *Oxford Essays in Jurisprudence, Second Series* (Oxford: Clarendon Press, 1973) [and in this volume, pp. 92–110—Ed.].

posed to make a difference to our calculations, which they fail to do if we hold—as utilitarians are supposed to maintain—that rights may be infringed if that is necessary to bring about the smallest increase in the general welfare. Perhaps there are no rights that may absolutely never be overridden; some rights, at least, may be infringed in order to prevent calamities, for example; but infringement of a right should always count against a policy, a law, or a course of action, even when considerations of the general welfare argue for infringement. And it is not necessarily the case that infringement of a right always detracts significantly from the general welfare. For such reasons, commitment to the general welfare standard seems to conflict with genuine acknowledgment of rights; utilitarianism seems positively to abhor them. In this paper I shall sketch how Mill challenges such a conclusion.

One strategy of response could be built upon the idea of "rule utilitarianism." In this century, utilitarianism was initially understood, by Moore and others, as requiring one always to promote the general welfare in the most efficient and productive manner possible, any failure to do so being judged as wrong, the breach of one's sole "moral obligation." Faced with objections that this "act utilitarianism" neglects ordinary moral obligations, which do not require one to "maximize utility" but indeed require contrary conduct, revisionists constructed new kinds of "utilitarian" principles. They required adherence to useful rules and excluded case-by-case appeal to the general welfare, hoping that these requirements would match the assumed obligations while still being based upon the general welfare. In the present context, one might extend this rebuttal by supposing that some useful rules would also confer rights, infringement of which would generally be prohibited, and infringement of which would never be warranted by direct appeal to the general welfare. Something like this is in fact suggested by Mill.

Mill's system does, in part, resemble a kind of rule utilitarianism, with the distinct advantage over recent theories that it explicitly acknowledges rights as well as obligations. It has a further, more general advantage. Recent rule-utilitarian theories seem either to have been concocted to avoid objections to act utilitarianism or else to offer an alternative but equally narrow interpretation of the general welfare standard. Both "act" and "rule" versions of utilitarianism seem arbitrarily to restrict the application of the general welfare standard to just one category of things—acts, say, or rules—among the many to which it might reasonably be applied. In contrast, Mill's endorsement of the general welfare standard leaves him free to judge all things by that measure. But he supplements it with analyses of moral judgments which commit him to acknowledging both moral rights and obligations.

For simplicity's sake, let us postpone examination of Mill's theory of rights and consider first his more famous (and initially simpler) principle of personal liberty.[3] Mill says that the only reasons we should entertain in support of coercive

[3]Mill's essay *On Liberty* appears consistent with his essay on *Utilitarianism* (written soon after) on all points relevant to the interpretation I am offering here. My interpretation of *On Liberty* does not so much ignore as render it unnecessary to hypothesize nonutilitarian tendencies in Mill's argument; for an alternative account, see Gerald Dworkin, "Paternalism," in Richard A. Wasserstrom, ed., *Morality and the Law* (Belmont, Calif.: Wadsworth, 1971), section V.

social interference is the prevention of harm to people other than the agent whose freedom may be limited. For example, we should not try to force a person to serve his own happiness or prevent a person from harming himself. In effect, Mill says that we should *not* apply the general welfare standard directly to such intervention. But how could Mill say this—without forsaking his commitment to the general welfare standard? Mill recognizes that his principle of liberty is not entailed by his "general happiness principle" taken by itself. The latter commits him in principle to approving paternalistic intervention that would serve the general welfare. And so Mill *argues* for his principle of liberty. But wouldn't such a principle be emptied of all practical significance by the tacit qualifications that are inevitably imposed by Mill's commitment to the general welfare?

These questions arise when we assume that Mill's commitment to the general welfare standard amounts to the idea that one is always morally bound to serve the general welfare in the most efficient and productive manner possible. His principle of liberty is then conceived of as a "summary rule," a rough guide to action that is meant to insure the closest approximation to the requirements laid down by his principle of utility. This is, I think, mistaken on several counts.

Let me suggest, first, that Mill be understood as reasoning along the following lines. The general welfare will best be served in the long run if we restrict social interference, by both legal and informal means, to the prevention of social harm. Experience shows that less limited intervention is very largely, and unavoidably, counterproductive. Even when we try our best to prevent people from harming themselves, for example, we are in all probability bound to fail. Before embarking on such intervention we are unable to distinguish the productive from the counterproductive efforts. We are able to do that later; but later is always too late. Since the stakes are high for those we coerce, and nonexistent for us, we *ought to make it a matter of principle* never to entertain reasons for interfering save the prevention of harm to others. The general welfare would best be served in the long run by our following such an inflexible rule.

Now this seems to me a perfectly intelligible position, and one even an act-utilitarian might consistently adopt. One need not reject the general welfare standard—as a basis, or even the sole basis, for evaluating things—in order to accept such a principle of liberty. Some possible objections ought however to be noted, though they cannot adequately be considered here. First, it may be said that this could not be a complete account of our objections to paternalism and other forms of social interference (so far as we object to them) because our convictions about the sanctity of liberty are much stronger than our warranted confidence in the factual assumptions required by Mill's argument. This seems to me, however, to prove nothing without independent validations of those judgments. Our moral convictions need justification; they are not self-certifying. If we are uncertain about the relevant facts, then we should retain at least an open mind about the relations between liberty and the general welfare.

Second, the argument attributed to Mill suggests that the general welfare will best be served only if we are something other than utilitarians, for it tells us *not* to apply the general welfare standard. The argument thus seems self-defeating for a utilitarian. But, while this problem might arise for utilitarianism in some other contexts, I do not think it need worry Mill right here. I might make it a matter of principle to avoid certain situations that I know will lead to choices that are self-destructive, though they will not seem such to me at the time. This is compatible with my continuing to appreciate my reasons for that policy. Mill's argument is similar. Indeed, one would expect the Mill of *On Liberty* to insist that we remind ourselves of the rationales for our rules and principles if we do not wish them to become ineffective dogmas. This presumably advises us to keep in mind the utilitarian foundation for the principle of liberty.

Third, it may be said that Mill's principle is too rigid and inflexible, that the general welfare would in fact be served better by a more complex principle, which incorporates some exceptions. It may be argued, for example, that paternalistic legislation within certain clearly defined limits should be tolerated.[4] But this is a point that Mill might easily accept—provided that any proposed qualifications on the principle of liberty would not lead to such abuse as to be counterproductive.

It should be clear, now, that the principle of liberty is no "summary rule," of the sort associated with act utilitarianism; nor is it one of those ideal rules of obligation obtained by applying some modern rule-utilitarian formula. It results from a direct application of the general welfare standard to the question, What sorts of reasons would it serve the general welfare for us to entertain when framing social rules?

Mill is not obliged to be either a rule utilitarian or an act utilitarian because he does not conceive of the general welfare standard in so limited a way. His principle concerns ends, specifically happiness, and provides the basis for evaluating other things in relation to that end. It does not concern acts or rules as such. It says nothing about right or wrong, duty or obligation. And it does not require one, in moral terms, to maximize the general welfare.

These points are indicated in Mill's "proof" of the principle of utility (where one would expect him to be careful at least in his formulation of his principle, even if his argument fails). In a typical passage Mill says: "The utilitarian doctrine is that happiness is desirable, and the only thing desirable, as an end; all other things being only desirable as means to that end" (chap. IV, par. 2).[5] At the end of the main part of his "proof" Mill says: "If so, happiness is the sole end of human action, and the promotion of it the test by which to judge of all human conduct; from whence it necessarily follows that it must be the criterion of morality, since a part is included in the whole" (chap. IV, par. 8). The relationship between moral judgments and the general welfare standard is then explained more fully by Mill in the next and longest chapter of *Utilitarianism*, which is devoted to the topic of rights and justice.[6]

[4] For some suggestions along these lines, see Gerald Dworkin, "Paternalism," section VI; and, on speech, see Joel Feinberg, "Limits to the Free Expression of Opinion," in Joel Feinberg and Hyman Gross, eds., *Philosophy of Law* (Encino, Calif.: Dickenson, 1975).

[5] All references in the text hereafter will cite chapters and paragraphs of *Utilitarianism*.

[6] I discuss this matter more fully in, "Mill's Theory of Morality," *Nous* 10 (1976): 101–120.

Mill maintains that judgments about the justice of acts are a specific form of moral appraisal: acts can be wrong without being unjust. To call an act unjust is to imply that it violates another's right, which is not true of all wrong acts. In a perfectly parallel manner, Mill maintains that moral judgments (about right and wrong, duty and obligation) are a proper subclass of act appraisals in general: acts can be negatively appraised—as inexpedient, undesirable, or regrettable, for example—without being regarded as immoral or wrong. To call an act wrong is to imply that "punishment" for it (loosely speaking) would be justified (chap. V, paras. 13–15).

Mill's distinction between immorality and mere "inexpediency" indicates that he is no act utilitarian and also that his general welfare standard does not lay down moral requirements. There must be some basis within Mill's system for appraising acts negatively even when they are not to be counted as wrong. This is either the general welfare standard or some other. But the general welfare standard is quite clearly Mill's basic, most comprehensive criterion. It therefore seems reasonable to infer that Mill would wish to rank acts according to their instrumental value (their promotion of the general welfare), *preferring* those that rank highest in a set of alternatives, without implying that a merely "inexpedient" act is wrong because it falls below the top of such a ranking and thus fails to serve the general welfare in the most productive and efficient manner possible.

According to Mill, to show that an act is wrong, and not merely inexpedient, one must go further and show that sanctions against it would be justified. For Mill says that to judge an act wrong is to judge that "punishment" of it would be fitting or justified.[7] The "punishment" or sanctions Mill has in mind include not just legal penalties but also public condemnation (both can be classified as "external sanctions") as well as guilt feelings or pangs of conscience (the "internal sanction").[8]

Now, Mill presents this as a conceptual point, independent of his commitment to the general welfare; but it has a bearing on our understanding of that standard. Mill distinguishes between general negative appraisals of the "inexpediency" of acts and moral judgments specifically condemning them as wrong. I have suggested that the criterion of "inexpediency" for Mill is an act's failure to promote the general welfare to the maximum degree possible. If so, this cannot be Mill's criterion of wrongness, for from the fact that an act is inexpedient in this sense it does not follow that sanctions against it could be justified. For sanctions have costs of the sort that a utilitarian always counts, and these costs attach to the distinct acts connected with sanctions. The justification of such acts presumably turns somehow upon *their* relation to the general welfare, not upon (or not alone upon) the relation of the act that is to be sanctioned to the general welfare. On Mill's view, therefore, the general welfare standard *can* be applied directly to acts, but then it simply determines their expediency (and enables one to rank them ac-

---

[7]For simplicity's sake, I shall understand Mill to mean "justified" or "warranted."
[8]Mill uses the terminology of "sanctions" in chapter III of *Utilitarianism*.

cordingly). However, this is not, according to Mill, a moral judgment, and it has no direct moral implications.[9]

Mill also seems to hold that a wrong act is the breach of a moral obligation, at least in the absence of some overriding obligation.[10] But what differentiates morality from mere expediency, as we have seen, is the justification of sanctions. Mill appears to regard the internal sanction as basic. His formulations imply that public disapproval may be justified even when legal sanctions are not, and that pangs of conscience may be warranted when no external sanctions can be justified. Mill suggests that greater costs and risks attach to social sanctions (which is plausible so long as conscience is not excessively demanding). It may also be observed that the justification of external sanctions involves an extra step, since they require distinct acts by other persons, while guilt feelings are triggered more or less automatically. Errors of judgment aside, to justify the operation of self-reproach in particular cases one must justify no more than the internalization of certain values. But to justify external sanctions one must also justify distinct acts by other persons, based on their corresponding values—acts ranging from expressions of disapproval to legal punishment. In Mill's view, then, to argue that an act is wrong is basically to argue that guilt feelings for it would be warranted. Other sanctions may be justified as well, depending on the stakes involved and on the circumstances.

Following Bentham, Mill clearly thinks of sanctions operating not just after an act, as responses to a wrong already done, but also beforehand, in order to discourage such conduct.[11] This conception presupposes that sanctions are attached to general rules, which serve as guides to conduct, and has its more natural application to rules of the social variety, to which external sanctions are also attached. We can combine this with the previous point as follows. Internal sanctions require that the corresponding values be "internalized," thoroughly accepted by the individual. For external sanctions to be justified they must work efficiently, and this requires that the corresponding values be shared widely, within, say, a given community; which amounts to the existence of a common moral code. A reconstruction of Mill's account of moral judgments, then, would go something like this. To argue for a moral obligation is to argue for the widespread internalization (within a community) of a value relevant to conduct; to show that an act

[9]The act-utilitarian reading of Mill is most strongly suggested in *Utilitarianism,* chapter II, paragraph 2. But, as D. G. Brown has noted, the passage is ambiguous; see his paper, "What is Mill's Principle of Utility?" *Canadian Journal of Philosophy* 3 (1973): 1–12.

[10]This paragraph has been revised in response to a very helpful comment by a reader for *Philosophy & Public Affairs,* for which I am grateful. Note, now, that Mill does not differentiate in *Utilitarianism* between duties and obligations. He may link both too closely with wrong actions, but he does not hold that an act is wrong if it simply breaches a moral obligation. This is because he recognizes that obligations can conflict. And when they do, rules or obligations are ranked by reference to the general welfare standard. Mill does not indicate that acts are so evaluated directly, even when obligations conflict; see the last paragraph of chapter II, as well as chapter V.

[11]Since Mill criticized Bentham's views extensively, but had only praise for Bentham's theory of punishment, I assume that Mill follows Bentham on all relevant points except where the evidence and the requirements of a coherent theory indicate the contrary.

is wrong is to show that it breaches such a rule, in the absence of an overriding obligation.

Mill thus suggests a fairly sophisticated version of what would now be called "rule utilitarianism"—except, of course, that he does not limit the general welfare standard to rules of conduct, any more than he limits it to acts. Following Bentham's conception of social rules and his theory of their justification, Mill also takes into account the costs of sanctions—the social price of regulating conduct—which most recent rule utilitarians have ignored.[12] Mill departs from Bentham on two important and related points. First, Mill acknowledges the internal sanction, conscience and guilt feelings, which Bentham had neglected, but which Mill thinks is fundamental to the idea of morality. Second, while Bentham analyzed the idea of obligation in terms of actual coercion or institutionally authorized coercion—which might not be justified—Mill analyzes obligation in terms of sanctions that could be justified. That is a much more plausible and promising conception than Bentham's.

I do not mean that Mill's account of moral judgments is adequate as it stands. For example, while Mill seems right in emphasizing the connections between judgments of one's own immoral conduct and guilt feelings, he seems to put the cart before the horse. For we usually think of determining whether guilt feelings would be justified by asking, first, whether one has acted immorally, while Mill finds out whether a given act is wrong by first calculating whether internal sanctions for such an act are justified. Perhaps Mill's analysis of moral judgments is misguided. But his general approach to these matters is instructive.

Since Mill's theory of obligation does not seem inconsistent with his general welfare standard, it seems to show that an advocate of the general welfare standard can take moral obligations seriously. For, on Mill's view, obligations alone determine whether an act is wrong; they alone lay down moral requirements. Even if the general welfare would be served by breaching an obligation, it does not follow, on Mill's account, that one would be morally justified in breaching it.

We are now in a position to consider Mill's account of rights. In distinguishing justice from morality in general, Mill says that obligations of justice in particular, but not all moral obligations, correspond with moral rights, An unjust act is the violation of another's right; but an act can be wrong without being unjust—without violating any person's right. Mill believes that we can act wrongly by failing to be generous or charitable or beneficent, and he treats the corresponding "virtues" as imposing "obligations"; but these do not correspond with anyone's rights. "No one has a moral right to our generosity or beneficence because we are not morally bound to practice those virtues towards any given individual" (chap. V, par. 15).

Though not all obligations involve corresponding rights, Mill seems to hold that rights entail corresponding obligations. Consequently, it seems reason-

---

[12]An exception is Richard Brandt; see especially his "A Utilitarian Theory of Excuses," *Philosophical Review* 68 (1969): 337–361.

able to interpret his explicit analysis of moral rights in terms of moral obligations. This analysis is presented as follows:

> When we call anything a person's right, we mean that he has a valid claim upon society to protect him in the possession of it, either by the force of law or by that of education and opinion. If he has what we consider a sufficient claim, on whatever account, to have something guaranteed him by society, we say he has a right to it [chap. V, par. 24].

After some elaboration Mill restates the point, and then goes one step further:

> To have a right, then, is, I conceive, to have something that society ought to defend me in the possession of. If the objector goes on to ask why it ought, I can give him no other reason than general utility [chap. V, par. 25].

Mill first analyzes ascriptions of rights; his analysis refers to arguments with conclusions of a certain type. After completing this account, Mill resumes his advocacy of utilitarianism; he indicates that, on his view, such arguments are sound if, and only if, they turn entirely upon the general welfare.

Mill holds that someone has a right when he ought to be treated in a certain way, which serves (or refrains from undermining) some interest of his. Combining this with Mill's theory of obligation, we get the view that someone has a moral right when another person or persons are under a beneficial moral obligation towards him;[13] or, in other words, when there are sufficient grounds for the widespread internalization of a value that requires corresponding ways of acting towards him.

Mill's approach seems to me significant. Someone who rejected the general welfare standard could consistently accept Mill's analysis of rights (or something like it) and use a different basis for validating the relevant claims. This is because his analysis of rights, like his analysis of moral obligations, is independent of the general welfare standard.

Now, if something like Mill's approach is correct, then we can say the following. If one's principles actually support the relevant sort of claim, then one is committed to the corresponding rights. Mill believes that some such claims are validated by the general welfare standard—that is, that it would serve the general welfare to protect individuals in certain ways—so he believes himself committed to moral rights. Mill's principle of liberty can be construed as a defense of some such rights, and its defense as an argument for—among other things—constitutional protections for them. Since Mill's belief is plausible, it is plausible to suppose that a utilitarian such as Mill—indeed, anyone who accepts the general welfare as

---

[13]For a fuller discussion of this sort of theory, see my "Rights, Claimants, and Beneficiaries," *American Philosophical Quarterly* 6 (1969): 173–185 [reprinted in this volume, pp. 58–77—Ed.].

a standard for evaluation—is committed to certain categories of rights. And it is vital to observe that this conclusion flows, not from a concocted version of "utilitarianism" designed to yield conclusions that external critics demanded, but from a reasonable interpretation of the general welfare standard coupled with a plausible analysis of rights.

Moreover, since Mill is not committed morally to maximizing welfare—to regarding the failure to so act as wrong—he is not committed to infringing rights whenever it would serve the general welfare in the smallest way to do so. Quite the contrary, since such an act would breach a moral obligation that Mill recognizes, and obligations may be breached only when other obligations override them. In this sense, Mill shows that a proponent of the general welfare standard—even a utilitarian—can take rights seriously.

Mill's account of rights is superior to Bentham's in ways that follow from the differences in their conceptions of obligation. Bentham also held that to have a right is to be someone who is supposed to benefit from another's obligation. But, as I have noted, Bentham analyzed obligation in terms of actual or authorized coercion, which might not be justified. This led to his notorious rejection of unenforced rights, including the rights that we invoke to argue for changes in the social order (as was done most famously in our Declaration of Independence and the French Declaration of the Rights of Man, both of which Bentham consequently criticized). Mill, however, is free to recognize such rights, which would be clearly in the spirit of his discussion.

It may also be noted that defects in Mill's account of obligation do not necessarily transfer to his account of rights. It is possible to understand both Bentham and Mill as embracing the idea that rights are to be understood in terms of beneficial obligations, and to interpret this in terms of an *adequate* account of obligation (whatever that may be). One could, of course, go further and say that the implications of the general welfare standard concerning moral rights cannot be fully understood without applying it to an adequate account of rights. Failing that, Mill has at least given us some reason to believe that utilitarians need not ignore or reject rights.

Let us now look at the specific commitments that Mill thinks utilitarians have towards moral rights. He holds that rules conferring rights take precedence over those that merely impose useful obligations, because they "concern the essentials of human well-being more nearly, and are therefore of more absolute obligation, than any other rules for the guidance of life" (chap. V, par. 32). In particular:

> The moral rules which forbid mankind to hurt one another (in which we must never forget to include wrongful interference with each other's freedom) are more vital to human well-being than any maxims, however important, which only point out the best mode of managing some department of human affairs [chap. V, par. 33].

According to Mill, our most important rights are to freedom of action and security of person; these concern our most vital interests, which must be respected or served if a minimally acceptable condition of life, in any setting, is to be possible. That position, I have tried to show, is not inconsistent with utilitarianism, and may in fact be part of a reasonably developed utilitarian theory. (Other rights concern, for example, specific debts or obligations that are due one and matters of desert.)

Mill's underlying reasoning may be understood as follows: An act is not wrong just because it fails to serve the general welfare to the maximum degree possible. This is because an act's being wrong involves the justification of sanctions, and sanctions (including internal sanctions) have unavoidable costs. The stakes must therefore be high enough so that the benefits to be derived from the redirection of behavior resulting from the existence of the sanctions (including the internalization of the corresponding values) exceed the costs entailed. But this applies to all moral obligations, including those "imperfect" obligations of benevolence which merely require generally helpful, charitable, or compassionate patterns of behavior. The obligations of justice are more demanding, and have greater costs attached, because they are "perfect." In the first place this means that they require one to behave towards certain other individuals in more or less determinate ways— that is, to serve or respect certain interests of theirs—on each and every occasion for so acting. In the second place this means that people are entitled to act in ways connected with their having rights: to demand respect for them, to challenge those who threaten to infringe them, to be indignant and perhaps noisy or uncooperative when their rights are violated or threatened, and so on. The obligations of justice are more demanding on the agent, since they do not leave one nearly as much choice as other moral obligations; they also involve greater liability to internal and external sanctions, as well as to demands by other persons upon one's conduct. This means that on a utilitarian reckoning they have special costs, which must be outweighed by the benefits they bring. The stakes must therefore be higher than for other moral obligations. Thus the interests that they are designed to serve must be more important. Rules concerning them will therefore generally take precedence over other moral rules. Such rights are not "inviolable," but their infringement will not easily be justified.

We can now make some further observations about the general nature of the rights that may be endorsed by the general welfare standard. In the first place, they may be characterized as morally fundamental, since they are grounded on a *non*moral standard and are not derived from some more fundamental moral principle.[14] In the second place, if Mill is correct about the importance to anyone of certain interests (such as personal liberty and security), regardless of particular social settings,[15] some of the rights endorsed by the general welfare standard could reasonably be characterized as "universal human" rights. Mill therefore gives us reason to believe, not only that the general welfare standard would not be hostile to such rights, but that it is positively committed to them—that is, to the sorts of

[14]In this respect they are just like the basic rights endorsed by John Rawls in *A Theory of Justice* (Cambridge, Mass.: Harvard University Press, 1971). Rawls' argument invokes self-interest, not the general interest, but on the view we have been considering the latter is no more a "moral" standard than the former.

[15]It is interesting to note that Rawls endorses such a notion with his use of "primary goods."

rights associated with the Declaration of Independence. If so, the general welfare standard cannot be blamed for any corresponding injustices that are condoned by arguments invoking the general welfare; for such arguments would simply be mistaken.

I do not wish to imply, however, that Mill's suggestions should be accepted without much more severe scrutiny. I merely wish to emphasize that the matter seems far from settled against the general welfare standard.

One final comment in defense of arguments for rights from the general welfare standard. These rights are grounded upon nonmoral values. This will seem unsatisfactory to someone who thinks that some basic rights, or the principles that proclaim them, are "self-evident," as the Declaration of Independence declares. Now, I am not sure what "self-evidence" amounts to, but I know of no account that makes it plausible to suppose that moral principles can somehow stand on their own feet, without any need for, or even possibility of, supporting argument. So I cannot see this as a serious objection to Mill.

A somewhat related and more familiar objection to Mill's manner of defending rights is to note that it relies upon the facts—not just too heavily, but at all. It is sometimes suggested, for example, that the general welfare standard must be rejected or severely limited because it is *logically* compatible with unjust arrangements. From any reasonable definition of human slavery, for example, it would not follow that such an institution could never satisfy the general welfare standard. It is therefore *logically possible* that enslaving some would sometimes serve the general welfare better than would any of the available alternatives. This objection does not rest on factual assumptions, and a utilitarian who tried to answer it by citing the *actual* disutility of human slavery would be accused of missing its point. Facts are simply irrelevant, for "basic" moral principles are involved.

A utilitarian might answer as follows. If moral principles independent of utilitarianism are assumed, the idea that the general welfare standard is valid is tacitly rejected at the outset; but that simply begs the question. At this point, any friend of the general welfare standard (even one who accepts other basic principles as well) might join in the rebuttal: Why should we assume that the principles of rights and justice are independent of the general welfare standard? Let us see the arguments for them, so that we can determine whether they are not actually grounded on and limited by considerations of utility.

Moreover, if facts cannot be called upon to help us interpret the general welfare standard, they must not be assumed by any objections to it. But it is difficult to see how facts can be excluded both from arguments for moral principles and from their applications. If moral principles are not regarded as self-evident, then they must be defended in some manner. The only plausible arguments that I know of in defense of moral principles—such as Rawls'—make extensive use of facts.[16] Moreover, most general principles require considerable information for

---

[16]A good example is Rawls' argument for his principles, which makes much more extravagant use of facts than Mill's.

their application to the varied circumstances of human life.[17] Someone who believes that facts are thus relevant to morality cannot reasonably object to the general welfare standard on the grounds of its unavoidable consideration of the facts. Until we have established principles of rights and justice on nonutilitarian grounds and also have shown that utilitarian arguments for them are ineffective, we must consider what proponents of the general welfare standard might have to say about such matters.

[17]This is true, not just of Rawls' principles, but, I think, of all principles of similar scope.

Bibliography

Benn, Stanley I. "Rights." In *Encyclopedia of Philosophy,* edited by Paul Edwards, Vol. 7, pp. 195–99. New York: Macmillan and Free Press, 1967.

Brown, Stuart M., Jr. "Inalienable Rights." *Philosophical Review* 64 (1955): 192–211.

Dworkin, Ronald. *Taking Rights Seriously.* Cambridge: Harvard University Press, 1977.

Feinberg, Joel. "Duties, Rights, and Claims." *American Philosophical Quarterly* 3 (1966): 137–44.

———. *Social Philosophy.* Chapters 4–6. Englewood Cliffs, N.J.: Prentice-Hall, 1973.

Frankena, William K. "Natural and Inalienable Rights." *Philosophical Review* 64 (1955): 212–32.

Hart, H. L. A. "Bentham." *Proceedings of the British Academy* 48 (1962): 297–320.

———. *Definition and Theory in Jurisprudence.* Oxford: Clarendon Press, 1953; also in *Law Quarterly Review* 70 (1954): 37–60.

Hohfeld, Wesley Newcomb. *Fundamental Legal Conceptions.* New Haven: Yale University Press, 1919; reprinted 1964.

Lyons, David. "The Correlativity of Rights and Duties." *Nous* 4 (1970): 45–55.

Macdonald, Margaret. "Natural Rights." *Proceedings of the Aristotelian Society* 47 (1946–47): 225–50.

Marshall, G. "Rights, Options, and Entitlements." In *Oxford Essays in Jurisprudence (Second Series),* edited by A. W. B. Simpson, pp. 228–41. Oxford: Clarendon Press, 1973.

McCloskey, H. J. "Rights." *Philosophical Quarterly* 15 (1965): 113–27.

Melden, A. I. *Rights and Persons.* Berkeley and Los Angeles: University of California Press, 1977.

————. *Rights and Right Conduct.* Oxford: Blackwell, 1959.

Nelson, William N. "Special Rights, General Rights, and Social Justice." *Philosophy & Public Affairs* 3 (1974): 410–30.

Ross, W. D. *The Right and The Good.* Appendix 1 to chapter 2. Oxford: Clarendon Press, 1930.

Scanlon, T. M. "Rights, Goals, and Fairness." *Erkenntnis* 11 (1977): 81–95.

Singer, Marcus G. "The Basis of Rights and Duties." *Philosophical Studies* 23 (1972): 48–57.

Vlastos, Gregory. "Justice and Equality." In *Social Justice,* edited by Richard B. Brandt, pp. 31–72. Englewood Cliffs, N.J.: Prentice-Hall, 1962.